# Schoolhouse of Cards

# Schoolhouse of Cards

An Inside Story of No Child
Left Behind and Why
America Needs a Real
Education Revolution

Eugene W. Hickok

ROWMAN & LITTLEFIELD PUBLISHERS, INC.
*Lanham* • *Boulder* • *New York* • *Toronto* • *Plymouth, UK*

Published by Rowman & Littlefield Publishers, Inc.
A wholly owned subsidiary of The Rowman & Littlefield Publishing Group, Inc.
4501 Forbes Boulevard, Suite 200, Lanham, Maryland 20706
http://www.rowmanlittlefield.com

Estover Road, Plymouth PL6 7PY, United Kingdom

British Library Cataloguing in Publication Information Available

**Library of Congress Cataloging-in-Publication Data**

Hickok, Eugene W.
  Schoolhouse of cards : an inside story of No Child Left Behind and why America needs a real education revolution / Eugene W. Hickok.
    p. cm.
  ISBN 978-1-4422-0524-6 (cloth : alk. paper) — ISBN 978-1-4422-0526-0 (electronic)
  1. Educational accountability—Law and legislation—United States. 2. United States. No Child Left Behind Act of 2001. 3. Education—Standards—United States. 4. Education--United States—Evaluation. 5. Educational equalization—United States. 6. Educational change—United States. I. Title.
  LB2806.22.H52 2010
  379.2'60973–dc22
                                                                  2010021277

Printed in the United States of America

# Contents

# November 2004

For members of the George W. Bush administration, the euphoria surrounding the president's 2004 reelection had hardly subsided a week after the campaign ended. Bush had emerged with a sense of confidence visible during an impromptu news conference, where he spoke of the "political capital" he had earned and his intent to spend it. During that conference, in response to a reporter's question about potential changes in his cabinet and administration, he alluded to the "great Washington parlor game" of rumor spreading about who was staying and who was going. That game had already begun, of course.

Secretary of Education Rod Paige took quiet satisfaction in Bush's victory. For most of the previous year, Paige had traveled tirelessly for the president, perhaps more than any other member of the cabinet. He had promised himself that he would not let education, the president's number one domestic accomplishment, bring Bush down. The president's No Child Left Behind initiative was Paige's legacy as well. And he could not let it be responsible for an electoral defeat.

In victory, Paige took the time to sit back and relax a bit. He cut back on his office hours and caught up on some reading. And he wondered about his own future. To his own surprise, he had become somewhat comfortable and confident as the secretary of education and was not thinking of leaving the post.

Earlier in the fall, Paige had informed his top lieutenants that the president had asked him to stay on, should he be reelected. According to the secretary, the president had chatted briefly with him and Housing Secretary Alphonzo Jackson during a White House barbeque for members of Congress held earlier in the summer of 2004, asking both to remain with his administration. Paige told his team he was inclined to do just that, for at least another year or so. He wanted to make sure the president's education agenda was secure and thought he would steer any amendments or changes to the No Child Left Behind Act himself. The campaign and election victory had buoyed his spirits as well, and he felt a renewed determination to finish the job in Washington.

Throughout Washington and on all the news outlets, the "parlor game" began. Would Secretary of State Colin Powell stay? What about Defense Secretary Donald Rumsfeld, who had suffered critical press over the war in Iraq and the prison scandal at Abu Ghraib? Would the president replace his attorney general, his economic team? Speculation and rumor were rampant. Paige had anticipated the process, felt comfortable and confident about his future, and placed a call to White House Chief of Staff Andy Card to cement things.

The call did not go as Paige had anticipated. He told Card he wanted to stay for about another year or year and a half and that the president had indicated his desire for the secretary to stay. Card suggested it would be better for Paige to complete the term. Paige said he would mull it over and get back to him. But something about the brief conversation had left him uncomfortable. Was Card saying that Paige needed to commit to completing another four-year term? That hardly seemed fair. The secretary, though in great health, was seventy-one years old and felt he should not have to make any long-term commitments. But was Card saying such a commitment was the condition for the president's keeping him on as secretary?

Rod Paige is a plain speaking and direct man, enormously admired for his success as an educator but not for his political skills. He is not good at the sorts of games most in national politics must be able to play in order to excel.

He decided he needed to get clarity from Card. This time, his call interrupted a meeting of the chief of staff and the president. Once again, briefly, Card hinted that Paige should complete the term. Once again Paige was left scratching his head. He was still unsure of Card's message.

Friday, November 12 was an ugly, gray, and rainy day in DC. By now Secretary Powell had announced his intention to step down. His deputy, Richard Armitage, followed suit. Paige was in his office that afternoon, discussing several projects with chief counsel and friend Brian Jones. They talked about a book he was working on and the possibility of lecturing at Howard University. In the background, Fox news was on. Many in important positions in Washington have found that keeping one eye on the television is often the best, perhaps only, way to know what is really going on in the government.

Susan Aspey, the Department of Education's press secretary asked permission to speak with the secretary. She had just received a phone inquiry from an Associated Press (AP) reporter who wanted to know if the rumor was true that Secretary of Education Rod Paige intended to resign his position. Aspey asked Paige if he wanted to confirm the rumor. He looked at her with some amazement, having become quite familiar with the Washington rumor machine and said he had no such intention. Aspey returned to her office and, following established procedures, called the White House Press Office to report on the AP inquiry and Paige's response. After getting the go-ahead from Trent Duffy at the White House, she would call the AP reporter back to nix the rumor. But when Aspey spoke with Duffy, he told her to confirm the rumor with the reporter. She was told, in other words, that Paige would indeed be stepping down.

Aspey was now caught in the most awkward of positions. She was to tell a national reporter that her boss was resigning, even though her boss had just told her he was not. It was classic inside hardball politics—and this White House's way of getting the message through to Paige that his time was up.

After getting off the phone with the reporter, Aspey again walked the long corridor to the secretary's office. As she walked in, Paige and Jones were hearing the news on Fox: the secretary of education intends to resign. All were dumbstruck. The secretary learned of his fate at about the same time as everyone else and from the same source: the media.

That afternoon and evening Secretary Rod Paige sought to work through his emotions. And the top management at the Department of Education was confused. His stepping down seemed at odds with what the president had asked of him, and it would cause Paige some embarrassment. For weeks he and his chief of staff, Anne Radice, had been telling senior managers at the department that he was staying at the president's request. (Bush's chief domestic-policy advisor at the time and next secretary of education, Margaret Spellings, denied the president ever asked Paige to stay and was outraged that Paige and his chief of staff were spreading such news around the department and the city.) That evening, he told his deputy, "I don't know what's going on."

It came down to this: Andy Card had told Paige to end his career with the current term. As Paige remembered it, when he had told Card about his interest in staying on the job for another year or so, Card had said something like, "Let's just complete the term." What he had meant, now so obvious to Paige, was the current term. At the time he had thought it meant that his remaining in the cabinet would require a commitment to stay until the end of the next term.

By Saturday evening, Paige had arrived at that place the White House had sought for him. After several conversations with close friends and advisors, he asked his under secretary, Ted McPhearson, and others to draft a letter of resignation for him to take a look at. On Monday morning, during his usual meeting with his closest advisors, he informed them of what they by now already knew: he was leaving. Finding it too difficult to do himself, he asked his chief of staff to read his letter of resignation. Trembling with emotion, she burst into tears. Paige threw his arms around her and asked his general counsel to read the letter.

With his resignation, Paige cited the long list of accomplishments during his tenure. Curiously, the first he noted with pride had little to do with No Child Left Behind, the president's education-reform agenda, or public education generally. He chose to highlight the department's clean audit, its first in years. Paige, first and foremost a manager, was proudest of an accomplishment few in Washington and few in the American education establishment knew or cared anything about.

Gathering their thoughts, Paige and his lieutenants next met with all the senior leadership of the department in the secretary's conference room. There, General Counsel Jones read the letter again. After an awkward moment of silence, the room erupted in applause.

In his letter of resignation, Paige offered to remain at his post until his successor was confirmed by the Senate. Within days of receiving his letter, the White House had chosen Paige's successor. Margaret Spellings was the president's domestic-policy advisor and close friend. Paige saw her nomination to replace him as yet another slap in his face. For almost four years the tension between the two had, at times, been impossible to hide and had contributed to numerous squabbles over policy and politics. Now she was to take his place. Secretary of Education Rod Paige, a man with a lifelong career at every level of education, was to be supplanted by a woman with only an undergraduate degree and a few years with the Texas Association of School Boards. Of course, she also had been Governor Bush's education advisor and a primary architect of President Bush's No Child Left Behind initiative. And Rod Paige's rival.

⸙

That period between the end of one term and the beginning of another—the transition—is usually dominated by talk of who is going and who is coming. Little substantive news is generated beyond that, primarily because the president-elect is assembling a team, and the members of Congress are mostly out of town. From mid-November until well into January, almost daily announcements were made regarding presidential personnel. In the end, nine of the fourteen cabinet members in the first Bush administration left, some voluntarily, some with encouragement. Only one personnel decision backfired: the selection of Bernard Karick to run the Department of Homeland Security. Citing his failure to properly report his employment of a housekeeper, he withdrew his name from consideration. Soon thereafter, however, allegations of a much more serious nature emerged.

As nominations for the cabinet were announced, the speculation surrounding confirmation struggles invariably followed. Some encountered modest trouble. White House Counsel and Attorney General designate Alberto Gonzales was grilled by the Senate Judiciary Committee for hours. His support of a legal memorandum referring to the Geneva Convention as "quaint" during a time of terrorism and his apparent endorsement of the torture of prisoners as appropriate under certain circumstances provided ample ammunition for critics. Similarly, National Security Advisor Condoleezza Rice, the president's choice to head the State Department, was questioned energetically by the Senate Foreign Relations Committee. After all, the nation was at war, and critics of the president had seen breakdowns in intelligence and diplomacy as the hallmarks of his foreign policy. Rice was confirmed after enduring some harsh interrogation.

In the end, all the president's nominees were confirmed, most with little trouble. Margaret Spellings danced through her confirmation hearings on January 6, and the Senate Committee on Health, Education, Labor, and Pensions (HELP) unanimously voted to recommend her confirmation later that same day. Where Rod Paige had run into his share of acrimony with the HELP Committee, Margaret Spellings seemed the darling of the members.

All during this time of transition, Paige sat on the sidelines trying to determine what he would do with the rest of his. After the initial shock surrounding his departure decision, he settled into a comfortable pattern of low-key activity. Only spending a few hours a day, if any, at the office, he found time to do what he wanted for the first time in years. He seemed to slip into the casual anonymity that former high-ranking government officials often fear—but Paige began to relish it. After all, for four years he had been on the ramparts in the "education wars," his name prominent in the media coverage of the issue. Now it was someone else's turn. But there was one more headline to be written about the outgoing education chief.

On January 7, 2005, the day after Margaret Spellings's confirmation hearing in the Senate, *USA Today* published a front-page story alleging that the Department of Education had contracted with a prominent African American conservative pundit, Armstrong Williams, to promote Bush's signature No Child Left Behind Act. It seems the department had paid Williams almost a quarter of a million dollars through a contract with its media consultant, Ketchum Consulting. Williams had not made public the nature of his relationship with the administration while, time and again, he told of his support for the education law on television and in print commentary. This gave the appearance of a commentator's accepting money, taxpayer money, to comment favorably on one of the president's major initiatives. Moreover, Paige and Williams were friends. It looked suspiciously like one friend helping another at taxpayer expense. It did not look good.

The story took on a life of its own. Williams immediately went on the defensive, attempting to clarify his role and apologizing for any inappropriate activity on his part. When he spoke glowingly of No Child Left Behind, that was honestly how he felt. But he admitted time and again, on any media outlet that would have him, that he should have disclosed his being paid by the department. He had exercised bad judgment. But Paige remained silent. As far as he was concerned, the arrangement was legal. His lawyers had signed off on it.

Into the second week of the controversy, major newspapers, syndicated columnists, and the White House itself criticized the department's actions. Members of Congress demanded an investigation. As similar agreements by other agencies were disclosed, the whole idea of government offices contracting with public relations firms and political pundits came under heavy scrutiny. Congress sought an investigation by their watchdog organization, the Government Accountability Office (GAO). The member of Congress most closely associated with No Child Left Behind and a vocal supporter of Paige, Republican John Boehner, chairman of the House committee that oversees the Department of Education, issued a statement condemning the arrangement and calling for an inquiry. When asked about the department's activity, the president said it was wrong and instructed his cabinet members not to engage in such conduct.

All the while, Paige remained silent. He did not feel he had done anything wrong. "First of all, Armstrong Williams and I are not good friends," he would tell his close advisors. "Williams came around trying to become my friend. He kept pushing himself on me." Moreover, he was convinced that what the department had done with Ketchum and Williams was lawful. "I asked the lawyers, stared them in the face, time and again, and they said it was legal."

The legality of the agreement remained subject to internal departmental debate for some time. The contracting of government agencies with public relations firms is both a legal and a long-standing practice in Washington. The department maintained that its contract with Ketchum was part of its larger strategy to get the word out about No Child Left Behind. Radio spots had been recorded and broadcast in various markets. Countless publications had been produced and distributed. According to law and regulation, all this activity is legal as long as an agency seeks only to provide the public with information about agency policies and programs. Propagandizing, or otherwise attempting to persuade the public to support agency policies, is against the law. Federal agencies can spend money to inform the public but not to sell citizens on their policies. Department officials, during hours of internal deliberations, defended their action along these lines. But a growing number of outside critics said the line between providing information and spreading propaganda had been crossed. Democrats and critics of the education law were having a field day. Media watchdogs pilloried Williams. So did many who typically supported the president.

Columnist George Will, no great fan of No Child Left Behind, pointedly criticized the Bush administration for engaging in questionable practices at taxpayer expense.

Concerning the contract with Armstrong Williams, officials within the department remained divided. The individual overseeing the contract, Director of Public Affairs John Gibbons, asserted the money was supposed to pay for advertisements explaining No Child Left Behind. Williams was to produce and distribute them through his public relations firm, Graham-Williams. Others in the department were not so sure. They pointed to language in the contract saying Williams was to promote No Child Left Behind to various audiences and groups whenever possible. And Williams himself had repeated publicly several times that he erred by not disclosing that he was being paid to express his support for the law. Gibbons, sorely shaken by the events, was convinced that any legal problem stemmed from Williams's independent actions, not the department's contract with Ketchum or Ketchum's contract with Graham-Williams. But even if Gibbons was correct, there was a deeper problem. Going over his records and trying to rationalize how events had transpired, Gibbons discovered that Williams had never even lived up to his part of the deal. The department had paid Williams for eight advertisements to be produced and distributed on radio and television. But only one could be found, and it was of amateurish quality. Even if Gibbons was right in his assertion that the department's activity was perfectly legal, his sloppy oversight of the contract, when revealed, meant the agency did not even get what it had paid for.

Things did not improve when Paige—at the insistence of his chief of staff and senior advisors and the pleading of White House officials, including Margaret Spellings—issued a one-page statement. Coming almost two weeks after the story broke and on the heels of hours of internal debate, with his advisors imploring him to say he was sorry, Paige's statement stopped well short of any apology. It asserted the legality of the actions taken, with an expression of "regret" for any perception of improper conduct that might injure the image or reputation of "the good men and women of the Department of Education." Paige then called for the department's inspector general to conduct an investigation. Despite his top advisors' pleas, Paige would not say he was sorry. He had apologized once before as secretary of education—after referring to the National Education Association as a "terrorist organization"—and the media had pounded on him for weeks; he was still paying a price. He was not about to let that happen again.

Paige's statement only secured the prominence of the controversy for weeks longer. At least one member of the Senate, Frank Lautenberg of New Jersey, threatened to put a hold Spellings's nomination in light of the allegations, although she had nothing to do with what had transpired. By that time, the GAO was commencing its investigation, as was the

Department of Education's own inspector general. Newspaper pundits and television talking heads were fulminating over the blurred relationship between government and public relations. As more allegations of questionable practices and agreements at other agencies were reported, the very credibility of the president came under question; his critics asserted he had "spun" much of his first term and used taxpayer dollars to pay for the "spinning."

The story behind how Armstrong WIlliams became a public affairs agency, and then a nightmare, for Rod Paige and the Bush administration's Department of Education is rooted in a problem that plagued Paige and his team at the department from day one. They had experienced incredible difficulty getting the word out about No Child Left Behind. The federal Department of Education was not equipped to conduct a major public relations campaign, unlike some other agencies. The Department of Health and Human Services, for example, annually budgets millions of dollars to develop and conduct large-scale campaigns to inform the public about everything from nutrition to disease prevention. The Department of Education had neither the staff nor the resources nor the talent to engage effectively in even a modest public outreach effort. Moreover, mounting such an effort seemed at odds with the culture of the agency.

In the past, the department's policies and programs spoke most directly to the public school community: teachers, administrators, and state and local officials. It seldom sought to reach a broader national audience. In addition, the new education law was very complex, spoke to education at the state and local levels, and was widely opposed by those very individuals and interest groups who would have to make the law work. The "education establishment"—teachers' unions, school board associations, school administrators, parent-teacher groups—had challenged its passage and its implementation. These highly organized, well-funded grassroots organizations had orchestrated an effective campaign to undermine the implementation of No Child Left Behind before the ink on the president's signature was dry. Paige's department was up against a very effective coalition, and he had been desperate to find help.

Over time, Paige had also felt assaulted by White House staff and members of Congress who had grown restless with his seeming inability to get an effective message out. Members in the House and Senate were being criticized by their constituents for supporting the law. Paige, in their eyes, had done little to help them respond. More than once he had been summoned to the Hill and lectured on his shortcomings and failure to counter the law's critics effectively. At the White House, Margaret Spellings had pounded relentlessly on Paige to be more proactive. In response, he hit the road, along with much of the senior leadership of the department, trying to sell No Child Left Behind as retail politics. But all the travel produced only modest returns. It might generate some positive local press when Paige visited a school, but a national campaign was needed to counter a growing national anxiety about the law, fed by its vocal and well-organized critics. And so the decision had been made in 2003 to hire a consultant who would help get the message out, particularly to the minority community, which stood to benefit so much from the new law's emphasis on the "achievement gap."

Ketchum, a well-respected, multi-million-dollar firm familiar with the ways of Washington, was hired to help spread the word. Then Gibbons instructed Ketchum to subcontract with Armstrong Williams through his own public relations firm, Graham-Williams. Williams seemed a good prospect to reach the minority community. An articulate, highly visible, African American conservative pundit, he did not have to be sold on the law's merits, and he liked Rod Paige. At the same time, however, he was a most unlikely candidate for the job. His audience was predominately white, middle-class, conservative, and Christian. His outreach to the minority community consisted primarily of the fact that he himself was black.

This did not seem to matter to Paige or to John Danielson, his chief of staff at the time the initial decision was made. For Williams possessed something else of interest to them as well. His partner was Stedman Graham, the "significant other" of Oprah Winfrey. Danielson had hatched the plan early in his tenure at the department: getting Rod Paige on *The Oprah Winfrey Show* would get the secretary and No Child Left Behind the sort of bounce needed to counter all the attacks. Paige and Danielson went to Williams to get to Graham to get to Oprah.

The Oprah connection never worked out. Neither did the Williams contract. Instead, Paige became enveloped in a public relations disaster that overshadowed all he had accomplished or worked toward during his tenure in Washington. On his way out the door, it threatened to leave an indelible stain on a remarkable career of public service in education.

January 20, 2005, dawned chilly and overcast. As President Bush took the oath of office for the second time, Rod Paige sat on the dais watching, as did his successor Margaret Spellings, along with administration officials old and new. After the inaugural ceremony, the president proceeded to a luncheon with members of Congress. Margaret Spellings was administered her oath of office. And Rod Paige left for Texas to go hunting.

This book tells the story of how the president and Congress changed, perhaps forever, the relationship of the nation's capital to the nation's schools. It is the story of President George W. Bush's personal commitment to improving education and how the resulting landmark legislation garnered strong bipartisan support in Congress even as it generated strong opposition among educators—the very men and women responsible for making the law work. Bush, contrary to his image as less than fully engaged, as all Texas swagger and twang and little substance, understood fully what he was trying to accomplish with No Child Left Behind. He knew every aspect of the law and kept well informed and engaged during its implementation. While the events of September 11, 2001, and the subsequent wars in Afghanistan and Iraq came to overshadow almost everything else that happened during Bush's presidency, he never lost sight of, or interest in, his education agenda.

How did it happen? How did education, primarily a state and local issue, become an important part of the presidential campaign of 2000? For years, Washington had meant little or nothing to the nation's education establishment. They looked to DC for money and the strings that came with it. But for most people, education revolved around state policy and money and local policy and money. Even after President Bill Clinton's Improving America's Schools initiative altered the federal education landscape, most of the nation's schools were barely affected, primarily because the Clinton administration did not implement the law faithfully. But that was to change under President Bush.

How did such a controversial and complex piece of legislation garner such strong bipartisan support in Congress? Bush's education initiative was the only bipartisan domestic-policy accomplishment of his entire presidency. Supported by liberal Democrats like Edward Kennedy, it aroused concerns among conservatives in the Republican Party. But a conservative from Ohio, Congressman John Boehner, led the fight to enact it in the House.

The man given the job of helping to lead a national discussion on education and to oversee the implementation of the law was an African American and veteran educator from Houston, Texas: Rod Paige. As he was a relative stranger to Washington, his naming by Bush generated tremendous excitement. For the first time ever, a real educator would be secretary of education. But Paige encountered troubles almost from the start of his time in office. The very traits that had endeared him to so many in education proved liabilities in Washington. And the challenges of managing the tensions among individuals at the White House, on Capitol Hill, and within his own department at times overwhelmed him and his senior leadership team.

Those tensions had an impact on the implementation of No Child Left Behind, undermining somewhat the potential success of the law. But the law itself was flawed. It could never deliver the result promised by its very name. No Child Left Behind represents an important milestone on the road to the sort of fundamental change needed in American education, but getting America's schools where they need to be will require far more transformative and imaginative change.

I filled a number of leadership positions in the Bush/Paige Department of Education, serving as under secretary, acting assistant secretary for elementary and secondary education, and deputy secretary of education. I was engaged in the process that created the education law and broadly oversaw its implementation. I attended meetings at the White House and on Capitol Hill that shaped the education debates during George W. Bush's first term. This book, then, is based on my remembrances, observations, insights, and opinions.

# 1

# The Idea

For more than a generation, American presidential politics has primarily comprised sound bytes and public-policy prescriptions. Presidential candidates and their ever-growing entourage of advisors, pollsters, speechwriters, and media managers dole out policy initiatives on a daily basis, driven by the need to define the news and get in front of the opposition. Presidential campaigns are fine-tuned machines that touch every voter, often frequently, and drive messages custom designed to attract specific audiences and constituencies.

This has not always been the case. Early in the history of the Republic, presidential contests were as much about governing philosophy as public policy. The two political parties emerged from two contrasting visions of where America should be going and how to get there. The Federalists, under George Washington and John Adams, saw the necessity of a strong national government with broad powers. They were challenged, and ultimately defeated, by Jeffersonian Republicans, who were wary of central authority and sought to ensure the vibrancy of the states by placing limits on the scope of national power. These contending views morphed, gradually, into political parties, a development that most of the Founding Fathers had hoped to avoid. Those parties, under a variety of names, although primarily as the Republicans and Democrats, have shaped the culture of American politics ever since.

Still, the parties came to dominate political discourse in this country by standing for something and nominating individuals to take that message to America. The earliest political conventions lasted for days and involved extensive debate about the parties' platforms. Candidates were "party men" and were chosen by the members of the convention assembled. There existed a coherence to the process that usually assured party and candidate

1

were one and the same. Once elected, the president governed with his party, which held either the majority or minority in Congress, and sought to advance his party's governing philosophy by supporting those measures that flowed from that philosophy.

This all began to change dramatically during the 1950s and 1960s, with the advent of the primary election system and the democratization of American politics generally. Accelerated by the evolution of the mass media, the changes in presidential politics yielded less a system of contending national parties and more a series of ongoing plebiscites whereby numerous candidates campaigned for popular support. By the time a party's nominating convention rolled around, the candidate attracting the most support among his party's primary voters was, by definition, the nominee. The party platform, ironed out long before the convention assembled, was the product of the plebiscite as well. The issues platforms addressed dealt more and more with the potential of electoral success and less with any political or governing philosophy. The nation's political parties became vehicles to achieve national political power through electoral success. What mattered was winning election. The conventions became little more than symbolic theater, and the campaigns emerged as vehicles to advance candidates and their policies rather than parties and their philosophies.

The two parties, over time, took somewhat different paths during the 1960s and 1970s, however. The GOP sought to retain a philosophical grounding and experienced a number of internal ideological struggles over its identity. The conservative wing of the party gained control in 1964, with the nomination of Barry Goldwater. His defeat that year set the conservative faction of the party back and paved the way for the more moderate "Main Street" wing of the party to dominate and to nominate Richard Nixon, who won the presidency in 1968. But the conservatives regrouped, and in 1976 they sought to take back the party with a compelling, albeit unsuccessful, attempt to get Ronald Reagan the nomination. Incumbent Gerald Ford fought off Reagan's challenge but lost to Jimmy Carter. Then, in 1980, the conservatives solidified their hold on the Republican Party. That continues today.

For the Democratic Party, winning election was less a function of warring ideological factions within the party and more a matter of cobbling together various interests and constituencies to create a majority in support of the party's presidential candidate. Democratic conventions focused on seating delegations reflective of the various traditional Democratic constituencies. Embracing long litanies of policies promoted by those constituencies, the party platform served not so much as a statement of what the party stood for as a laundry list of constituent and interest group policy preferences. The approach worked in 1964 and 1976. But by the 1980s the Democratic Party was bereft of any philosophical roots. Bill Clinton won in 1992 by claiming to be a "New Democrat"; he also benefited from conservative Republican disenchantment with George H. W. Bush and the independent candidacy of H. Ross Perot. But Clinton failed to define the Democratic Party as anything more than the sum of its parts, and the GOP ascended, albeit barely, in 2000.

By the time Gov. George W. Bush decided to formally announce his intention to run for the White House, he was the anointed candidate of the Republican Party. Even before he was reelected governor of Texas in 1998, the pundits and prophets of American politics had him going for the gold. A December 1997 *National Review* article opined that Bush's nomination seemed all but inevitable.[1] While a number of other contenders sought to get a foothold on the nomination—Gary Bauer, Lamar Alexander, Pat Buchanan, Alan Keyes, John McCain, John Kasich—Bush was attracting the support of the party leadership. In an unparalleled development, the nation's Republican governors flocked around Bush and supported his candidacy. So, too, did a majority of Republicans in Congress. Before the first primary vote was caste, Bush seemed the party's inevitable nominee.

All of this was driven by a number of factors. First and foremost was the GOP desire to end the Clinton era and to defeat the equally inevitable Democratic nominee, Vice President Al Gore. In addition, the Republican Party was emerging as the nation's majority party in both houses of Congress. Under the leadership of Newt Gingrich of Georgia, the GOP took control of the House of Representatives in 1994 for the first time in forty years. As Speaker of the House, Gingrich led a Republican revolution under a "contract with America" that effectively challenged President Clinton's ability to govern and led pundits to ponder whether Clinton was even "relevant" anymore. Clinton rebounded, but the remainder of his tenure was clouded by political and personal issues that Republicans exploited to political advantage. Having a Republican in the White House would complete the revolution begun earlier, solidifying the party's governing authority for the first time in generations. Add to this Bush's electoral and governing success in Texas, working with both Republicans and Democrats, and his attractiveness as a candidate becomes obvious.

As it turned out, Bush stumbled a bit early on in his bid for the nomination. He won the Iowa caucuses but lost the New Hampshire primary to John McCain. But in the South Carolina primary Bush prevailed, and by mid-March his nomination seemed assured.

Both before and during the primary season, Bush delivered a number of speeches outlining his thinking in a number of areas. Several of them focused on education. They were not laden with a lot of public policy; rather, the speeches sought to present the governor's ideas about what needed to happen in American education. They reflected his experience in Texas and laid the foundation for what later became No Child Left Behind. They also harkened back, in their tone, content, and delivery, to an earlier time in American politics. Bush was trying to lay an intellectual and philosophical foundation for his future education policies. He was seeking to establish a Republican national education philosophy. The specifics would come later.

Accountability had to be the primary focus of education reform, Bush repeatedly argued in speech after speech. Public schools needed to be held accountable for the performance of their students. And there should be consequences for failure and rewards for success. Bush provided the broad parameters of what a strong accountability system might look like, with its requisite testing and academic standards. He argued that student performance needed to be "disaggregated" to expose the achievement gaps among students of differing socioeconomic groups. Bush contended that these gaps were unacceptable and pernicious, that they were brought about by a willful indifference on the part of people, and that we needed to expect more of all our students, including those who underperform chronically.

In late March 2000, Bush proposed a $5 billion, five-year program to address what he saw as a national literacy crisis among children. This would become Reading First, a key provision of the No Child Left Behind Act.[2] But most of his education speeches stuck to broader themes and stayed away from discrete policy proposals. In them Bush argued that parents need to have more of a say in their child's education and more alternatives when confronted with poorly performing schools. While offering few specifics, he talked about getting help to kids who were experiencing problems in math. And he alluded to school choice for parents of kids stuck in failing schools, though he refrained from mentioning "vouchers." In addition, he talked about the need for more and better research into "what works" in education. In what would become a continuing theme going forward, Bush spoke of the need to develop "scientifically based" research and to make sure federal dollars only pay for things proven to work in the classroom. He cited the generation-long reading research conducted by the National Institutes of Health and asserted that making sure every child can read should be a national priority.

In other speeches Bush emphasized teacher quality and the important link between teaching and student achievement. In presentations laden with praise for the teaching profession, he discussed the need to make sure every child has a qualified teacher, someone who has studied the discipline and knows how to teach it. He coupled this with calls for ongoing local control in American education. Being a governor, Bush understood well that Washington does not have all the answers and that education is primarily a local and state concern. He saw a greater role for the national government in education—one that complemented local control rather than usurping it.

In other speeches he spoke to such themes as character, citizenship, and safety in America's schools. Referencing the spate of school shootings then plaguing the country, he said that schools should be safe havens, that parents need to know whether their child's school is safe, and that they must have options if it is not. He talked about the need to identify "unsafe" schools as being every bit as great as the need to identify "poor performing" schools and about the need for parents to have alternatives for their children in those schools.[3]

Setting Bush's education speeches apart was both their content and their lack of it. They were thoughtful and well crafted. They spoke to broad themes rather than specific policies. They touched upon issues that have rubbed edges raw in the education establishment for years—the need to hold schools (and by implication teachers and administrators) accountable and for better-qualified teachers, the idea of expanding schooling options for parents, the problem of school violence. But Bush refrained from offering specific suggestions or remedies. Rather, he sought to establish his credibility as a thoughtful and informed student of American education who understood the concerns of parents and taxpayers and saw a need for national action.

The speeches set him apart from both his Republican and Democratic rivals in several ways. The Republican Party had for years criticized the Department of Education and ridiculed the federal role in education, while simultaneously calling for such controversial reforms as vouchers. As recently as 1996, GOP presidential candidate Bob Dole, senator from Kansas, had attacked the nation's teachers' unions during his convention acceptance speech. And calls to dismantle the federal Department of Education go back to the Reagan years. Bush was having none of that. He was positioning himself as the thoughtful critic of education who saw a need for a federal role. His speeches attacked no one and blamed no one. They were positive and hopeful and comprehensive.

Countering the Republicans, the Democrats, under Clinton and now Gore, continued to extol the virtues of the education policies they had been offering up for almost a decade. They pointed to the need to reduce class size, the need for school uniforms, the need for better professional development for teachers. They embraced a spate of policy initiatives that rang with authenticity (who could be against smaller student-teacher ratios?) and had been embraced by the education establishment. Gore talked about accountability as well and pointed to the fact that, with President Clinton, he had pushed Congress to reauthorize the Elementary and Secondary Education Act in 1994, requiring states to test students at least once at the elementary, middle, and high school levels. Their themes were familiar, safe, tried, and true.

Also setting Bush apart from his rivals in both political parties was how he chose his audience. Education has almost always been a winning issue for Democrats nationwide. The teachers' unions have always supported Democratic candidates with both votes and money. And Democrats have earned that support, advancing policies that speak to the interests and concerns of the education establishment. Smaller classes mean more teachers. More teachers means more union members. By courting the education establishment, Democrats have succeeded in controlling the terms of the education debate and won the loyalty of educators, often winning elections as well. It is very smart politics. Republicans, on the other hand, by pushing a much more negative set of proposals—get rid of the Department of Education, give vouchers to parents for private school choice—not only alienated the education establishment but offered little in the way of a positive alternative to the Democrats. Republicans chose to enrage the opposition while never finding a constituency for their policy prescriptions.

George W. Bush, on the other hand, sought to broaden both the discussion and the audience. He chose to speak to everyday people, not just the education establishment, and to speak in terms they understood. His strategy aimed to tap popular sentiment about education. He understood that the American people care about their kids and their schools. He understood that teachers are, by and large, respected by parents. And he knew that years of perceived GOP attacks on education had not succeeded. For this reason, he went out his way to become identified positively with teachers and students. But even when appearing at schools, he would address his comments to parents, taxpayers, and business leaders and touch upon those themes he knew would resonate with them. He chose to get beyond the traditional audience for education politics, the education establishment, without ignoring or criticizing that establishment.[4] But Bush recognized that the real constituency for education reform will never be educators. The real constituents are the people who rely on public schools to educate their children, to train their employees, and to ensure the health and vitality of their communities. He knew how to change the terms of the education debate. He had learned that in Texas.

What came to be called the "Texas miracle" in education started long before George W. Bush became governor of Texas. The Texas education wars began in the 1980s, when Ross Perot sought to stir the pot with his criticisms of high school football and the need for Texans to get serious about improving the performance of the state's school. For more than a decade, under three governors, education was a dominant political issue—one that crossed party lines. When Bush challenged incumbent governor Ann Richards in 1994, he tried to take the issue away from her. During his campaign he stuck religiously to a few key themes: improving public education, reforming the juvenile-justice and welfare systems, and changing the state's tort laws. In an election that surprised everyone but Bush, Richards was easily defeated. Bush advisor Mark McKinnon would later recall that, despite the odds against him and all that was seemingly in Richards's favor, Bush "beat her like a red-headed stepchild."[5]

In office, Governor Bush sought to build on and institutionalize his predecessors' changes in education. He created an accountability system that emphasized testing based on state academic standards. He sought to establish a policy aimed at stopping the practice of social promotion, requiring students to pass a grade-level proficiency test in order to leave grades three, five, and eight. A centerpiece of his accountability plan tied teacher and administrator success to test scores on the Texas Assessment of Academic Skills (TAAS). During Bush's governorship, Houston superintendent Rod Paige received a number of $25,000 bonuses, in part for raising student test scores. Bush also pushed for safer schools and the ability to remove disruptive students from classrooms. And he established an early-reading program.

The governor's partner during this time, Margaret La Montagne, had joined his staff in January 1995. She quickly caught his eye, becoming a senior advisor.[6] Her portfolio was education, and she reported directly to Bush. La Montagne was key to Bush's success in education reform. She had worked for years for the Texas Association of School Boards and knew her way around the rough terrain of Texas education politics. And she knew that success in mastering that terrain would require bipartisanship and cooperation with the education establishment.

With the Democrats controlling both houses of the state legislature and occupying a constitutionally weak governorship, Bush proved adept at reaching across the aisle, developing a particularly good working relationship with the Speaker of the state house of representatives. He also made peace with the leadership of the state's teachers' unions, often seeking the public counsel of Gayle Fallon of the Houston Federation of Teachers. And he forged a strong partnership with the Texas business leadership through the work of Charles Miller, one the governor's appointees to the board of the University of Texas System. Miller, a multimillionaire, was attracted to Bush's commitment to accountability and his interest in continuing and building on previous governors' reform efforts.

The bipartisan reach across the aisles inclusive strategy was buttressed somewhat by money. Texas teachers welcomed Bush's emphasis on education and experienced raises during his time in office. But as governor, Bush tended to emphasize improving teachers' skills more than he did increasing their compensation. School boards benefited from Bush's decision to give them greater authority and autonomy, while decreasing the influence of the Texas Education Agency.[7] Riding a booming economy, the governor sought to pour significant new money into public education as a way of purchasing educators support for his initiatives. During his tenure as governor, state education spending rose 55 percent.[8] The strategy worked. Not only did Bush get the reforms he wanted, but they had the effect he wanted: schools began to improve.

As the presidential campaign heated up after the primaries and leading up to the conventions, education became a major issue. This in and of itself was unique since education represents a rather modest percentage of the federal budget and remains primarily a state and local issue. But Bush made it a national one, and Gore had no choice but to reciprocate and to treat it as such as well. And as the issue drew increased attention from both campaigns, Bush's record in Texas drew increased scrutiny from his critics and opponents. Predictably, the "Texas miracle" was being dubbed a mirage by some, including some well-respected education analysts and think tanks.

Writing in the *Washington Post* in September 2000, John Mintz reported that a growing number of skeptics were saying that "Texas' standardized tests are too easy and that aggressive test-drilling inflates children's scores and turns some Texas schools into drab factories for test preparation." He pointed to evidence suggesting the performance of Texas students on the TAAS was not reflected on other national tests, such as the National Assessment of Educational Progress (NAEP), and that the achievement gap was not narrowing, as the Bush campaign was claiming. Walter Haney of Boston College was quoted as saying, "The Texas miracle in education is a myth." Haney contended that the accountability system Bush had installed led to higher dropout rates by "mostly minorities," which in turn led to higher scores. The article went on to echo the growing chorus of critics who argued that a focus on taking tests narrows the curriculum, places too much pressure on students and teachers, and turns classrooms into nothing more than test-prep centers. In the same article, Bush's education advisor, Margaret La Montagne, stated, "If kids are practicing long division so they can do well on the test, then fine."[9]

In response, Jay Greene of the Manhattan Institute reported that "something very surprising happened in Texas during the 1990s: students stayed in school and learned more." Greene was reacting to what had become known as the "Texas miracle." What made it a miracle, of course, was that Texas was one of a handful (maybe two) states demonstrating real progress in public education.

This may not sound like such a surprising thing to say about education, but it is. The normal pattern in education has been that, despite a huge increase in resources over the past few decades and despite endless reform efforts, student achievement fails to improve significantly. Between 1961 and 1998, real per-pupil spending in public elementary and secondary schools has more than tripled, from $2,294 to $6,915. According to the NAEP, which is the most reliable long-term measure of educational achievement, test scores have hardly changed during this time of incredible spending growth.

According to Greene, Texas was bucking the national long-term trend. "Not only were the increases large," he argued, "but they occurred across the board demographically." NAEP math scores for Texas thirteen-year-olds climbed twelve points from 1990 to 1996. For black thirteen-year-olds, the increase was thirteen points; for Hispanics, it was eleven. "These are larger gains in six years than the U.S. has experienced over twenty years," Greene exclaimed. "The overall pattern in Texas is one of significant progress in student achievement, especially in math skills."

Citing a host of critics arguing that the miracle was really a myth, Greene ended his analysis by asserting that the Texas school-accountability system was the reason for education progress in the state.

What accounts for the Texas education miracle? Most of the reforms touted by teacher unions and their fellow travelers are unlikely explanations for increased student achievement in Texas during the 1990s. Reducing class size does not appear to explain the gains either. . . . Increasing per-pupil spending does not appear to explain the gains. . . . Increasing teaching qualifications does not appear to explain the gains. . . . Nor is a change in student demographics in Texas, the teacher union's favorite excuse for student performance, a likely explanation given that average student characteristics have changed little in Texas during the 1990s.

For Greene the conclusion was clear: "The most obvious explanation for the significant increase in student achievement in Texas is TAAS, a comprehensive system of measuring student achievement and holding students and schools accountable for the results." TAAS worked because it forced teachers "to teach their students how to read, write and do arithmetic." This was possible in Texas, he reasoned, because the "teacher unions were weak and senior government officials were determined to keep up the pressure." He doubted whether other states with stronger education establishments could see similar results under a similar system of accountability. In any event, the progress in Texas, begun before Bush but nourished and expanded by him, was real.[10]

The debate continued off and on for the remainder of the campaign. The assertion was made, with some accuracy, that while Texas students were improving, the reforms responsible for the improvements were in place before Bush was governor. Kevin Fullerton wrote in the *Austin Chronicle*, for example, "Much of what has helped to strengthen Texas' school system was in place before Bush ever became governor."[11]

But a report issued by the highly respected RAND Corporation caused the Bush campaign the most indigestion. Issued in October 2000, at the height of the campaign, the report questioned the performance of Texas students. While scores on the TAAS had indeed improved over time, the improvements could not be replicated on other national tests, such as the NAEP, calling the validity of the "Texas miracle" into question. The RAND report was also critical of how the Texas accountability system was administered and of the practice in Texas of giving teachers the questions on the TAAS each year after the test itself has been administered. "Although there is a new version of the exam each year, one version looks a lot like another in terms of the types of questions asked, terminology and graphics used, content areas covered," the report concluded. The clear implication was that teachers used the old tests as crib sheets for the next test. Reuters reported RAND researcher Stephen Kline as saying, "I think the 'Texas miracle' is a myth."

Curiously, the report came on the heels of an earlier RAND study that hailed the improvement of Texas students on TAAS. Now it, too, was brought into question. Predictably, the Bush campaign had hailed that earlier report and pointed with some satisfaction to its source as a well-established, highly regarded institution. Now it had to backtrack a bit and question RAND's reputation.

Predictably, Vice President Al Gore hopped on behind the RAND report in an attempt to regain the traditional Democratic advantage on education. Speaking to a crowd in Nashville, he sought to mix advocacy for his education plans with criticisms of Bush's record in Texas. Throughout the campaign, Gore had stuck to traditional Democratic education themes: small class size, teacher professional development, lifelong learning, more money. Now he stepped up his attack on Bush. Referring to the RAND report, Gore told the audience, "The study reported that, contrary to all we've been told, the achievement gap for Texas students has not narrowed, it has widened. The study called the claim that the achievement gap was closing in Texas, and I quote, 'false.'"[12]

The waning days of the campaign saw a flurry of activity in both camps of the education debate, with experts and advocates trotted out to counter the opponent's experts and advocates. After the election, with no clear victor, education, along with all the issues that had dominated the campaign, seemed to slide from view as the nation focused on ballots, hanging chads, and litigation in Florida.

⌒∞⌒

Throughout the previous year, as the primaries approached the November election, Bush's stump speech on education followed his core message. Calling himself a compassionate conservative, he harped on the need to hold schools accountable, keep control local, give parents more options, and make sure kids can read. He repeated over and over again the need to address the achievement gap between low-income and minority students and their more affluent white peers. He argued that the nation needed to expect more from its schools and from all its students. And he repeatedly employed a phrase that became the best of his campaign, calling upon the country to end "the soft bigotry of low expectations." It became an almost mind-numbing repetition—but it worked. Education was his issue, and it was a winning one.

Democrats sought time and again to counter Bush's message but were unable to get traction by returning time and again to old ideas. Republicans, both supporters of the governor and competitors for the nomination, were also caught somewhat off base. Conservatives, perhaps particularly those supportive of Bush, privately sniped at the "compassionate conservative" talk—resenting the implication that conservatives were not compassionate but that Bush's brand of conservatism was. Nor did they quite know what to make of all the fuss over education. It was hardly even a national issue, to their way of thinking, after all. But Bush made it one, and the polls consistently gave him the advantage on it.

While the details of Bush's education initiative would not be unveiled until after he became president, his staff had begun assembling the plan early in the campaign. Margaret La Montagne and Sandy Kress, a friend of the governor and former member of the Dallas school board, relied heavily on their experience in Texas. They dispatched junior members of the team, Nina Rees and Sarah Youseff, to research what other states were doing and keep track of emerging policies. By the summer of 2000, Bush was providing more specifics in his education speeches and growing more comfortable with each delivery. It was clear that accountability was the primary message.

Testing has been a part of education since the first teacher met the first student. And it has been a part of federal education policy since 1994, when the Improving America's Schools Act called for testing students at least once in elementary, middle, and high school. During the 1990s, the accountability movement had spread among the states, surely encouraged by the 1994 legislation. States enacted academic standards in various disciplines and began the process of aligning curriculum and test to those standards. By the campaign of 2000, the standards-and-accountability movement was nothing new to American education, but Bush sought to take it to the next level. He would have every state do what Texas and a very few other states were doing: test every student in grades three through eight every year in reading and math. According to Bush, annual testing was critical to educational improvement. Arguing that "what's tested gets taught," Bush maintained that tests forced the schools to get serious about instruction and student achievement. He countered critics who foresaw too much testing and "teaching to the tests" by asserting that testing was the only way to get an objective, comparable measure of student achievement. And annual testing was necessary because "a student could fall years behind before you know it" otherwise. He joked with his audiences about how much students hate testing, referring to his own lackluster performance as a student. He tended to ignore the critics, focusing on his ideas rather than their concerns. And he constantly sought to maintain an optimistic tone: high expectations for all students, opportunities and results for all kids.

Bush went into the nation's urban centers with this hopeful message, seeking to undermine the hold the Democrats have always had in the cities and in minority and low-income communities. Again, while not taking on his detractors directly, he talked about the schools his audiences sent their children to and the need to "raise our expectations." He sought to appeal directly to these voters, unlike any of his Republican or Democratic competitors, by talking of the "soft bigotry of low expectations" and the need to confront the achievement gap in American education so that all children might succeed. In these speeches he dwelled upon the need to "disaggregate" tests scores by socioeconomic criteria in order to uncover the achievement gap. As Bush said countless times, "If you don't disaggregate, the achievement gap gets hidden in the averages." A school could mask an achievement gap among, say, African American students with its overall strong performance. Disaggregating would force public schools to deal with the problem. This message began to resonate among traditionally Democratic audiences frustrated and disenchanted with their children's schools. And Bush did not argue for abandoning those schools with vouchers but for improving them with accountability.

More importantly, the message was about kids, rhetorically at least. In 1994, the reauthorization of the Elementary and Secondary Education Act had been about "improving America's schools." Bush sought to put a human face on the education challenge. Schools matter because of the students in them. His mantra targeted the hearts of voters by focusing on their children: leave no child behind.

Ironically, early on in the internal deliberations over the Bush education plan, the decision was made to make the school the unit of academic accountability rather than the student. Public schools exist to teach all children. Determining how well schools discharge that responsibility was a sensible way to focus accountability efforts. Of course, schools must educate a diverse student body. The typical public elementary school in this country might have students with several non-English native languages, a broad array of learning disabilities, and disadvantaged, low-income family backgrounds, or no family at all. Was it fair to assume a school with these sorts of challenges could perform as well as, say, a school in a wealthy suburb, where the vast majority of students are white and come from middle-class or higher families that have resources? Why not make the unit of academic accountability the student? Why not focus on the improvement in a student's achievement from year to year?

This would become the subject of intense debate during the early congressional discussions of Bush's plan. But during the campaign, Bush aides dismissed the idea. First of all, few states had data on student achievement that went beyond the school level and was student specific. Texas and North Carolina did. But most states had refrained from enacting student-level performance systems due to concerns about privacy and costs. The idea of Uncle Sam forcing states down this road was dismissed out of hand. It would be too expensive and politically controversial. Moreover, such an accountability system would set the student up as an excuse for failure. School officials would point to the character and makeup of their student bodies and whine about the challenges of getting their kids to read. Or they would point out that one student or another had made progress, while not yet working at grade level.

This was also to emerge as a key component of Bush's plans for school accountability. The goal would become ensuring that every student is performing at grade level in reading and math; that is, third graders are reading at a third-grade level, and so forth. Again, the idea had a certain basic appeal that was hard to argue against. Later, critics would assert that this goal is unrealistic, that it is not possible for every child in every school to perform at grade level. What about special education students or non-English-speaking students? Does improving student achievement not count? But for Bush and his team, grade level was the key. All they were asking of America's schools was to make sure America's children were performing at grade level!

Side by side with his emphasis on accountability was his constant deference to local control. As he was a governor, this had a certain authenticity that resonated with his Republican and gubernatorial colleagues. His speeches included throwaway lines like, "Washington doesn't educate kids, teachers do," and "The farther away you are from a school, the less you know about how it works and the less influence you should have over the education that school provides." The truth, of course, was that as Bush kept pushing his education ideas, a large federal role seemed to take shape. Still, Bush held firmly to the local-control principle and wove it throughout his ideas for No Child Left Behind.

For candidate Bush, public school accountability would be a national policy implemented according to state direction. Following the lead set in the 1994 reauthorization, states would establish the broad parameters for school accountability. States would enact academic standards in reading and math—something every state was already doing in 2000. States would test their students on those standards—something states were already supposed to be doing by 2000. States would establish, administer, and develop ways to employ the tests to get at student and school achievement. As long as every child in grades three through eight in every school was tested every year, the states would have discretion as to how that was accomplished. For Bush, this was local control.

There were some immediate problems with all of this, however. Most states were only just getting engaged in the standards-setting process, and very few were testing all students in all schools in the grades designated. So, while on paper the Bush plan seemed to dovetail nicely with what President Clinton had established in 1994, the reality was quite different. Bush's ideas would push states hard, giving critics plenty of ammunition with regard to just how much local control was left to them. Moreover, all of this would cost money. The campaign put off all discussion of financing the education initiative, however. The high ground was accountability, called for by Washington but designed and implemented by the states.

As the campaign moved forward, more bits and pieces of the education puzzle were put into place. There should be report cards for schools, school districts, and states. These report cards should tell parents and taxpayers their schools' rank on the state's accountability system. They should provide the sort of "transparency" that allows citizens to understand whether their schools are doing the job or not. Citing a need to appeal to teachers, the campaign started talking about the importance of the profession while embracing the call for a "highly qualified teacher" in every classroom. Explaining what that meant was put off until later. But then, how could one take issue with the principle? And the best teachers should be assigned to the most academically needy students. Again, how this would be accomplished was reserved for later discussion. Returning to a theme he had embraced early in the campaign, Bush asserted that schools with a record of violence must be identified and parents notified; accomplishing both objectives would be left up to the states.

All of this was somewhat new to a Republican Party so persistently opposed to a large federal role in education. Most of it was hardly new at the state or local level. The GOP was used to harping on the need for competition in the public education monopoly, not building on that monopoly. The Bush campaign had a response for that: give parents choices when their kids are in failing schools. The details could be worked out later. But public and private school choice, charter schools, magnet schools, and tutoring services were all offered up as options and alternatives a President Bush would provide parents.

Reading was a constant theme in Bush's education speeches during the campaign. In Texas, he had continued a reading initiative begun by his predecessor that was having an impact. Citing the need to improve the "science of education" so that the nation only paid for "what we know works" in teaching and learning, Bush talked of the science of teaching reading.

He would reference the work of the National Institutes of Health and its outspoken research director Reid Lyon. He would talk of the importance of making sure children learn how to read at an early age, tying good reading instruction with the need to measure student performance. He would point to the fact that Washington already paid for reading instruction and support but was not getting what it paid for. Scores were low nationwide and unacceptably low among Hispanic, African American, and low-income children. "The research tells us how to teach reading so children can read at grade level. We should only pay for teaching that we know works," Bush asserted often. Again, this had a certain immediate appeal: only pay for what works. But this would entail limiting choices at the state and local levels. Rather than sending to the states millions of dollars to support reading instruction and programs that the state and local education agencies would decide how to spend, Bush talked of telling them how to spend it. This seemed at odds with the principle of local control but appealed to those who felt schools waste taxpayer money and do not educate kids.

As a package, Bush's education-reform proposals had a certain commonsense appeal: getting every child on grade level, ensuring that every school is progressing toward that goal every year and that families in poorly performing schools get help, ending achievement gaps among kids, and spending taxpayer dollars only on those programs that really work. Just as importantly, the way Bush spoke of his proposals made it difficult to oppose them, at least rhetorically. His message was about the possibilities of American education—the hope and the promise. He did not attack the education establishment. He did not point out its failures. Rather, candidate Bush talked about its potential and the potential of every child.

Bush's constant reference to the achievement gaps in American education set him dramatically apart from any of his competitors as well as any previous national education-reform initiatives. Others, among them Bill Clinton, had spoken about accountability, about the need for academic standards and testing. Clinton had even called for disaggregating test scores by race, ethnicity, and other categories in order to look at how various socioeconomic groups compared on student achievement. But he had not required states to report the information. More importantly, the Clinton administration had been restrained generally in its enforcement of federal education policy. Most states had therefore not acted to comply with Clinton's Improving America's Schools Act. Few were doing in 2000 what Washington had required of them since 1994.

Against this backdrop, Bush's emphasis on education must have seemed merely like more of the same potentially coming from Washington. But there was a difference. Bush cared personally and passionately about the issue. It was really the only domestic issue that mattered to him. He found the achievement gap personally troubling, and his constant reference to it was intentional, even if it was questionable politically. "The soft bigotry of low expectations" was, to Bush, the root of many of the nation's economic, racial, and urban problems. But it was also something that few in public life were willing to confront directly. Bush would make it impossible not to confront the problem.

Ironically, of course, here was a Republican seeking to force the country to confront an issue that affected primarily traditional Democratic constituencies. The victims of the achievement gap were minority (primarily African American and Hispanic), low-income, and non-English-speaking students. They were enrolled primarily in urban and very rural schools in high-poverty neighborhoods and areas. They were the descendents of generations of traditionally Democratic voters, if their families voted at all, and the children of relative newcomers to this country. Bush's education campaign focused on the need to make sure these children were not left behind. Here was a Republican presidential candidate embracing and espousing policies that would seem more natural to his opponent's party and seeking to speak to families that were certainly more at home there. In the end, it was good politics and generated enormous positive energy for the nascent Bush administration. But for Bush it was more than good politics. It was the right thing to do. Typically, however, Bush failed to win over many minority voters with his call to end the achievement gap. In time, as his proposals wound their way through a Republican Congress, he found they encountered problems with members of his own party as well.

cᴑᴂᴐ

There can be little argument with the assertion that Americans care about, and are willing to spend their hard-earned money on, public education. Most of the money that goes to America's public schools comes from state and local revenues, not Washington. In 2001, federal dollars devoted to K–12 education averaged maybe 7 percent of what states spent on it. Most states at that time devoted approximately 16 percent of their budgets to K–12 public education. In 2001, almost 30 percent of Michigan's budget was earmarked for its public schools. Approximately 10 percent of Alaska's budget went to public education.

The national average per-pupil expenditure in public education was $7,614. New Jersey spent the most on a per-pupil basis ($11,848), followed closely by New York ($10,924). Arizona spent the least on a per-pupil basis of any state in the Union at the time ($5,814). Washington DC, then home to perhaps the most poorly performing school district in the nation, spent upward of $11,700 per student.[13]

Public education is expensive business, and it is more expensive in cities than in towns. The average per-pupil expenditure in the nation's urban areas was around $8,300. In the nation's suburbs it was a little less, around

$8,000. In rural America public education costs still a bit less, about $7,500 on a per-pupil basis.

Considered in total, Americans spent more on their children's public schools than just about any other country on earth. Only Switzerland, Norway, Austria, and Denmark spent more on a per-pupil basis. Public education is a huge enterprise in this country, exceeding $418 billion in 2001.

Where does all this money go? How do state, local, and federal taxpayer dollars translate into education expenditures? If one were to look into school district budgets in 2001, on average 51 percent of the spending went to instruction. A little more than 27 percent underwrote such things as administration, support services, operations, and maintenance. Capital expenditures ate up about 11 percent of the typical school district budget. The remainder went to such things as transportation and instructional staff support. These school district budgets, generally, were approved by popularly elected school boards at school board meetings all across America. It is almost an annual ritual, sometimes attended with some controversy, often not.

But while school district budgets can help to explain where the taxpayer's money goes, they do not provide much information regarding how dollars translate into learning. In 2001, that was impossible to determine in America. It seemed Americans were willing to pay their taxes, and America's schools were willing to spend the taxpayers' money, but almost no one could explain what sort of educational return the taxpayers' got for their investment. School officials could explain what they spent money on and defend their budgets and requests for more money each year, but they could not say what educational difference a dollar made. And few were ever asked to do so. Public education was a necessity, and taxpayers recognized that.

But while relating expenditures to educational outcomes at the school or school district level might have been a subject best left to mystics, the evidence available on student performance across the country was troubling. The results of NAEP scores, often referred to as the "nation's report card," were troubling. The majority of America's fourth and eighth graders were scoring either at basic or below basic levels in both reading and math. Approximately 40 percent of the nation's fourth graders and about 70 percent of its eighth graders were underachieving in math. Reading scores were a little better, but there was almost no improvement in the scores between fourth and eighth grades. Fewer than one-third of America's fourth and eighth graders were considered proficient or better in the subjects tested. Proficient, meaning competent in the discipline tested, was not a very high standard to which to aspire. And the scores were even lower in urban schools, where per-pupil expenditures were generally higher.

On an international basis, American students were well behind many of their peers in other countries. In math, the United States was outperformed by such nations as Singapore, South Korea, and Japan and on a par with

England and Bulgaria. In science, the United States was on a par with Latvia and Bulgaria and far below Singapore, Japan, and South Korea. And the news was compounded by the fact that test scores for American students became less competitive the longer they were in school. In other words, America's fourth graders performed better against international competition than America's eighth graders. As one pundit has often quipped, "The longer our kids stay in school, the dumber they get."[14] While the nation outspent most others on a per-pupil basis, its students were less than competitive with those of most of the nations tested.

In 2001, there was almost no way to determine the cause of such mediocre performance. Plenty of excuses were offered, but few explanations. One might have been teacher quality—it might have been the case that too many of America's children were being taught by underprepared teachers—but there was no way to know that. Teacher preparation and professional development were almost completely determined by state policy. States determined what constituted appropriate credentials for teachers, and institutions of higher education had a monopoly on training teachers. Once teachers were prepared, their assignment to schools was almost completely driven by local decision making and, more often than not, by local contracts. In other words, it was next to impossible to determine a good teacher from a not-so-good teacher and, therefore, very difficult to make sure the better teachers were assigned where the need was greatest. It was assumed, generally, that a certified teacher was competent and better than a noncertified teacher, but there was no evidence available to support that proposition. Most importantly, there was no evidence available to demonstrate a teacher's impact on student learning. In 2001, American education was the subject of debate, discord, conversation, and controversy. There was a sense, fed by much of the available information on spending and results, that the nation was not doing very well.

How could this be so? How could the wealthiest nation on earth produce such a mediocre system of public education? The United States is a world leader in per-pupil spending on elementary and secondary education. Yet, it trails behind much of the rest of the world when it comes to student performance. Americans, generous when it comes to supporting education, care deeply about their schools and the education America's children receive. Public opinion polls consistently report this. So, if it were a matter of money and concern, public education in America would be excellent. Instead, while excellent schools and superior performing students exist in this country, they appear to be the exception rather than the rule. There are "islands of excellence, surrounded by a sea of mediocrity," as Rod Paige has put it. And in some places, in some schools, mediocrity is a generous term. In some places, in some schools, failure is the norm, and a generation or more of young people are the victims.

There are surely many possible explanations for this. Perhaps Paul Houston of the American Association of School Administrators is correct. Perhaps we have come to expect something from our system of public education that the system was not designed to do: "provide a better education for all" rather than merely a "good education for some."[15] If that is the case, then merely pouring additional resources into that system will not do the trick. The system itself has to undergo change in order to respond to what is now expected of it. Perhaps it is not really a "system" problem at all but a wider social problem. The world in which public schools exist today differs dramatically from the world into which public education was born over a century and a half ago. Ask any teacher or principal in any school anywhere in America: "Our students come to us with lots of problems." "Parents don't care and aren't supportive." "We are asked to be lots of things for our kids—parent, therapist, counselor, brother, sister, nutritionist, disciplinarian, nurse—I signed on to be a teacher." The litany goes on with almost dulling familiarity. And it is all true, of course.

But if the above hypothesis is true, then it would seem the system must be altered to respond to the world in which it exists, for that world is not going to change to accommodate the system. If there ever was a time when Mom and Dad and Johnny and Sally gathered around the dinner table every evening and discussed how things went at school that day, a time when parents packed parent-teacher association meetings, helped their children with their homework, volunteered in the school library, and attended meetings of the school board religiously, then those idyllic days are long gone. And they will not return. If, in our national subconscious, we conjure up a utopian world of a *Leave It to Beaver* America, it is the stuff of fantasy. America has never been like that. And it surely is not today.

But America is a wealthy country, and Americans care about, and want the best for, their children. America's educators work hard, are underpaid and undervalued, and care about their students. Our mediocre performance is not due to a lack of caring or effort. If it is not resources, effort, interest, or concern, then what is holding America's schools and her children back?

⊂◈⊃

Imagine you have been asked to interview for the position of CEO of an organization in a medium-sized city or town. When you arrive, you get a tour of the organization. Its physical infrastructure is in excellent condition, although improvements are needed. As you learn more about the organization, you discover some interesting and important things. The organization's annual operating budget is one of the largest of any business in town, as is its payroll. As you ask about basic management issues, you learn that the employees of this organization are highly educated, many possessing advanced degrees. You learn that once employees have been with the organization for two or three years and demonstrated a certain level of competence, they are virtually guaranteed their jobs for as long they want them—though it is uncertain how an employee's competence is demonstrated. The employees are loyal to the organization too; several have worked there for over twenty or twenty-five years. You learn, as well, that in this organization, every employee is guaranteed a pay increase every year. When you inquire, you find out that the salary increases are tied to length of service. In other words, every year every employee gets a pay raise, and those who have been there the longest get paid the most. Moreover, in this organization, in the name of "job equity," employees are all paid according to a scale based almost solely on length of service. Job specialties, extra effort for the organization, community service, and so forth: none of these influences employee compensation. Nor does lack of effort or poor performance. Those who come early, work hard, and leave late are paid the same as employees who arrive late, do the minimum, and leave early. In this organization, all are treated "equally," compensation is tied to years of service, and jobs are guaranteed for life. When you ask why employee performance is not a factor, you are told that measuring their performance is almost impossible and that most indicators discussed in the past are inadequate or distorted. You are told the organization has no control over the "raw material" it has to work with; therefore, it is unfair to make distinctions among employees based upon how productive they are with that "raw material."

As you size things up, you find the organization intriguing—and surely a management challenge. The facilities and the payroll and operating budget suggest adequate resources, although it could always use more. You ask some questions: "Can management incentives be introduced to encourage greater productivity among employees?" "Can exceptions to the compensation plan be made to accommodate high-demand, low-supply specialties the organization might need and to reward outstanding effort that contributes to the welfare of the organization?" "Can basic hours of operation be changed to accommodate community needs?" "Can the size and compensation of the workforce be changed to reflect changing economic conditions?" "If appropriate performance indicators can be developed, can they be implemented and employee compensation, or a fraction of it, be tied to those indicators?" The response to each of you inquiries is, "Probably not." Those questions would have to be put before the organization's board of directors, which shapes the contours of the organization's working arrangement with its employees. You would report directly to that board of directors.

Now things are getting interesting. You meet the board. All nine members seem competent, committed to the organization and its purpose. They seem to reflect a cross section of the community, as well, and are relatively well-known there. "Can I attend a meeting of the board, to get a flavor of how they work?" All meetings are open to the public, but it seems few ever attend. Curious, since the board has oversight of such a large organization with a large budget. You ask members of the board the same sorts of question you asked earlier, and they respond the same way: "That's not the way we operate." "It's been tried elsewhere and hasn't worked." "It would be impossible to win such concessions from our employees." "We've always done it this way."

You have heard enough. You cannot sign on as CEO of an organization that leaves little or no room for sound management practices. And you cannot work for a board of directors that abdicates its fiduciary responsibilities.

As you begin to leave, the members of the board seem surprised by your lack of interest and decision not to pursue the position. It is handsomely packaged, with a very large salary, benefits, and prestige in the community. More importantly, you would be "in charge" of what many feel is the single most important organization in the town, one responsible for its very welfare, its economic and community development, its future. You do not take the job.

While the scenario is somewhat exaggerated, it paints, for the most part, an accurate picture of what the organization of public education in America looks like—and it is not a pretty picture. Basic management principles are absent and rejected. Because of this, anyone sincerely interested in improving the management of the system is hamstrung. It is a system that encourages conformity and rewards complacency—or, at the very least, does not penalize it. It is a system that prizes artificial and empty collegiality over productivity and innovation and thus underproduces and stifles creativity. And yet, it is a system the American people have willingly paid for, for generations. It is a system that will determine America's competitiveness, and that of every community in America and every American, in a competitive world. That much is at stake.

But let us look at that organization from the viewpoint of one who is interested in becoming a public school teacher. All the research tells us the vast majority of those who seek to enter the teaching profession do so for the "right" reasons. They care about children, want to help them succeed, and are driven by high purpose and idealism to the classroom. Many come from families of educators, no doubt growing up in homes that foster a respect and admiration for those who teach. "America's teachers are America's heroes," Rod Paige has said. Perhaps. Given the world in which they work, "heroic" might be an apt description of the sort of effort it takes to succeed.

Before becoming a teacher in a public school in America, you must become certified. This certification credential, designed, regulated, and designated by state action, is your "license" to teach. Getting certified is comparable to a doctor's taking the boards or a lawyer's passing the bar exam. Somewhat.

When you enroll in the school of education at the university, you are told what it will take to become a teacher. The courses you take toward your major in elementary education are all taught in the school of education. After your third semester in college, when you have decided go into teaching, you rarely set foot in a classroom in the school of arts and sciences. Education becomes your passion. Many of the courses you take focus on effective practices, curriculum and instruction, classroom management, education theory, and child psychology. You are taught by career educators, most of whom possess doctorates in education and have taught generations of teachers. They instill in you a passion for the profession you have chosen.

Toward the end of your undergraduate career, you are a student teacher at an elementary school not far from the university. The experience is somewhat sobering. The teacher you are placed with is a pro, with ten years of service under her belt. She gives you your freedom almost from the moment you enter her classroom. But she is a mentor as well. She helps you learn to manage the gap between the theory of the university classroom and the reality of the elementary school classroom. The students need constant attention and direction. There are countless classroom disruptions, with children picking on one another or just not paying attention. Their performance on daily exercises in reading and math is as variable as the families they come from. The diversity of the neighborhood in which the school sits is on display in your classroom: it is multiethnic, with several native languages, some poverty, no real wealth, and some single-parent households. But for the six weeks you spend at the school, these are "your kids." And with the help of your mentor, you manage to find your way and to help your students find theirs. The experience only serves to whet your appetite even more for the profession you have chosen.

As an undergraduate you excel. Your graduating grade point average hovers around an A–. Not bad, considering your score on the Scholastic Aptitude Test (SAT), the test you took to get into the university, had been mediocre. And you surprise yourself a bit with your performance on the state's certification tests. Since your chosen field is elementary education, you do not have to take any certification exams in specific disciplines, such as math, history, or science. You do take a "general knowledge" test that you ace. And so, as a freshly minted college graduate with a major in elementary education and a state teaching certificate, you strike out to achieve your dream.

Years into your career, all of your passion now sounds like the naïve exuberance of youth. The profession does not turn out to be the stuff of your dreams. You start at a good elementary school in the city, teaching fourth grade. Your students are a challenge on every front. Your colleagues are collegial at first. But as you begin your career, they watch you warily. They tell you to pace yourself, to work with your kids but not to get too close to them. As you do both and try to foster a sense of family in your classroom, you find yourself working long hours and using your own money to help supply the classroom with what you feel is needed but the school cannot afford to make available. And your classroom is everything you feel it should be—full of color, rich in books and activities. Your efforts begin paying off too. Your students respond, and their families show an interest missing in other classrooms.

But as your efforts increase, they seem to have the opposite effect on many of your colleagues. They do not appreciate the way you show them up with your enthusiasm, dedication, and willingness to extend any effort to help your kids. You know they feel you will "get over it" as the routine of daily life in the classroom gradually makes the effort you put in unsustainable. They are right. The psychic rewards of seeing your children improve are important, but after a few years in the profession, psychic income is not enough. Extra hours and effort may produce educational results for your students but not enough additional income for you. While your salary increases with each year of teaching, in some years even eclipsing the rate of inflation, it does not, in your opinion, reflect the effort you put into your job, especially compared to what your "colleagues" do. Moreover, teaching has become almost a solitary profession for you. Days are not filled with a lot of interaction with your fellow teachers, sharing ideas and helping one another. Rather, each day gradually acquires a dull rhythm of managing the classroom, playground, and cafeteria. And as the years go by, the management becomes more difficult rather than easier, as might be expected as one gains experience. The job gets tougher, the rewards seem fewer, and satisfaction gradually disappears.

As the years go by, you find yourself pushed in too many directions. The love for your students compels you to continue to extend yourself too much. Your need to earn more money leads you to work on graduate degrees during the summers, as well as to take a part-time job. You take advantage of every opportunity for professional development you can. Although you find much of it a waste of time, it means more income and usually provides some modest dividend in your classroom. But as the daily grind and pressure begin to spill over more and more into your personal life, you realized it is time to do something else. And so, seven years after you began teaching, you abandon that career for another that will pay better, that will refresh your soul as well as your pocketbook.

Much of this is, of course, an exaggeration—but only up to a point. Most of the young men and women who go to college to become teachers do not take many courses in academic departments or disciplines. They take their courses in schools and departments of education. They take math for educators and science for educators. The average grade point average for students in America's education schools is higher than it is for their peers in the arts and sciences, particularly the sciences. Yet, the average SAT scores of students entering those schools of education is usually much lower.[16] Most of America's aspiring teachers spend only a number of weeks in a real public school classroom as undergraduate student teachers—this is a limited, measured, monitored, and artificial experience.

Among the states, acquiring a license to teach usually consists of overcoming a number of state-imposed hurdles aimed at ensuring that anyone who enters a public school classroom in that state is at least minimally qualified to teach the students in it. It is a *de minimus* qualification. Surely some states have more rigorous certification requirements than others, but no state can be said to have anything approaching a rigorous teacher-certification policy. It is a threshold. While some states have enacted policies aimed at ensuring licensed educators acquire advanced degrees and professional development in order to keep those licenses and stay in the classroom, no state has enacted policies seeking to relate teacher licensure and retention to student achievement. It is a bureaucratic process, not an educational one.

Indeed, an understanding of the relationship between how hard one works at teaching and how well students perform seems nonexistent in American public education. Neither is there much sense of any relationship in place between work effort and salary. Because of this, there is little incentive to ensure students excel or to go the extra mile for them. There are incentives to stay in the profession. Each year brings some additional income. But those things that attract individuals to teaching—that sense of purpose, of making a difference, of helping young people—gradually are overcome by the nature of the work and the system in which it takes place. It is true that most of those who go into teaching either leave after a few years or remain in the profession for the long haul. Those who leave often cite salary as a reason, but they also often cite the teaching profession. It is not what they expected. They leave it unfulfilled and disappointed. And they leave behind students who will never benefit from what these teachers might have contributed to their lives.

Curiously, states have consistently made it very difficult for men and women to go into the teaching profession unless they choose to do so when they begin their college career. An individual who has pursued a career in engineering, for example, and decides he would like to teach high school math often (depending on state policy) has to complete the same undergraduate coursework in education and go through the same certification process as any teacher in that state. This often takes years to do, which is hardly an incentive to go into teaching in mid-career. And yet, many such individuals are more qualified to teach than teachers certified by the state and already in the classroom. In American public education there is no solid, reliable, identifiable relationship between teacher certification and teacher quality. Licensure matters. Teacher quality does not. It is almost as though good teaching takes place in spite of the system.

⁓

The transition from the Bush campaign to the Bush administration was compacted, of course, by the conditions that surrounded the presidential election of 2000. The Supreme Court decided the issue with its ruling in *Bush v. Gore*, handed down on December 12, 2000, having heard oral arguments in the case the day before. Bush and his transition team, then, had about a month and a half to organize an administration and prepare to govern.

In truth, the Bush transition team had been conducting very secret operations since mid-November in hopeful anticipation of ultimate victory. But they had been very discreet, not wanting to create the popular impression that they felt victory was a forgone conclusion. Still, not long after the December decision, the president-elect began announcing his cabinet choices. His choice to oversee the federal Department of Education, and by implication his number one domestic priority, was the product of some internal deliberations and squabbling among his closest advisors. Margaret La Montagne had primary ownership of education for Governor Bush and was not about to relinquish it to any secretary of education. But she also understood she was in no position even to be considered for that job. Moreover, she was inclined to stay by the president-elect's side, should she be asked and should she agree to join the administration in Washington. Sandy Kress, a longtime Bush education advisor and lifelong Democrat, was already engaged with La Montagne in drafting bits and pieces of what would become a blue print for No Child Left Behind and had been since well before the election was decided. He had determined he would, if asked, join the administration as an informal, unpaid, in-house consultant and counsel to work on the education plan. Both La Montagne and Kress sought for the president-elect an education secretary who would be seen as an advocate for children and education reform, had some credentials within the education community, and, most of all, understood that the White House would steer education policy and politics, not the secretary and not the department.

A number of names surfaced during the curtailed transition period. They were leaked by transition team staff in an effort to gauge popular reaction. In truth, only two individuals received serious consideration: Lisa Graham Keegan, a former Arizona secretary of education, and Roderick Paige, the current superintendent of schools in Houston, Texas. Both were well-known in education circles. Keegan had a reputation as a maverick who favored such hot-button issues as vouchers and charter schools. She had been among a small band of state education leaders who had formed a reform-minded organization, the Education Leaders Council, aimed at shaking up the status quo. Attractive, intelligent, articulate, and politically savvy, she had been in the Arizona House of Representatives before becoming a national education-reform personality. She was well-known to La Montagne, Kress, and the president-elect and liked by them. So was Rod Paige.

Paige had an altogether different reputation and background from Keegan. An African American who had grown up in the segregated South, Paige had deep roots in almost every aspect of education. With a doctoral degree from Indiana University in physical education, Paige had been a college football coach, professor, and education school dean. But he had acquired something of a reformer's reputation while serving on the school board of the Houston Independent School District and then as its superintendent. A major urban school district, it had experienced improvement under Paige's watch and was seen as something of a model for urban districts across the country. Bush, La Montagne, and Kress had watched Paige's success in Houston and called upon his expertise frequently in Texas. It only made sense that they would consider him for the secretary's job. He was a known quantity with a real record of success. And he was African American, which would send the right message from a new administration eager to close the achievement gap. He could talk from experience and to an audience that remained skeptical of the new president and his party. He was not a politician. He was an educator—respected, experienced, and accomplished.

Keegan met with the transition team in December and felt things had gone well. In the top-secret environment of the transition, every effort was made to keep the press and public uninformed of the final names Bush was considering for key administration positions. For each major job, a number of names were assembled and vetted. From these, a handful might be invited to meet with some of Bush's advisors. Of that handful, a precious few would be invited to meet with the president-elect. Keegan hardly needed a meeting since she was well-known to and liked by Bush's inner circle and Bush himself. But in December she traveled to Austin for the obligatory session. Upon returning to her home outside of Phoenix, she told family and some close friends that she thought she had the job. Somehow this got back to La Montagne and the transition team, and they were outraged. The vow of secrecy had been shattered—and with it their trust in Keegan to be a true team player—ending her chance to become Bush's secretary of education.

Something else, however, had undermined any chance Keegan might have had at getting the job: her personality. Keegan was an outspoken education reformer who enjoyed a strong reputation as a public speaker. The columnist George Will had once touted her for vice presidential consideration. She enjoyed the spotlight and performed well in it. This presented a problem for La Montagne. She did not want a secretary of education who might exercise too much independent judgment or garner too much publicity. Education policy and politics were going to be driven by the president and White House. In this administration the secretary would carry out the orders of others. La Montagne questioned whether Keegan would be too difficult to manage. The president-elect had been inclined to go with Keegan, but the fact that she had spoken publicly of her visit and interview, coupled with La Montagne's lobbying against her and for Rod Paige, convinced him to look elsewhere.

Paige's session with the team and Bush had gone well. He had the added advantages of having been a family friend for some time and being a Texan. That was not an unimportant aspect of his personal resume. The level of loyalty and trust among Bush's inner circle derived, in no small degree, from the fact that many he relied upon the most were Texans he had known for a long time. Karl Rove, Harriet Miers, Alberto Gonzales, La Montagne, and Kress: all were Texans with ties to Bush going back many years. Paige could claim similar status. His selection appeared solid. But Paige was a bit stunned by the sudden turn of events and wanted to slow things down a bit. He needed to "get his head around this," as he would later say. He was honored to be considered, of course, but he was unsure what the nature would be of his relationship with the new White House, with La Montagne and Kress, both of whom he knew and knew about.

As Paige warmed to the prospect of becoming a member of a president's cabinet, he also understood he would be coming in from a position of some weakness. He knew little about the U.S. Department of Education, and he knew even less about Washington politics. He would need around him people he could trust and who understood how he thought, acted, and worked. He informed La Montagne that he would want to bring with him to Washington his closest advisors from the Houston school district: Terry Abbott, his public-affairs officer, and Susan Sclafani, his chief academic officer. La Montagne bristled at the idea of someone being considered for the president-elect's cabinet placing conditions on accepting the job. In her mind, the new White House would decide who worked in the agencies, not the new cabinet officers. Moreover, neither Abbott nor Sclafani was a seasoned veteran of national education policy and politics. Even worse, Sclafani, albeit a very successful and respected educator, was a Democrat. Paige would not budge though. After a number of exchanges, some a bit heated, he got his way. It was the first of a number of such confrontations with La Montagne that would come to define his relationship with the White House during his time as secretary.

In late December 2000, only weeks before the newly elected president was to take his oath of office, George W. Bush introduced Roderick Paige to the nation as his choice for secretary of education. It was a more important personnel announcement than usual because of the importance the new president planned to place on education. Paige was the third African American named to the cabinet, behind Colin Powell and Condoleezza Rice. And most in the education community hailed his selection as an inspired choice.

The days following the announcement were a blur for Paige. Suddenly he was a national figure, something of a celebrity, barraged with both congratulations and information. He began almost around-the-clock meetings and briefings about his new duties and responsibilities. Suddenly his life was no longer his own. The education transition team, led by Bill Hansen, a longtime Washington education insider who had served in President George H. W. Bush's administration, embraced Paige and began the process of preparing him for the confirmation hearings that would come as soon as the new Congress was seated and before the January 20 inaugural. Paige studied briefing books, began a series of courtesy visits to senators' offices, and tried to adjust to living out of a suitcase in a cramped and musty old Holiday Inn located directly across the street from his new post at the Department of Education. And he spent a considerable amount of time, as much as he could find, alone. He preferred solitude and quiet to read and reflect. He was not at home in most social settings and found it hard to make easy conversation. And yet, his life would now be defined by the need to "mix and mingle" and "meet and greet" and make appearances and shake hands and seem very interested in whatever anyone said.

Washington, sadly, places a premium on men and women's ability to play an elaborate game of charades. The conversations among elected and appointed officials are full of the courtesies and accoutrements of rank and station. One is expected to be deferential to office and rank, to attend social functions and to be seen. It is a world that tends to reward pretense and affectation almost as much as it respects power and influence, a world that responds to seniority and polish, loyalty and contacts. It is also a world in which a relatively small number of men and women, still mostly men, define the pulse of business and how it gets done. These are the ultimate Washington insiders, those who have seen countless presidential administrations come and go, worked with countless congresses, Republican and Democratic, and know one another on a first-name basis. It is composed of a handful in Congress who have been around the longest, members of the interest group and trade associations who have worked the system for years, and the K Street lobbyists who shape each budget and policy that winds it way through the legislative labyrinth. It is a world to which Rod Paige was entirely new and almost completely unsuited.

When Paige answers his phone, he says one word: "Paige." He prefers to make his own phone calls rather than have an aide do it. He likes three meals a day, usually peppering his entrée with hot sauce. He works out most early mornings and goes to church on Sundays. On rare occasions he will have a glass of wine. He speaks briskly, walks briskly, and is not given to small talk. He is a quiet man of few words, tending to straight talk, reflection, and common sense. He is not an impressive public speaker but can speak with passion regarding those things he cares and knows the most about. He can get angry at incompetence. He seldom shows his emotions.

Almost everything about Rod Paige made him ill suited and ill prepared for the job he was about to enter. And that is what made him so appealing a choice for it. He was not ready for Washington, but nor was Washington ready for him.

After weeks of preparation, Paige appeared before the Senate Committee on Health, Education, Labor, and Pensions (HELP) for his confirmation. For over two hours, with Hansen seated directly behind him, he tried to respond to the senators' queries. His straightforward manner and no nonsense ways impressed the committee. Its chairman, taciturn senator from Vermont Jim Jeffords, liked what he saw and heard. It pleased him that the nominee was an educator rather than a politician. His counterpart, Senator Ted Kennedy of Massachusetts, was also pleased by the nomination, although he sought during his questioning of Paige to determine just how wedded he was to any notion of private school choice or vouchers as part of the president-elect's education-reform agenda. Paige, while a supporter of school choice broadly defined, demurred on the issue of vouchers. The hearings were uneventful. Paige would be confirmed.

It came as no surprise to anyone on the transition team that Paige would experience few problems during the confirmation process. They had worked hard to ensure this, just as the president-elect had worked hard to establish good relationships with those members of the House and Senate engaged in education policy and politics on both sides of the aisle. Having survived a very divisive election, Bush sought to establish some credentials as a healer. For him, education was best understood as a bipartisan issue—much as he had shaped it while governor of Texas. Not long after the December Supreme Court decision, he had invited members of Congress from both sides of the aisle down to Austin to discuss education issues and get a sense of where they stood on things. At this meeting and many others held in Washington, Bush sought to establish a working relationship with the Republican and Democratic education leadership in both chambers. He was particularly eager to cement good feelings with Kennedy and George Miller, the Democratic minority chair of the education committee in the House. Calling the tall, white-haired Californian "Jorge Grande," Bush embraced the congressman and was deferential to him, citing his years of experience on the Hill and his national education credentials. Bush's effusiveness, conviviality, and good nature charmed Kennedy as well. The choice of Paige as secretary of education only seemed to provide further evidence to Kennedy and Miller that this new president was not going to fit the mold of his GOP predecessors when it came to education. Bush was determined to demonstrate he could bring both parties together and pass landmark education legislation early in his first term. He would rely on other policies, such as tax cuts, to cement his already strong relationship with the Republican base.

On January 21, 2001, President George W. Bush traveled to the U.S. Department of Education to oversee the swearing in of his secretary of education, Rod Paige. Only hours earlier he had talked of the importance of education in his inaugural address. He had wanted to punctuate the emphasis he planned to place on the issue by going to the department for the ceremony. Surrounded by family and friends, some old and some new, Paige became the nation's seventh secretary of education and its first who was, by credentials and experience, an actual educator. It was an exciting and historic moment.

After the ceremony and reception, Paige and his chief of staff, Terry Abbott, took the elevator to the seventh floor, where the secretary's office was located. Still somewhat numbed by the crush of events, Paige now looked out his office windows at the broad sweep of the Mall. He could see from the Washington Monument to Capitol Hill. The Smithsonian's National Air and Space Museum was directly across the street. It seemed almost unreal for a man from such humble origins to find himself in such impressive surroundings. He was driven by an almost overwhelming sense of obligation to make sure he accomplished everything President Bush asked of him. His humility was matched by his sense of obligation, duty, and loyalty.

Just down the hall from Paige's office sat Beth Ann Bryan. A Texan and close friend of the Bushes, Margaret La Montagne, and Sandy Kress and an acquaintance of Paige's, she had been assigned by the White House to help the new secretary as a senior advisor. In truth, her primary job was to make sure Paige did what the White House wanted. From the moment he became secretary of education, Rod Paige was destined to play a supporting and sometimes modest role in the administration's education-reform effort. The power, authority, and decision making would be driven by La Montagne and Kress from the White House. And it did not take long for Paige to figure that out.

# 2

---

# January 2001

The East Room of the White House, the largest room in the executive mansion, is where state dinners are staged, where presidents host important events of state. It is where, on January 23, 2001, President George W. Bush unveiled his signature domestic initiative: No Child Left Behind. Gathered in the East Room were about two hundred invited guests from across the country. Many were educators, some of whom had been advisors, formal and informal, to the Bush campaign and provided input on the proposal along the way. Members of Congress were there, both from the House and the Senate, both Republicans and Democrats. Members of the infant Bush administration stood to the rear of the crowd, watching their new president in his first public performance since the inauguration.

Only a few days before, Bush had delivered his inaugural speech to a Washington drenched in a cold rain and to a nation still bitterly divided over the election. No president of the United States had ever come to office as George W. Bush did—by a decision of the Supreme Court. He was, of course, well aware of this and sensitive to the pain half the nation felt about him delivering the speech that day rather than Al Gore. He had instructed his speech writers to craft a speech that would appeal to the hearts of all Americans. The themes he touched on were timeless and beyond politics: civility, courage, compassion, and character. No single public-policy issue dominated; instead, he spoke of a number of priorities his administration would address. In retrospect, it was a prescient speech, covering issues he would confront with success and failure in the years to follow.

"We will reform Social Security and Medicare," he said, "sparing our children from struggles we have the power to prevent." "And we will reduce taxes." Perhaps anticipating other struggles yet to come, the president as-serted, "We will build our defenses beyond challenge, lest weakness invite challenge. We will confront weapons of mass destruction, so that a new century is spared new horrors. The enemies of liberty and our country should make no mistake: America remains engaged in the world by history and by choice, shaping a balance of power that favors freedom." And he spoke of America's children. "Every child must be taught" those principles that bind our nation, "that unite and lead us onward." He spoke of the need to "turn the hearts of children toward knowledge and character" and to "reclaim America's schools, before ignorance and apathy claim more young lives."

It was a memorable inaugural address. Now, three days into his presi-dency, he stood in the East Room eager to make good on the concerns he had addressed that day. Standing next to him was his new secretary of education, Roderick Paige.

Paige's ascension to the cabinet was the product of extended internal discussion during the shortened transition after the Supreme Court had decided the election the previous December. His name had not figured prominently in the media, although it had appeared. Paige had emerged within the Bush inner circle as the consensus candidate for a number of reasons. When chosen, he was the superintendent of the Houston Indepen-dent School District, the fifth largest in the country. On his watch, student achievement improved, graduation rates increased, dropout rates declined, and the business community began to gain some confidence in the public schools of the city. He had seen education from just about every angle. Paige's life story, however, was compelling as well. In Rod Paige, George W. Bush found an able, accomplished practitioner who favored the sort of education reform Bush did and could speak to a broad constituency in a language its members would understand. He knew Paige would be a loyal soldier, reach out to the minority community, and do whatever needed to be done.

Just days earlier, Paige had been sworn in by the president of the United States at the Department of Education. Now he stood in the White House introducing the president. Anyone familiar with Paige's life history had to be impressed and happy for him. His voice trembled a bit as he spoke of his new boss: "Today he takes the first step towards becoming the educa-tion president by proposing to the Congress a strong program to improve America's schools," Paige said, as the enormity of the responsibilities he had just agreed to take on was surely dawning on him finally. And with that, the president began to describe to the assembled audience his ideas for leaving no child behind.

Among those assembled was the man who would oversee much of the process of turning the president's initiative into law. Sandy Kress first met

George W. Bush as he was preparing to run for governor of Texas. Kress, a Democrat at the time, was on the Dallas School Board and had acquired a reputation as a reformer. They developed a friendship. Kress, after withstanding criticism as chairman of the Dallas School Board, moved to Austin in 1997, where his work with the prestigious law firm of Akin, Gump, Strauss & Feld focused on education law, policy, and politics. He developed a broad array of clients in education, business, and industry and had become a major player in the education world, primarily in Texas, and an advisor to Democrats and Republicans alike. Now he was going to join the new Bush administration as an informal, unpaid advisor to the president. Bush liked his bipartisanship, trusted him, and was going to rely on him to make No Child Left Behind a reality.

The audience in the East Room was peppered with folks from Texas that day. And the president enjoyed greeting some of his friends who had made the trek to DC. Among them was Charles Miller. Only two years earlier, Governor Bush had appointed Miller to a six-year term on the Board of Regents of the University of Texas System—if not the most prestigious post in Texas, certainly one of the most desirable. He was a very successful investor, who over the years had acquired a fortune and emerged as one of Texas's more prominent business, community, and philanthropic leaders. He had chaired the state's largest business organization: the Greater Houston Partnership. And he had been actively engaged in almost every aspect of education in the state. In addition to his association with the Texas University System, Miller had started the Charter School Resource Center of Texas, worked with the Center for the Study of Community, the Texas Medical Center, and the Jesse H. Jones Graduate School at Rice University, chaired the Texas Educational Economic Policy Center, and served on the governor's Select Committee on Public Education.

Miller's influence in Texas was extensive. In education reform it stretched back to the early efforts of H. Ross Perot and ran through several governors. In Houston, where he lived, he had helped put Rod Paige on the Houston Independent School District school board, then helped to make sure he became superintendent. Paige respected the man. Miller had encouraged the president to name Paige to the cabinet.

Another Texan stood at the entrance to the East Room, out of sight of the reporters and most of the audience. She preferred staying out of the limelight, in the background, out of the headlines. Today was a big day for the president. But it was a big day for Margaret La Montagne too. This education initiative was very much her baby. It had been given birth during the campaign and now it was going to Congress. She was going to be there every step of the way, as the president's domestic-policy advisor. La Montagne now had an office in the West Wing of the White House. Endless conversations with George W. Bush about improving education were about to become the focus of a new national conversation about improving America's schools.

The president began that conversation three days after assuming office.

> This is an important moment for my administration because I spent such a long amount of time campaigning on education reform. It's been the hallmark of my time as governor of Texas. My focus will be on making sure every child is educated, as the president of the United States as well. Both parties have been talking about education reform for quite a while. It's time to come together to get it done so that we can truthfully say in America, "No child will be left behind—not one single child."

As the presidential campaign had unfurled, American education seemed to watch from the sidelines. On this day, even as the president began to discuss his vision for national education policy before the invited audience of public officials, educators, and friends, approximately 54 million students were sitting in approximately ninety-three thousand schools all across America. The great majority of those students, about 89 percent, were sitting in public elementary and secondary schools. The number of schools had increased in the previous decade, after years of decline. The number of elementary schools increased 9 percent between 1990 and 2000. The number of middle schools increased 27 percent during the same period. Those patterns mirrored enrollment trends, as years of decreases with the maturation of the "baby boom generation" were followed by increases, with record levels of enrollment in the mid-1990s.

The profile of America's students reflected the profile of America. Of the more than 47.44 million students enrolled in public schools, over 60 percent were white, approximately 17 percent were either black or Hispanic, 4 percent were Asian, and a little over 1 percent were Native American. Almost 3 million teachers sat in America's classrooms, with the vast majority, more than 97 percent, belonging to one of two national teacher organizations: the National Education Association (NEA) and the American Federation of Teachers. Just as the number of students in America's public schools had increased during the previous decade by over 13 percent, so too had the number of teachers in those schools by almost 24 percent. Nationwide, the student-teacher ratio was about sixteen to one. The average teacher salary was $44,604.

An impressive percentage of the teachers in America's public schools possessed a master's degree: 41 percent. But black and Hispanic and poor kids were less likely to be taught by those teachers.

America's students felt a little safer in their schools in 2001 than they had only a few years earlier. In 1995, fewer than 10 percent of all students reported being the victim of a crime while at school. In 2001, that percentage was cut in half. Dropout rates had declined as well. In 1990, the dropout rate nationally hovered around 12 percent; in 2001 it was closer to 11 percent. It remained higher for blacks, although only barely. But while the dropout rate for Hispanics had declined dramatically, it was still unacceptably high: 32 to 27 percent.[1]

In the audience at the White House that day were representatives of all the major education organizations: the leadership of both teachers' unions, the nation's local school boards and state boards of education, the various state departments of education and their chiefs, and the organization that represented administrators in the fifteen hundred school districts in the country. Most had watched and participated in the recent presidential campaign with a combination of emotions. It is always good when education receives the sort of prominence in national politics that it did that year. But this also meant that the world in which these people operated would change, perhaps dramatically. They would be directly affected by what the president was saying—even should he not be able to turn his ideas into law. As the transition from president-elect to incumbent had progressed, and as Bush put his education leadership in place, most had offered polite but tempered reactions.

Bob Chase, president of the 2.7 million member NEA, struck a conciliatory note after his organization had supported Vice President Al Gore in the election: "Historic moments like President Bush's inauguration and Secretary Paige's confirmation remind us that we are one American family. And public education is an issue in the next session of congress that can unite our nation."[2]

The Association of State Boards of Education had issued a statement from its executive director expressing delight "that the Senate has moved so expeditiously and overwhelmingly in confirming Dr. Rod Paige."[3]

Sandra Feldman, of the American Federation of Teachers, had issued a similar statement, offering her organization's support to both Bush and Paige as the issue of improving American education was to take center stage.

Only Paul Houston, leader of the American Association of School Administrators, seemed defensive. He had grown tired of all the criticism the public school system had endured in recent years. "Public education is not in decline," he asserted in an open letter to the president. "We do not have a failed system. . . . We have changed the mission from a good education for some to a better education for all, but we haven't done enough to change the infrastructure or the resource allocation to make that happen." Speaking directly to the president, he asserted that "the measure of your leadership in education will rest on your courage to confront the issue of equity." And in a curious passage, he encouraged the president to not be afraid to fail. "The willingness to fail has made America great," Houston proclaimed.[4]

It might be said that one need look no farther than the performance of America's schools to probe the accuracy of Houston's curious claim. For as President Bush was addressing the audience that day at the White House, America's schools and America's students were flirting with the "willingness to fail" Houston found so commendable.

∼≫∽

Surely there are many, many reasons for the lamentable performance of so many public schools in America. Schools are asked to do so much more than educate kids. Kids come to school with so many problems. Parents do not care. There are not enough resources. The list is long. But few cite one of the chief challenges to securing quality public education in this country. The system, as it currently exists, seems almost perfectly designed to resist reform and to perpetuate the status quo. It flies in the face of even the most elementary principles of sound management and prizes regulation and compliance over innovation, opportunity, and results.

As George W. Bush spoke to his audience at the White House, American public education was approaching a crossroads. For most of the previous decade, public confidence in the system had been continually eroding. In virtually every state, governors and legislatures and state boards of education and state school chiefs had offered a broad menu of reform options. Many had taken root. Most were well intentioned but untested. And with each call for reform, the criticism of the education status quo was implicit, if not explicit. Gradually professional educators had grown tired, frustrated, and angry about the seemingly unrelenting scrutiny and attacks. Public education interest groups and associations organized public relations campaigns to counter not only the mounting criticism but the reform efforts as well. All this time, during the 1990s, record spending went for public education in almost every state in the nation. Ironically, in other words, as the American people questioned the value and quality of public education more than ever, they simultaneously spent more and more money on it.

Criticism of public education is as old as public education itself. Each generation has complained that students are underperforming, teachers underworked, administrators overpaid, and taxes to underwrite the schools too high. The chorus reached something of a crescendo with the publication of *A Nation at Risk* in 1983. Responding to then education secretary Terrel Bell's observation that America's schools were not doing an adequate job of preparing young people for the workforce, the report cited public education as a "national security risk" and made the bold and disturbing assertion that "if an unfriendly foreign power had attempted to impose on America the mediocre education performance that exists today, we might have viewed it as an act of war."[5] The report focused national attention on the plight of public education and created a flurry of activity, primarily in the academy, where sides were drawn and scholars and pundits dueled one another over just how bad or not bad the nation's public school were. But, in reality, more heat than light was created. Now, almost two decades later, public education was once again paramount in the minds of the American people, fed by a presidential campaign and now by a president who seemed set on doing something serious.

Of course, while adults everywhere seemed to be choosing sides in the escalating debate, students everywhere were doing what students have always done. In growing numbers, they attended America's schools, which led to building more schools. The issue of school construction and building renovation only served to fuel the debate further. The poor infrastructure of most urban public schools competed for funds with the growing appetite of the relatively palatial and expanding suburban districts. School construction is big business in America. About $52 billion was spent on school construction and facility maintenance, replacing equipment, and servicing debt the year President Bush assumed office.[6]

One would think, nevertheless, that the need for more classrooms and more teachers was at a breaking point, given the rhetoric surrounding the public education debates. A numbing pattern of assertions declared what was needed to fix the education problem. "Smaller class sizes" ran with "fix the teacher shortage." "Higher teacher salaries" competed with "stiffen certification requirements." "Improve technology in schools" ran up against "get back to basics." And meanwhile, students just went to school.

The problem, of course, was that in 2001, students in America's schools were not performing very well. On virtually every indicator of student achievement, the majority of the nation's students were below proficient, according to the National Assessment of Educational Progress. In some subgroups—minority and low-income students—upwards of 60 percent were not performing at grade level in such fundamental disciplines as reading and math. The achievement gap between African American students and their white peers was startling, as was the gap between Hispanics and whites. Most troubling was the fact that this had been the case for almost a generation.

In 2001, according to some reports, the high school dropout rates ranged from close to 8 percent for whites, 11 percent for African Americans, and 27 percent for Hispanics. But the dropout rates, which had been improving for a few years, were about grow.[7] There did not exist an agreed-upon way to calculate high school graduation rates. But one scholar argued that in 1998 the graduation rate for all of America's high schools hovered at around 71 percent, with African American and Hispanic rates much lower than that of their white peers.[8]

In 2001, no state in the nation could report to its taxpayers an accurate high school graduation rate for its students. Estimates ranged, however, from a high of 93 percent in Wisconsin to a low of 54 percent in Georgia.[9] No state had reliable information, but the perception was growing that a dropout problem existed. In some urban school districts, student attrition and truancy seemed such a problem that class size was hardly an issue, so few students showed up. While every state had policies for teacher licensure, few states could report with any accuracy the percentage of teachers in their schools who possessed appropriate credentials to teach. It was virtually impossible to determine how much taxpayers spent on reading instruction. But a majority of America's students were not reading at grade level. The same could be said for math. Billions of dollars were directed toward special education and "at risk" children. But it was next to impossible to determine how those dollars paid off in terms of children's learning.[10]

In 2001, the mediocre to poor performance of K–12 public education was reflected in what was happening to postsecondary and higher education in the United States. The six-year graduation rate hovered at around 50 percent. For blacks it was below 40 percent. The three-year completion rate for an associate's degree was about 30 percent. A ninth grader had about a 37 percent chance of going to college by age nineteen. The percentage of high school graduates going directly to college was around 57 percent. But attrition rates were growing, and the number of remedial and "developmental" courses being offered by colleges and universities was up dramatically. In the early 1980s, a little more than 50 percent of the nation's colleges and universities offered remedial or developmental courses for credit. In 2001, that number had risen to almost 80 percent. Over this same period, while the enrollment in remedial courses had remained steady, the amount of time spent in such courses had increased.[11]

The president and his advisors were well versed in the unacceptable status quo in American education. Bush stepped forward to make his statement.

> We must confront the scandal of illiteracy in America, seen most clearly in high-poverty schools, where nearly 70 percent of fourth graders are unable to read at a basic level. We must address the low standing of America's test scores amongst industrialized nations in math and science, the very subjects most likely to affect our future competitiveness. We must focus the spending of federal tax dollars on things that work. Too often we have spent without regard for results, without judging success or failure from year to year.

From there he began to describe the broad contours of his ideas to fix America's schools—ideas hatched in Texas, fine-tuned during the campaign, and deeply embedded in the initiative he was now sending to Congress. "First," the president said, "children must be tested every year in reading and math. Every single year." He followed with a second principle for education reform: "The agents of reform must be schools and school districts, not bureaucracies. Teachers and principals, local and state leaders must have the responsibility to succeed and the flexibility to innovate." Next, the president asserted the importance of setting higher standards and higher expectations, especially for "low-income schools," and promised, "Once failing schools are identified, we will help them improve." Finally, he enumerated his fourth principle: "When schools do not teach and will not change, parents and students must have other options."

The president sprinkled references to lawmakers present as he outlined his plans: George Miller, Democrat from California, and his Republican counterpart from Ohio, John Boehner, the chairman of the House Education and Workforce Committee; Judd Gregg, senator from New Hampshire, who sat on the HELP Committee; and Joe Lieberman of Connecticut, who had only months earlier tried to defeat Bush alongside Vice President Al Gore. The president challenged the Congress to take up the issue immediately, "because I know we need to act by this summer so that the people at the local level can take our initiatives and plan for the school year beginning next fall." It was an audacious proposition. And then he closed.

> We've got one thing in mind: an education system that's responsive to the children, an education system that educates every child, an education system that I'm confident can exist; one that's based upon sound fundamental curriculum, one that starts teaching children to read early in life, one that focuses on systems that do work, one that heralds our teachers and makes sure they've got the necessary tools to teach, but one that says every child can learn. And in this great land called America, no child will be left behind.

Who could argue with that? And that was the point. By staking out the lofty moral imperative that every child can learn and repeating the mantra of "No Child Left Behind," the president rhetorically disarmed potential opponents almost immediately. It simply became nearly impossible to take issue with the fundamental premise and promise of the president's education-reform ideas. Those who might challenge where the administration wanted to go with education reform would have to focus on the details behind the bold promise. How could America's teachers not believe every child can learn? How could superintendents espouse anything less than that? The No Child Left Behind idea became, from the outset, almost inextricably entwined with the idea of the promise of America. "And in this great land called America, no child will be left behind." Quietly, beyond the television cameras and off the record, educators everywhere shook their heads. It was a noble idea that sounded good. But anyone the least familiar with public education in America in 2001 knew it was little more than that: a noble idea.

⸙

President Bush staked out a position on education that changed the terms of the national debate. By merging two fundamental principles in American thought—equality and opportunity—he was able to appeal to those sentiments in the American people. Every child can learn. Every child can perform at grade level. This was the sort of equality held up by the president. Prior to this time, equality in education was about per-pupil spending and ending segregation. Suddenly it was about every child succeeding. Success in the classroom was the prerequisite to success in life. Opportunity was created through education. No Child Left Behind became, from the moment Bush first introduced it, synonymous with securing the American dream

By emphasizing the child over the public education system, he was able to put a face on an issue—education reform—that had persistently preoccupied public attention for decades. His was a positive message. Rather than focusing on the problems with the status quo in American education, Bush chose to emphasize the possibilities. Even as he held up discouraging test scores as evidence of the need for change, he employed them to speak to the possibilities rather than dwell on the inadequacies of the system. With the No Child Left Behind initiative, George W. Bush was able to accomplish what none of his Republican predecessors had been able to do: he made education a Republican issue. Only a few years earlier, the platform of the party had called for the elimination of the U.S. Department of Education. George W. Bush would embrace it, expand the federal role in education, and upset the traditional political coalitions that had formed around the issue of education for generations. On this day in the East Room of the White House, the conversation about education reform began to change, and it would take months for those who had traditionally been at the center of that conversation to catch up.

Talk of reform in public education is as old as public education in America itself. The public's perception and opinion of public schools has almost always been critical, even while public support for public schools has always been very strong. The American people consider public education essential to the democracy. Yet, they simultaneously feel schools are not getting the job done. When asked to consider fundamental change to the public education system—vouchers, for example—the American people are skeptical; fearful that such changes will hurt public education. What explains this?[12] What is behind the apparent "love-hate" relationship Americans have with public education?

Unlike virtually any other social institution or field of public policy, everyone knows something about education. Think about it. When discussing issues like the environment, energy, transportation, health care, and national defense, unless we have a particular insight or knowledge of the subject, we tend to listen to others, to defer to the experts. But everyone has an opinion about education because everyone went to school. Everyone knows someone connected to education—a teacher, school board member, administrator, student. Everyone pays taxes that help pay for the construction and operation of schools. Education is something everyone can relate to, has an opinion about, pays for.

Interestingly, how one is related to public education tends to shape opinions about the schools. Parents with children in school tend to care a great deal about their child's school and usually feel pretty good about it. If they are critical, they tend to voice their concerns and act to address them. They may be quite critical of public education generally, yet believe their child's school to be a good one.[13] Older citizens, with grown or no children, tend to be more critical of the system generally. This is important. As the nation's baby boomers retire, their swollen numbers will be responsible for footing the bill for America's schools. Yet, if current patterns hold, they will pay those bills with ever-decreasing satisfaction with the system. In other words, if current trends continue, Americans' confidence in American public education will continue to erode.

Because reforming public education has been a perennial theme in American public life, suggestions for reform have come and gone like waves on a beach. Indeed, the pattern has been of one education-reform fad following another, one trend replacing another. The list is long and familiar: open classrooms, Montessori schools, junior high morphing into middle school, magnet schools, team teaching, small schools to consolidated high schools to small schools. Instructional theories have abounded, each with its following and research literature. Teachers of reading gather annually to do battle over the best way to teach Johnny to read. The "reading wars" spill over into other disciplines as well: social sciences versus social studies, the relevance of history, the apparent irrelevance of trigonometry, the questionable need to master the elements of grammar, teaching as mentoring, instruction as tyranny.

Most all of this has been irrelevant to parents. They just want their children to learn and do well in school. And much of it has come across as nonsense to taxpayers, who foot the bills and just want to know if the schools are getting the job done. And that has been the crux of the problem. It has been difficult over the years to determine, on any objective scale, whether the schools have been getting the job done. For most parents, schools get the job done if their child does well.

For generations of parents, choosing a home has involved checking out the local schools, meaning their reputation. Good neighborhoods have good schools. It seems real estate agents have been, for generations, the arbiters of school quality. It all revolves around the general "sense" of how good a school is. Vague indicators are used, of course: high school graduation rates, what the graduates do after high school, class size, and so forth. Once assigned to a school, the challenge becomes making sure your child gets the "best" teacher. And determination of the best teacher is, again, a product of reputation. Every school has its share of desirable and not-so-desirable teachers, and parents know this and angle accordingly. But none of this is based on anything other than reputation. There are precious little data relating teaching to student achievement, teaching style to student learning. "Good" teachers are those students and parents feel good about. They are the teachers that seem to care about the kids, listen to the parents, and give the children the attention they need.

For much of its history in America, the quality of public education has been a matter of impression, reputation, and sentiment. People know a good school when they see one, and a troubled school is too obvious to miss. Good teachers are known by their reputation. Word of mouth has been the currency of choice in public schools.

The problem with this, of course, is that no one really knows much about what works and what does not in education. No one really knows how good a school is, how well students are doing. The grades students receive for their coursework are the product of the subjective judgment of their teachers. They do not translate across schools and districts or, often, even within schools. An A at this high school might be a C at another. What gets taught in a classroom is decided by the teacher in the classroom, as is what gets tested. And determining student achievement has been left to the discretion of educators.

One would think that research in education might provide better, more reliable indicators about teacher, school, and student performance. But education research, or what passes for research, is notoriously impressionistic as well. Unlike the "hard" sciences, education research tends to be anecdotal, observational, and historical. The techniques associated with science—control groups, longitudinal studies, scientifically based methods—are seldom applied in education research. As a result, schools of education have only helped to institutionalize the problem. They prepare America's teachers based on how they have always prepared America's teachers, with little reliance on evidence of what works and what does not, beyond theories of learning and classroom management. Public education on a mass scale has existed in this country for almost two hundred years. Yet, the "science" of education remains to be born. With the possible exception of reading, we have no real knowledge of how to teach subjects so that students will learn. It is stunning that we have done as well as we have. Or as well as we think we have.

The initiative President Bush outlined in the White House on January 23 held the promise of changing all of this. The emphasis on accountability, if taken seriously, had the potential to introduce objective, measurable data on student and school performance on a broad scale for the first time ever. The emphasis on teacher quality held similar promise. Again, for the first time ever, teacher preparation and certification would emphasize knowledge of the discipline to be taught. And that would be determined through objective data as well. The president would extend this to research in education, arguing that the principles and methods of scientific inquiry should be applied to education and that public dollars should only underwrite methods of instruction that have been proven to work. At one level, it all seemed pretty commonsensical. Teachers need to know what they teach. Student achievement should be measured objectively and should be comparable across schools and disciplines around the country over time.

The call for accountability and objectivity in education did not begin that day in Washington. Rather, for the previous decade, it had been growing within the states, where education reform had been a hot issue for years. Since the early 1990s, two reform movements had taken root in most of the states that could provide the president with political cover for his own initiatives. The charter school movement represented a growing alternative to the traditional public school system and provided the president with some leverage against an obstinate public education community. His support for charter schools and for more options for parents could tap a sentiment growing among the states. The accountability movement gave the president the ability to merge a national education-reform message with movements already underway at the state level. The fact that he, as governor of Texas, had been a strong advocate for that message gave him instant credibility with governors everywhere, regardless of political affiliation.

Charter schools are semi-independent public schools. They began in Minnesota in the early 1990s, and by the time Bush arrived in the White House, they existed in thirty-seven states, Puerto Rico, and the District of Columbia. Currently more than 1.5 million students attend forty-six hundred charter schools in forty states.[14] Regulated by state law, each charter school is overseen by its own board of directors, which is legally responsible for the operation of the school and making sure it adheres to its charter, the statement of policies and practices that define the school. Most charter schools have discreet missions; many embrace certain curricula and learning philosophies and employ both traditional and nontraditional teaching methods. They began as an alternative to the typical public school, usually fashioned by individuals unhappy with the status quo in a neighborhood. The school charter represents something like a contract with the families who send their children there and with the public school district in which the charter school exists. Once the charter is granted, usually by the local school district or some other charter-granting entity within a state, the school operates independently from the school district, reporting to its own board. The charter school board then must be able to demonstrate to the school district authorities that the school has lived up to its contract.

The supporters of charter schools say they represent freedom and choice in public education and opportunities for innovation and creativity. Parents of children in charter schools tend to be more involved with the school and their children's education. Teachers in charter schools tend to be certified, as are those in regular public schools. But they do not necessarily have to be. It is not unusual to find a professional musician teaching music rather than a certified music teacher, a professional dancer teaching dance. Students in charter schools tend to be low-income, minority, and at risk—a bit more so than their peers in traditional public schools. The vast majority of charter schools are elementary schools.[15]

Opponents of the charter school movement assert that it undermines public education, that it is creating a "dual" public education system, and that charter schools are not held accountable to the extent regular schools are. They argue that taxpayer dollars going to support charter schools are needed in regular public schools. And they point to the fact that students in charter schools do no better than their peers in traditional schools on standardized tests.

Charter schools have emerged as the primary public school alternative to regular public schools. Because they are indeed public schools, they do not represent any additional costs to families, such as tuition at nonpublic schools. As public schools, charter schools must abide by state and federal laws governing accountability in both student achievement and financial management. Unlike traditional schools, however, when charter schools fail, in management or educational practice, they can be closed, their charters not renewed. And parents can withdraw their children from charter schools should they be dissatisfied. Mismanaged or poorly performing traditional public schools usually do not close, and parents with students enrolled in them cannot just withdraw their children and enroll them in another school of their choice. At base, charter schools are created in response to a demand in the community that the public school system is not responding to. They are schools defined by the community. In contrast, most traditional public schools are defined by the system they are a part of, and parents have to respond to the needs of that system as well.

The public school accountability movement paralleled the charter school movement during the 1990s. Every state was engaged in some version of school accountability. States developed academic standards, as well as testing based on them, and instituted various approaches to evaluating student and school performance. Most states tested students periodically; some tested every year. In about one-third of the states, students had to pass a state test in order to graduate or go on to the next grade. In some states, rewards and sanction for schools were tied to school and student performance. And everywhere, it seemed, the emphasis was on achievement and reporting results. By 2001, then, the drive for accountability in public education was maturing, and the time was right for a national initiative building on state action.

Interestingly, that initiative had been encouraged at the national level by Bush's predecessor, Bill Clinton. When the Elementary and Secondary Education Act was reauthorized during Clinton's term in 1994, it called for state academic standards and testing in elementary, middle, and high schools. It also called for disaggregating test data to uncover achievement gaps among student groups. Called the Improving America's Schools Act, it was hailed by Clinton and his secretary of education, Richard Riley, as a fundamental change in American public education. There is no question that the act strengthened the standards-and-accountability movement. However, Clinton's Department of Education had not done much to enforce the act among the states. Few had accountability systems in accord with the federal statute. Most had portions of systems in place. Indeed, when President Bush entered office in 2001, only eleven states were fully compliant with federal law. The Clinton administration had granted waivers or extensions and "compliance agreements" to most of the states. The accountability movement that did exist, then, was almost exclusively due to state and local action. Washington was almost irrelevant to it. That was about to change.

The president's education-reform initiative was given top billing by the Republican Congress. It was to be the first bill introduced in the new House of Representatives: House Resolution 1. The symbolism was important. This president wanted education to be seen as his highest domestic priority. He provided additional evidence of this with his initial budget request to Congress, which included major increases for education funding: 11 percent. Bush was eager to establish his "education president" credentials, and in doing so he reversed years of Republican animus toward the U.S. Department of Education and conservative squeamishness over too much federal spending on education. The president, in pushing for major education reform coupled with major funding increases, was following a political strategy that he had employed as governor of Texas.

As governor, Bush also had inherited education-reform efforts begun earlier. The standards-and-accountability movement was well underway. Governor Bush built his reforms on those already in place and increased the state's financial support of public education in dramatic fashion, much of it going to improve teachers' salaries. He formed coalitions with the education establishment, which was willing to support his reform agenda in return for the new money.

As president, Bush would seek to achieve similar results with a similar strategy. He would seek to embrace reform while reaching out to a national education establishment that was, at best, wary of his reform ideas.

He would demonstrate his commitment to that establishment with more money—the traditional way Washington demonstrates its commitment to almost anything. And he would seek to reach out to that establishment through his new secretary of education, who was of the establishment, honored by it, and knew his way around it. The president felt improving public education could only happen if those engaged in it bought into the idea. And he would seek to do just that—buy their support.

Bush decided early on that he would adhere to another strategy that had worked well for him in Texas: bipartisanship. As governor, Bush had received high marks from state Democrats and Republicans alike. He had become close to a number of Democratic legislative leaders, such as the Speaker of the Texas House. Moreover, Bush saw education as a bipartisan issue, one that crossed party lines and could create coalitions among traditional rivals. Prior to his inauguration, he had invited Republican and Democratic senators and congressmen to Texas to discuss education reform and had reached out to Democrats. Part of this was his attempt to heal the wounds rubbed raw by the presidential election. But the president's commitment to bipartisanship was real, rooted in his political experience and his approach to education. He considered it critical to success in education reform. It was a strategy that stood in stark contrast to the one he chose to follow as he pursued tax cuts. There the partisan divide was deep and the rhetoric at times vicious. With education, he would seek higher moral ground and common political ground.

As the audience gradually moved out of the East Room and onto the White House grounds, the sense of excitement was almost palpable. Here was a new president and new administration and what seemed a new and fresh and determined call to improve America's schools. Here was a president who wanted to reach across the aisle to political opponents and seek their counsel and help, a president who wanted to demonstrate that Republicans care about education and are willing to spend money on it.

Every new president enjoys a honeymoon on entering the office. Bush, given the way he obtained the office, surely was not going to enjoy much of one. But on this day in January 2001, it seemed everyone felt good about what he wanted to do for American education. For the moment, it seemed everything might be possible. That moment did not last very long.

# 3

## An American Law

It is difficult to overstate the difficulty of transforming a presidential campaign into a presidential administration. The challenge has multiplied over the years, as the size and complexity of the executive branch of government have increased. Then there are the hours and resources that go into finding qualified and willing individuals to serve in the administration.

This has proven more difficult in the modern age of American politics. Once upon a time, individuals seeking public positions made their aims known to candidates and party leaders, and a "spoils system" rewarded those who had loyally supported the winning candidate. An individual's skills and experience pertaining to an office were less important than political affiliation and loyalty. This began to change, somewhat dramatically, in the late 1800s with the introduction of the civil service system and evolution of a professional public service; since then, men and women who work for the government have been considered career employees rather than political appointees and hold their positions due to the skills and expertise they possess. These are the men and women who make up the bureaucracy so often railed against by elected officials. But in truth, they make the government work. The government does not have to be reinvented with each new presidential administration in large part because of the presence of a career civil service. Of course, career civil servants often present challenges to political appointees seeking to advance an administration's policy agenda. It is commonplace for a tension to exist within the bureaucracy that can frustrate both political leaders and career employees, both convinced of the rightness of their position.

For the nascent Bush administration, the challenges were augmented by the shortened transition period, the bad blood created by the election and

Supreme Court decision, and the fact that the process of finding, nominating, and confirming men and women for high-ranking political positions within the bureaucracy is becoming more and more time-consuming. It took an average of fifty-two days to go from nomination to confirmation to appointment in President Bill Clinton's first administration. The average would exceed 112 days for nominees to President George W. Bush's.[1] This was due, in part, to the increase in the number of positions requiring confirmation by the Senate.[2] Each name has to be scrubbed, and each individual must go through some sort of background check by the FBI. The process is long, expensive, and labor-intensive. And many of the most qualified men and women, finding the whole process irritating and somewhat offensive, are put off by it.

For the individuals who would become part of the political leadership of Bush and Rod Paige's Department of Education, the pattern of presidential appointment was long and predictable. First would come an announcement from the White House of the president's intention to nominate an individual, followed, usually weeks later, by another White House announcement of the president's nomination of that person. Then, sometimes after months of making the rounds in the Senate, the chamber might confirm that person during some usually innocuous vote to clean up any unfinished business. After Senate confirmation would come the actual appointment by the president. In the end, only two of Bush's top-level nominees, other than Paige, even appeared before the Senate Committee on Health, Education, Labor, and Pensions (HELP) for confirmation hearings. Most were confirmed without much comment or notice. Only one, Gerald Reynolds, was refused confirmation. He was assistant secretary for civil rights at the department for almost two years under a recess appointment by President Bush.

During the time between nomination and appointment, those selected to join the Bush education team were cloistered in cubicles throughout the department's main offices spanning a block across from the Smithsonian's National Air and Space Museum and overlooking the National Mall. As nominees, they were not allowed to do anything official and were generally limited in any policy or administrative role they might play. In other words, nominees were allowed to work with staff to secure their confirmation and could offer informal advice on a range of issues, but they were forbidden from carrying out any duties that might be related to the official business of government.

Because of this, Rod Paige was the only confirmed member of the Bush education team from January though late June. He had his chief of staff, Terry Abbott, who did not require senatorial confirmation, and a handful of other advisors who likewise did not require confirmation; among them were Beth Ann Bryan and Susan Sclafani, as well as Clay Boothby, installed by the White House to help steer the confirmation of the president's nominees, and Lindsey Kozberg, who oversaw the press shop. But for months, the offices that would oversee virtually every operation of the U.S. Department of Education, including the development and implementation of No Child Left Behind, should it become law, were officially vacant. The president had introduced his landmark education initiative in January, and there was nobody in place in the department to carry it forward for months afterward. Paige had neither a deputy secretary or under secretary nor any assistant secretaries. And yet, here he had been asked to bring his president's education priorities to fruition. Or so it seemed.

In truth, as Paige worked with his skeleton staff and the Office of Presidential Personnel to assemble an administration, the White House became fully engaged in beginning the campaign to get Congress to pass the president's education-reform plan. Paige, always interested in management and organization theory, was looking at various organization charts and interviewing countless people for top positions in the department, while Margaret La Montagne, Sandy Kress, and a handful of others at the White House were beginning conversations with House and Senate Republicans and Democrats on the broad contours of No Child Left Behind. Almost from the beginning, then, Rod Paige was on the fringes of the politics and policy debates that would go into making No Child Left Behind a reality. He may have been secretary of education, but he was not going to oversee the president's education-reform initiative. From time to time he would be enlisted to travel up to the Hill to meet with members or to attend functions related to his office. And he traveled extensively as the administration's very visible point man on education. But he was barely engaged in the formulation of the policies that would go into No Child Left Behind. Paige was to be the administration's symbol and front man on the issue.

The fact that he was not actively engaged in policy formulation disturbed Paige a great deal. Neither Kress nor La Montagne had experience in the trenches; neither knew how education and schools work. And all of them were new to Washington and the politics of Capitol Hill. But Paige was hesitant to make an issue of things early in his tenure. He would bide his time, assemble his team at the department, and see what developed. He had enough to do getting his administration in place.

By the early spring of 2001, the bare bones of that team were finally coming together. Every morning, Paige would meet for breakfast with a small group of his gathering cadre of presidential nominees to discuss where things were and what lay ahead. It was his way of getting some chemistry going among his developing management team and learning what they were doing. Paige's management style was formal and informal at the same time. He sought to establish a decision-making process within the department that mirrored the process he had put in place in Houston. The individual with ownership of an issue was to write a decision memo outlining it and the pros and cons. This memo was to be circulated to the relevant officers within the department. At an appointed time, all would gather to make a decision. It was all about chain of command and information flow.

On the other hand, Paige did not stand on ceremony much. The department's statutory organization chart did not sit well with him. So, after much study and thought, Paige drew up a revised one. He placed three offices together at the very top of the chart: those of the secretary, deputy secretary, and under secretary. Paige wanted the three offices to act as one as often possible: "No one of us is as smart as all of us," he would often say. He hoped that the three would work as one, ensuring a seamless decision-making process and smooth oversight of the administration of the department, even when Paige was away on travel. Even before his top lieutenants had been confirmed, he found himself seeking and depending on their counsel.

It was the counsel of Paige's lieutenants that produced the first of many confrontations with La Montagne and the White House. While the discussions about No Child Left Behind were getting well underway on the Hill, little real progress was being made. It was, through the spring of 2001, really a matter of White House and Hill staff getting to know one another and developing relationships. Sandy Kress had been assigned the role of policy point man for the administration and spent hours in the department with policy experts, learning what he could of existing elementary and secondary education law and regulations and exploring various ways in which the administration might get at issues of accountability and testing. Kress enjoyed the long discussions with the department's career policy experts and attorneys. He likened them to graduate seminars on national education policy. But Paige grew more and more disturbed by the idea of Kress coming to the department and engaging in those discussions without even letting the secretary's office know. He saw it as disrespectful and undercutting of his authority.

What really began to bother Paige and his senior staff, though, was the way Kress would request time on the schedule to brief Paige and his team on where things stood in negotiations with the Hill. Usually coming on a Friday, Kress would appear in the secretary's dining room to join Paige and assembled staff for breakfast and briefing. Always respectful, Kress would inform those in attendance of the conversations on the various issues and his thoughts on things, and he would solicit Paige's reactions and input. The sessions were brief, perfunctory, and, in Paige's mind, pointless and bothersome. He felt he and his team should be doing what Kress was doing. He saw through Kress's feigned respect during the briefings, always saying he would defer to Paige, of course, given his experience and office. It was insulting, thought Paige.

His most senior and closest advisors, except for Beth Ann Bryan, agreed. In their eyes, Kress's actions undermined the very authority of the secretary of education. They recognized that he acted on instructions from the White House—from La Montagne—and they realized that they all had to defer to White House decision making on both process and policy, but it struck them as bad form on the part of the White House to remove Paige from any serious input on No Child Left Behind. More importantly, if word got out that Paige was not actively engaged in deliberations with the White House and the Hill on No Child Left Behind, his stature and authority as a member of Bush's cabinet would crumble. Paige needed to assert himself and establish his authority as secretary of education, they felt, and he needed to do that soon.

Every presidential administration establishes its own way of managing things, which usually evolves from a combination of factors. Most administrations seek to act according to strict chains of command and operating principles and procedures. But personality always plays a part—the personality of the president, of his advisors, and of those responsible for pursuing the administration's agenda. Then there are events—some foreseen, many not—that shape the way the administration operates, often changing established patterns and norms and creating cycles of advisors rising in status or falling. It was still early in Bush's term, and those management principles and organizational policies were still evolving. Paige and his senior advisors felt there was still time for the secretary to establish his authority within the White House and with the president. They were not even sure Bush was aware of the way Kress and La Montagne were acting as administration emissaries on the Hill.

One of Paige's top aides sought counsel from Bill Bennett, himself a former secretary of education in the Reagan administration. Bennett was an admirer of Paige and of Bush and understood what the new secretary was going through and up against. He had himself once taken action to establish his own bona fides with the White House when he was in the cabinet. As secretary of education, Bennett was an outspoken critic of the education system, its many interest groups and professional associations, and its unions: "the Blob," as he was fond of labeling it. He also felt the Department of Education was overly supported by the Democratic Congress and sought decreases in education appropriations. This established his uniqueness among cabinet secretaries generally, who almost always seek to grow the budgets of their agencies. But it sat well with the only person Bennett felt obligated to satisfy: Ronald Reagan.

Once, as the budget process was getting underway, Bennett was on the phone with a junior staffer, Deborah Steelman, at the Office of Management and Budget (OMB), which was responsible for putting together the president's budget request for Congress. After he had laid out his intention to seek an appropriations decrease or, at the very least, level funding, the staffer shot back that Bennett's plan was not going to happen and that she and the folks at OMB would decide the secretary's budget request. Bennett asked the staffer's name and said he would be over immediately to discuss the issue with the director of OMB.

Bennett, OMB director James Miller, and Steelman gathered in the director's office in the Old Executive Office Building next to the White House. Bennett wasted no time and minced no words. Rising in his seat and staring only at Miller, he said he thought it was important for both the director and his staff to understand that he was the secretary of education, a member of the president's cabinet, and that he, not some staffer at OMB, would decide what he would seek from Congress by way of a budget, subject only to the president's approval. Miller blanched. Steelman shrank in her seat. Bennett left the room. He never had another problem asserting his authority again. And he got the budget request he wanted.[3]

According to Bennett, Paige had to do something similar now. He had to get to President Bush and establish his own bona fides with this White House and this administration. Rumors were already circulating around Washington, according to Bennett, that Paige was not really in charge, that Margaret La Montagne was.

The top aide conveyed Bennett's advice to Paige and his small coterie of close advisors, even relating the story about Bennett's run-in at OMB. Paige, himself a "big Bill Bennett fan," was encouraged to make a similar move. He called La Montagne's office seeking a meeting with her and then with the president.

The meeting with President Bush never happened. La Montagne would not allow it. When Paige brought up his concerns about Kress sidestepping the department and his office, she cut him off, saying this was the way the president wanted it done. According to La Montagne, Paige was getting briefed on a regular basis and would be brought into more direct deliberations when they reached the appropriate stage. It was too early to concern a member of the cabinet with things. And besides, she asserted, Paige had an organization to put together. His time would be better spent on running the Department of Education.

Paige relented and returned to the department to convey the essence of the discussion to his senior aides. La Montagne had made some sense, he admitted, and so he had not pressed the meeting with the president. Both of his most senior advisors, the nominees for deputy and under secretary, were very sure Paige should have pushed for the meeting. Paige's deputy-designate, Bill Hansen, was an old Washington hand and could see a disturbing pattern emerging that would relegate his boss to the sidelines if he did not do something about it. But neither pushed Paige on the issue. After all, he had been in the room with La Montagne, he had had the conversation, and he was doing what he felt he should do. For the time being, all agreed it would be wiser to let things play out.

For this White House, control of the executive branch was a very high priority. They employed a "command-and-control" approach, limiting tightly the discretion that might be vested in members of the president's cabinet and White House staff. Only a relative few, close to and trusted by Bush and his inner circle, were allowed to exercise much independence and judgment.

⋉∞⋊

The House and Senate are two very different institutions that work in very different ways and fulfill two very different purposes in Congress. The House, run by rules and procedures, is a cumbersome and slow-moving assembly that relies heavily upon the structure of committees and sub-committees, institutional and party leadership, and consensus making at each step in the legislative process. All of these came into play during the deliberations and debate over No Child Left Behind in the House. The fact that Bush's education initiative was House Resolution 1 spoke to the priority the president attached to the proposal and the willingness of the Speaker of the House, Denny Hastert of Illinois, to go along with it. It would be more than embarrassing to Hastert not to be able to pass an education-reform bill coming from a president of his political party. The fact that the Republican Party had enjoyed an edge over the Democrats on the education issue during the 2000 election gave the Democrats in the House (and the Senate) every incentive to try to reestablish it as their political property. To do that, they would need to demonstrate that they could shape education policy going forward. For a while, traditional lines on this issue in the House of Representatives were crossed and procedures rebuffed. Republican and Democratic staff on the education commit-tee met and discussed the issues regularly, trying to find what common ground they could to take back to the two ranking members, George Miller and John Boehner. It would fall to them to marshal the support they would then need to pass the initiative through the committee and then the floor of the House.

The Senate, a smaller and clubbier institution than the House, operates on different principles. In the Senate certain norms have evolved over time that help the institution go about its business. While, as in the House, there are rules and a committee system, in the Senate great deference is paid to every member of the chamber, which operates on the assumption that all the members agree to proceed to the business at hand. Unanimous consent agreements mark the flow of business. One senator can object and stop things, at least temporarily. A single senator can put a hold on a presidential nomination, for example. In the Senate, a minority, forty, can bloc legislation and make it impossible to conduct business. The filibuster is unique to the Senate and speaks to the importance placed upon the equal and special status each senator enjoys. That is not to say that some senators do not have more influence than others—chairmen have prerogatives over committee business—but because of the size of the chamber and crush of legislative business, every member has a chance to chair either a committee or subcommittee, and so they have an incentive to accommodate one another. Party leadership matters, of course, but not as much as senatorial courtesy and collegiality. In the closely divided Senate of 2001, courtesy and collegiality, along with the desire of both parties to retain the edge on education, created a chemistry that, initially anyway, seemed dedicated to making sure something was accomplished.

The White House had a friend in Congressman John Boehner of Ohio, and that was a very good thing. Boehner chaired the House Education and Workforce Committee, which would oversee education policy and the No Child Left Behind Act. Boehner, well-liked and respected by his colleagues on both sides of the aisle, was a veteran of Washington ways. Only recently he had been among the very few vying for leadership in the Republican caucus. Having failed to get the post, he looked upon his chairmanship as a chance to demonstrate leadership and get something done that would recommend him to his colleagues. And he cared about the issue of education—more, it seemed than even he realized.

John Boehner was first elected to the House of Representatives in 1990, after serving six years on the Ohio legislature. A self-described "son of a saloon keeper" and one of twelve siblings, Boehner came from somewhat humble origins. But he had acquired a talent for politics over the years. Low key, confident, a chain-smoker often found sneaking a cigarette before and after meetings, he had the ability to reach across the aisle and work with even the most liberal of his Democratic colleagues. An avid golfer, he was well known to, and well supported by, the K Street lobbyists, who helped finance his campaigns and not a few golf outings. But Boehner was not seduced by Washington politics. He knew how things worked and could get things done, but he was not caught up in it all. He had remained grounded in spite of the power and influence he wielded. And he was a good Republican. Now with President Bush embracing education as his highest domestic priority, John Boehner was about to see his time in the sun. He would make the most of it.

Boehner's counterpart on the House Education and Workforce Committee was George Miller, Democrat from California. Well grounded in liberal California tradition, Miller had devoted much of his career to education and youth issues. Tall and imposing, with a mountain of grey hair, he had grown tired of the traditional education establishment's siren song requesting more money and was less seduced by the teachers' unions than in his youth. He saw in George W. Bush someone who seemed genuinely interested in improving education with a track record of success in Texas.

In Miller, Bush saw a Democrat he could work with and befriend; the president referred to him in Spanish as "Jorge Grande," or "Big George." From the outset, the two struck up a relationship of rough respect. And Boehner, seeing a chance to forge a bipartisan consensus for some sort of major education bill, quickly sought to embrace Miller as his bridge to the Left in the House.

The politics were altogether different in the Senate, where the GOP held a very slender majority, and the committee leadership was less convinced of both the president's education-reform ideas and his sincerity regarding reform. Leading the Senate HELP Committee was taciturn senator from Vermont Jim Jeffords. Barely a Republican, he found himself more and more at odds with the politics and policies of his own party. He fancied himself something of an expert on education issues and was particularly interested in special education. But he was uncomfortable with the talk emanating from the Bush team, with its embrace of vouchers and school choice and running on about accountability. He had grown wary of conservatives agitating for fundamental change in American education and viewed Bush with suspicion. The nascent administration was also wary of Jeffords—that was for sure. They saw him as a weak leader, wobbly on the issues of concern to them, and too easily manipulated by the education establishment. As a result, they tended to ignore Jeffords rather than court him, as they did others like Miller in the House and Ted Kennedy in the Senate, both Democrats. Instead, they looked to another Republican New Englander for help in the education cause, New Hampshire's Judd Gregg. Gregg, second in seniority to Jeffords on the committee, was a true conservative and a Bush fan. The president and his team saw him as a solid ally and advocate in the Senate.

The senior senator from Massachusetts, Ted Kennedy, was the minority chairman of the HELP Committee. Here again, Bush thought he had someone he could work with. After all, Bush had something of a national reputation for his ability to forge bipartisan coalitions in Texas, particularly regarding education. Contrary to the prevailing consensus within the Republican Party, Bush saw Kennedy as sincere in his interest in advancing children's issues and susceptible to the sort of political wooing he had practiced in Texas. Bush reached out early and often to Kennedy as a man he could work with and who commanded great respect in the Democratic Party and in the Senate. He would be the administration's bridge to the Left in the Senate.

That bridge quickly became critical. Jeffords, alienated from the Bush administration almost immediately, quickly became a vocal critic of the president's ideas. He felt the real problem in education revolved around special education, and he demanded the administration dramatically increase spending on it. The Bush team chose to ignore him, focusing on Gregg and Kennedy, Boehner and Miller. In addition, the administration decided early on to establish an informal working group on the Senate side led by Sandy Kress, bypassing the traditional approach of working directly with Jeffords's staff on the Senate HELP Committee. When the White House snubbed Jeffords by not inviting him to a "Teacher of the Year" ceremony, it was the last straw. He announced that he was no longer a Republican. With that, the Democrats gained the majority in the Senate, Kennedy became chairman of the HELP Committee, and Gregg became the minority chair. Suddenly, bipartisanship became more important than ever.

While the early positioning on the education-reform effort was underway, the Bush administration was simultaneously pushing hard for its other primary domestic initiative: tax cuts. This was "red meat" for Bush's base and something akin to sacred ground among the GOP faithful. The Democrats in Congress were just about equally determined to oppose the new president on his tax policy. The administration decided early on that this would be their bow to those who had elected Bush. They would follow a strong partisan path to achieve their tax-cut victory. Over several weeks of sometimes bruising politics, they triumphed, even while some in the party wondered about the wisdom of the policy. Jim Jeffords was among the Republicans in the Senate who openly distanced himself from the president on the tax-cut issue, one of the many that led to his estrangement from the party and the administration.

Another contentious issue, this one relating to Bush's education agenda, also bothered Jeffords and many on the Democratic side of the aisle in both the House and the Senate. Among the provisions embraced in the administration's initial draft of No Child Left Behind was private school choice, or vouchers. Bush proposed to make vouchers available to students stuck in persistently failing schools. Most in the administration were ambivalent about the concept of private school choice, which had never been a part of Governor Bush's education agenda in Texas. Moreover, the president's domestic-policy advisor and primary education confidante, Margaret La Montagne, was somewhat outspoken in her antipathy for vouchers. She was, at heart, a public education advocate. To her way of thinking, vouchers were anti–public education and represented a threat to public schools. But many on the conservative side of the GOP embraced the idea, which was seen as something of a staple among conservative education-reform advocates. It was included in the original package of education-reform policies Bush sent to the Hill, therefore, as a bow to the conservatives in Congress more than anything else. Bush did not care much about its success or failure; La Montagne surely would not mind its failure.

But many in the administration and in Congress embraced private school choice and saw it as a central component of true education reform. Among those were Secretary Paige and his newly named, yet still unconfirmed, top lieutenants. Paige had instituted something of a school-choice policy while superintendent in Houston, which he saw as a healthy way to introduce competition into the system. His aides embraced vouchers as essential to introducing real reform into a poorly performing system. They saw the issue within a broader philosophical prism of empowering individuals and families by giving them greater control over their educational choices. School choice, in a sense, was one of the hallmarks of the nation's approach to higher education, after all. And taxpayer dollars underwrote students enrolled in private and even sectarian institutions of higher and postsecondary learning, helping to create a world-class higher education sector. The GI Bill was, to their way of thinking, a huge voucher program that benefited millions and transformed America after World War II. Private school choice at the elementary and secondary levels held out the same promise of helping students stuck in failing schools, empowering families with greater control over the education of their children, and potentially transforming public education in the process.

Vouchers were equally important to the relatively few, but vocal and influential, conservatives in the House and Senate who were having a difficult time understanding how a newly elected "conservative" president could embrace a larger role for Washington in education. Only a few years earlier, the Republican Party had campaigned to dismantle the U.S. Department of Education and return greater control to the state and local levels. Now they were being asked to work with a Republican president who would expand, perhaps considerably, the national government's authority over the nation's schools. They might be willing to accept such an expansion, however reluctantly, if it was coupled with policies that also gave greater freedom and control to parents.

At the same time, vouchers were considered a deal breaker among Democrats in the Congress. For years, the education establishment had fought furiously to defeat voucher initiatives among the states, with great success. Small, pilot programs had sprung up, most notably in Milwaukee, Wisconsin, and Cleveland, Ohio. And some success had been attributed to those programs. Some studies reported that student achievement was improving and students in both the private and public schools in those cities were doing better. But other studies questioned the educational benefits of school-choice programs. The evidence was mixed. And the nation's teachers' unions and education establishment had drawn a line in the sand years before and were determined to defeat any voucher program anywhere. They had made their concerns known to their allies in Congress and within the Bush administration very early the opening discussions about No Child Left Behind.

The voucher issue itself had emerged only briefly during Paige's confirmation hearings before the Senate. During those otherwise nonconfrontational and noneventful hearings, when Senator Kennedy had inquired into his views on school choice and vouchers, Paige had responded with a half-hearted endorsement of the idea but sought to convince the senator that vouchers were not essential to improving schools and that he was not committed to the concept. Kennedy seemed satisfied with Paige's response.

As the preliminary conversations around Bush's education initiative began to gain greater focus, however, the voucher issue became something nobody could ignore. For conservatives it was an essential price to be paid for their support of a greater role for Washington in education; indeed, they might seek even greater concessions before signing on with the president. For others, in both parties and chambers, vouchers were a nonstarter. As long as the president included them in his package of proposals, the package would go nowhere. It quickly became evident that the administration would have to make a decision sooner rather than later about the issue. The political calculus was relatively simple in the end: keeping vouchers might satisfy a handful in Congress who were wary of the Bush education-reform agenda, while getting rid of them would advance the possibility of broader, bipartisan support for it. It was a no-brainer.

As the discussions intensified, with administration emissaries scurrying around Washington trying to engage various groups on various issues, Paige's two top advisors encouraged him to go the president and push to keep private school choice in the education-reform package. It was way too early to compromise on such a fundamental issue, they argued. Moreover, it would appear that the president was more interested in responding to Democrats and the education establishment than those in his own party. Besides, they reasoned, Paige was perfectly positioned to appeal to the president on the issue, given his background and record. For his part, Paige was not pleased to see the administration buckling to pressure to scrap his voucher idea. Again, he would seek a meeting with the president, which would never take place. Again, Paige was rebuffed by Margaret La Montagne.

At about the same time that he had decided to lobby the president personally on vouchers, one of Paige's aides had received a phone call from former education secretary William Bennett, who was trying to determine where Paige stood on the issue and to encourage the new secretary to be bold in his support for vouchers. Bennett was told that Paige indeed supported vouchers and was bothered by all the speculation that the president was about to discard the school-choice provisions in order to appease Democrats. Bennett, heartened by the news, encouraged the aide to continue to press Paige to push for a meeting with the president. And the aide told Bennett that he was free to spread the word that the new secretary was pro–school choice and was trying to make the case within the administration.[4]

Bennett did just that. Within a few days a Robert Novak column appeared in the *Washington Post* reporting Paige's, and his deputy's, consternation over the possible surrender on vouchers.[5] The story helped to solidify Paige's standing among conservatives and school-choice advocates but exposed a disagreement within the administration, which infuriated a White House already establishing its reputation for message control and discipline. Paige himself was torn: he did indeed support vouchers and personally liked being out front on an issue so dear to conservatives, but he did not want to appear disloyal to the president. His ambivalence was erased, however, by a difficult conversation with Margaret La Montagne, who, in a heated exchange, let Paige know that he was not going to be meeting with the president on this issue, that the issue had been settled and the president had made up his mind, and that neither she nor the president liked the idea of airing internal disagreements publicly. La Montagne was quick to point out that Paige was there to carry out the decisions of the White House, and should she or the president want his advice or opinion, they would seek it.

The conversation shook Paige. He did not want to appear disloyal. He immediately called Novak on the phone to tell him his story was wrong, that there was no disagreement within the administration on the voucher issue, and demanded to know where Novak got his bad information. Novak shot right back that he had his sources and would not retract the story. With their voices rising, the conversation ended abruptly. Paige was upset now. And he had reason to be. His authority as secretary of education within the administration had been cut off at the knees by La Montagne, and his position had been exposed by a nationally syndicated columnist. It was becoming apparent that La Montagne would call the shots, not the secretary of education, and that he would be relegated to doing her bidding. That was tough enough to swallow. But now the story was out there that he had sought and failed to get a key provision into the education-reform package. Here was a member of the president's cabinet who, early in the administration's tenure, had suffered a defeat on an issue he cared deeply about. His credibility was dealt a serious blow, both within and outside the administration. The rumors began to circulate that Paige was not really a player.

In addition to adopting a bipartisan approach to his education strategy, Bush sought to give Congress some ownership of his No Child Left Behind initiative. He had started that process in the White House just days after the inauguration, when he introduced his ideas as a blueprint for reform rather than actual draft legislation. Reaching out to Congress, Bush promised bipartisan education reform would be the "cornerstone of my administration" and welcomed ideas from members of the House and Senate. This was the president's invitation to dialogue and compromise. It was also Bush's way of making sure Congress would shoulder some heavy responsibility for getting something done. As he had reached out to both sides of the aisle asking for ideas and input, it would become more difficult for Congress to walk away from education reform. By offering a blueprint rather specific legislation, Bush left his team room to negotiate and compromise and left the myriad, troubling details for Congress to iron out.

The blueprint itself, embracing the four principles of education reform that Bush had pushed during the campaign, emphasized testing and accountability above all else. The president would have states establish academic standards and test students annually on them. States would identify schools failing to make adequate yearly progress (AYP) and develop strategies to help them turn around. In addition, they would address issues relating to teacher quality and options for children trapped in troubled schools. While it was Bush's blueprint, much of it resembled various proposals that had been floating about Congress for some time. Indeed, the testing and accountability ideas had been espoused only a few years earlier under the Clinton administration. This, again, was a conscious decision by Bush. In his blueprint, most members of Congress could find something worth supporting, leaving most of the debate for those few more novel and controversial ideas that the president supported but seemed willing to compromise on.

The most obvious of these was the voucher proposal, which died an early death. In addition, however, the president, in a bow to federalism, sought to establish education block grants, allowing states greater flexibility and discretion in the distribution of federal education monies. As with vouchers, the politics surrounding block grants tended to adhere to party lines, with liberal Democrats opposing the idea and conservative Republicans embracing it. And as with vouchers, the president, in the end, compromised on the concept, leaving in place a multiplicity of funding streams going to the states with rules and regulations attached to them. States would be left with only a modicum of independent authority in the implementation of No Child Left Behind.

Bush's strategy—bipartisanship, a willingness to compromise, bestowing ownership of the education issue in both the House and the Senate, and working around the less supportive Jeffords in the Senate—yielded relatively quick gains. It was easier in the House, with both Boehner and Miller very engaged and rules and procedures limiting the interference of discontented members on both sides of the aisle. Still, the broad consensus in both chambers, along with the energetic and indefatigable efforts of Kress, produced results. By the end of March, both the House and the Senate had moved separate versions of No Child Left Behind out of committee. In the House, the version had the stamp of the chamber's leadership, as well as of the administration. In the Senate, the committee's bill, which Jeffords had steered, was replaced at the last moment with one more in line with the president's wishes and authored by the rump negotiating team Kress had helped to oversee.

After the committees had acted, the debate over the specifics of No Child Left Behind became more acrimonious. In the Senate the issue was measuring adequate yearly progress for schools and the time line for all students to achieve proficiency in reading and math. Jeffords felt the policies being proposed in the Senate were too aggressive and unrealistic. Some argued that under the sort of accountability regime envisioned in the Senate language, virtually every school in America would fail to make adequate yearly progress, which the public surely would not accept, thereby undermining the whole accountability movement. In the House, there was greater receptivity to holding the line on accountability. Both Boehner and Miller were more than willing to hold schools' feet to the fire.

Recognizing a need to keep things moving, the administration worked on compromise language in the Senate that extended the time line for requiring all students to make proficiency from ten to twelve years and allowed states to measure schools' progress as an average over three-year periods rather than at a single point in time, thus mitigating the threat of huge numbers of schools failing to make AYP.

During this time a compromise on school choice was achieved as well. Recognizing the depth of the voucher controversy and unwilling to sacrifice accountability at the altar of school choice, the administration sought a middle ground. They found it with public school choice and after-school tutoring programs. The thinking was that kids stuck in failing schools should be able to transfer to public schools that work and to access free tutoring, called supplemental educational services. Conservatives were unhappy. Liberals were wary. But the middle seemed mollified.

The testing provisions of the emerging No Child Left Behind became contentious when conservative congressman Pete Hoekstra of Michigan joined arms with the very liberal Barney Frank of Massachusetts in an attempt to amend the bill in the House to eliminate testing altogether. For a while, the move proved popular enough, particularly among state and local policy makers and educators, to derail the bill altogether. But testing was essential to the president's proposals and the Hoekstra-Frank proposal was beaten back after a strong effort by the administration.

As spring moved toward summer and the two chambers debated different versions of the president's education-reform package, members from both parties attempted to insert their favored provisions into the legislation. Gregg in the Senate continued to push for vouchers, as did Boehner in the House. Congressman Miller sought to strengthen the highly qualified teacher provisions. Senator Jeffords, by this time increasingly frustrated by the administration's treatment of him, had announced his defection from the Republican Party. While his departure lost the GOP control of that chamber, Bush's by now very strong relationship with Kennedy seemed to ensure it would have a minimal impact on negotiations. In late May, the House passed its version of No Child Left Behind. The Senate followed during the second week of June. The summer would be consumed with the work of a conference committee that would seek to reconcile the two measures and send a final bill to the House and the Senate before the end of the year.

As the Congress began to take up Bush's education-reform agenda and other Bush initiatives, La Montagne and Paige were also going about the task of creating an education department molded in the president's image. By early spring of 2001, the skeleton of that department was in place. In addition to the secretary and his two closest lieutenants, the deputy secretary, and under secretary, the White House had chosen a bright African American conservative to become the number one lawyer at the department. Brian Jones was no stranger to Washington. A graduate of Georgetown University Law Center and a veteran of judiciary committee service in the Senate, Jones was a rising star within the GOP. While he would not be confirmed for months, he quickly earned the trust and respect of Paige and his leadership team. For years going forward, it was Brian Jones, more than any other person within the department, on whom Paige would rely for counsel, advice, and friendship.

Other important positions within the department were gradually filled by men and women jointly agreed upon by Paige and La Montagne. The process for selecting top departmental managers had been established early. The White House would assemble a list of potential nominees for each position and send it over to the department. Paige would meet with those the White House wanted seriously considered. Both La Montagne and Paige had to agree on each of the major appointments; either could veto a name. As individuals were vetted, interviewed, and selected, the White House would announce the president's intention to nominate them, which he would then do. Most began employment as consultants pending their final Senate confirmation and appointment. In the end, only two nominees even appeared before the Senate HELP Committee for confirmation hearings: Jones, for general counsel, and Jerry Reynolds to head the department's Office for Civil Rights. Jones was confirmed; Reynolds was not and eventually received a recess appointment from the president.

The men and women appointed to the senior positions in the Bush Department of Education were, by and large, professional educators who had spent careers in the field. They were not politicians. In some cases, they had little or no management experience. They were chosen because of their resumes, experience, backgrounds, and potential to contribute to the president's agenda. Their political leanings did not seem important. Bob Pasternack, a lighthearted, gregarious special education official from the state of New Mexico was a liberal Democrat. But he was also a good friend of Reid Lyon, the reigning "reading czar" at the National Institutes of Health, in whom Bush and La Montagne had great confidence. Pasternack became assistant secretary for special education and, almost from the beginning, established a reputation for managerial incompetence and political naiveté. His relationship within the senior leadership team ebbed and flowed with his performance. During senior staff meetings, for a while held weekly and chaired by Paige, Pasternack would end each meeting reading some joke from his BlackBerry. Often the jokes were sexual in nature, generating an uncomfortable giggle among those in attendance. It was a pattern of conduct that either endeared Pasternack to others or repulsed them. Pasternack would not survive the entire first term of the Bush administration; nor would he oversee the reauthorization of the one federal law he supposedly cared the most about: the Individuals with Disabilities Education Act.

On the other hand, the president's appointee as assistant secretary for vocational and adult education, Carol D'Amico, was a hard core conservative Republican, a friend of the president's budget director, Mitch Daniels, and someone dedicated to both the president's education agenda and transforming vocational education. An astute politician and strong manager, D'Amico openly challenged the bureaucracy within the department and sought to engage the White House and Paige in entertaining radical ideas about the way the government oversaw and underwrote job training and adult education. But she quickly learned that her issue held little interest with the Bush administration. She also quickly found out that those who were interested in her issues were rivals over at the Department of Labor who coveted her offices, responsibilities, and programs. D'Amico fought hard within both the department and the administration to get an agenda of positive change established. But she never gained any traction. She left before the first Bush term ended to become a major leader in Indiana's impressive community college system.

Perhaps the single most important office within the department was the office that would have to oversee the day-to-day implementation of Bush's education agenda, should it become law. The Office of Elementary and Secondary Education would have to make No Child Left Behind a reality. Up to now, its influence upon national K–12 education policy had been marginal, as had the influence of the federal government generally. But the president's agenda held out the possibility of a greatly expanded federal education presence. Whoever became assistant secretary for elementary and secondary education would potentially wield great influence and oversee billions of dollars and hundreds of programs. Susan Neuman, a university professor and nationally recognized expert on early childhood and reading instruction, was chosen, in part, again, through the influence of Reid Lyon and due to her impressive credentials. Reading was to become a primary emphasis under Bush, and Neuman was thought to bring unquestionable expertise. She did, and together with La Montagne and Beth Ann Bryan, Paige's senior advisor and White House confidante, Neuman sought to exert her influence immediately. Convinced state and local education policy makers were ignorant or incompetent regarding reading instruction, and driven by data that continued to show most students in America reading at relatively poor performance levels, she sought to take control of the issue. She surrounded herself with talented, younger men and women equally dedicated to turning the reading problem around. Fierce in her determination and stubborn in her thinking that nothing should stand in her way, she quickly became a managerial martinet, distrustful of all but a handful within the department, who demanded that her subordinates always clear any communications inside or out of the department through her personally. Neuman quickly became a thorn in the side to Paige and his leadership team, but she had the trust of the White House and often went around Paige and others in developing her policies and management style. As time went by, Neuman would create a culture of confusion, mismanagement, and error that ultimately led to her downfall as assistant secretary and almost cost the administration the heart of its No Child Left Behind legacy. For senior leadership in the department, she became the poster child for the disconnect between the ivory tower and the hardball world of politics and policy. She had no business being in Washington.

Many others would join the Department of Education, coming from various places and positions, drawn by a chance to serve, loyalty to the president, and the excitement and possibility of a position in a new administration. Laurie Rich had served Governor Bush as his advocate in Washington. Now she would work with governors and state education leaders and state legislators to advance President Bush's education agenda. Russ Whitehurst would oversee a revamped institute of educational science and be responsible for building a better research base for education policy. Whitehurst came from the State University of New York, Stony Brook, with an excellent reputation. His job, by design, was insulated from much of the everyday politics that colors most government jobs in the department, and so his academic credentials and background were not as much of a disadvantage as they had been for Neuman.

It took months to name someone to lead the department's efforts in postsecondary and higher education, reflecting the administration's relative lack of interest in and knowledge of that important aspect of education in America. The White House, therefore the department, was totally focused on K–12 education, even though the federal Higher Education Act would need to be reauthorized within a few years and represented literally billions of dollars in student aid and higher education programs and policies. Sally Stroup, a veteran of the Hill and an official with the University of Phoenix, the nation's largest for-profit provider of postsecondary education, arrived late in the first year of the administration and was given broad discretion, primarily because few cared or had the time to care. That would change, of course.

Within the Department of Education, individuals arrived to take up the administration's effort at changing the way English-language instruction is conducted in the United States and the relationship of special education to general education, to oversee day-to-day bureaucratic operations within the department, and to establish the president's initiative to ensure that community and faith-based organizations qualified for federal funds. They became assistant secretaries, deputy assistant secretaries, and directors and took a host of other titles and positions that make up the modern bureaucratic establishment in Washington. They came from various walks of life with various levels of experience, many with their own agendas. They entered a department that was to receive greater attention and scrutiny than any education department since the institution's creation during the Carter administration. What was typically a marginal issue at the national level was to become the dominant domestic issue for the Bush administration, and the talent and abilities of the men and women at the Department of Education would be sorely tested.

By late summer of 2001, then, much of the Bush education team was assembling, going through the motions of nomination and confirmation, filling out forms and visiting senators and getting established professionally and personally in Washington DC and its environs. And by late summer of 2001, the president's education proposal was languishing on Capitol Hill, the victim of partisan squabbling, House and Senate rivalries, and summer doldrums.

The Jeffords defection, while it shifted the majority in the Senate to the Democrats, did little to change the dynamic in the chamber regarding No Child Left Behind. The two major players had always been Kennedy and Gregg, a very unlikely alliance and an uncomfortable one for both senators. It was held together by constant stroking on the part of officials in the White House and loyalty to the president on the part of Gregg and his staff. Gregg himself harbored serious misgivings about the whole enterprise, having for years argued for local control in education and school choice, which had been sacrificed early in the deliberations on the Hill. But he wanted to help this new Republican president and besides, to his way of thinking, his home state of New Hampshire had very good schools, and so the new federal initiative very likely would not have much of an impact there. The problems in American schools were in the urban areas. That was the emphasis, he thought. That was where the achievement gap looms large. Not in New Hampshire where there are no large urban areas and relatively few minorities.

If Gregg was less than fully committed to the president's education-reform package, Kennedy and his staff were fully engaged. He relished the role of chairman of the committee and the chance to be the focus once again of so much attention. The fact that the Senate was so closely divided meant Kennedy would by definition have to temper his more liberal impulses in order to secure enough support for a bill to survive in the chamber. But that was fine with him. He instructed his staff to continue to work with Republican staff to seek common ground.

In the House, both Boehner and Miller were very engaged, and their staffs met constantly to iron out policies. It was a good working relationship that, while at times fractious, was held together by the commitment both Boehner and Miller had made to each other. Both were determined to overcome partisan differences and to find common ground on this issue, and they had instructed their staffs to follow that line. The long held suspicions and animosities did not disappear, surely. But gradually a chemistry developed that moved deliberations along.

The "Big Four"—Kennedy, Gregg, Boehner, and Miller—would steer the conference committee charged with working out the differences between the two chambers. And it was an unusually large conference committee. All the members of the HELP Committee in the Senate, including Jeffords, were appointed to it, along with centrist Democrats and moderate Republicans. From the House were eight Republicans and six Democrats. From the administration, La Montagne and Kress would serve as point players.

Sandy Kress, by now a familiar and very visible participant in the No Child Left Behind negotiations, was personally deeply committed to the president's education agenda. As an uncompensated consultant to the White House, he spent most weeks in Washington, away from his home and family in Austin. With no other distractions while in the city, he devoted most days and evenings to discussions over virtually every aspect of the legislation that was evolving in the House and the Senate. He became a familiar fixture on the Hill and within the Department of Education. And by the summer of 2001, he was beginning to get on the nerves of Boehner and Miller, many of the staff that would work for the conference committee, and much of the leadership of the department. Gradually, Kress's role was diminished. La Montagne, and later Paige, would play a larger part.

The conference committee had considerable ground to cover. There were more than two thousand discrepancies between the House and Senate versions of the legislation. On top of that, the partisanship that had so driven the president's tax package earlier in the session spilled over into the day-to-day business of the Congress, undermining the spirit of bipartisanship so essential to No Child Left Behind. And then there was the fact that staffs were working on issues with which they had very little experience, issues relating to student testing and accountability and measuring school progress. These issues might come before a state legislature or state board of education all the time, but they were new, complex, and difficult to decipher for House and Senate staff huddled in Washington. It was over these sorts of issues that the spirit of cooperation began to break down, with rivalries forming within and among House and Senate staff. Nobody quite knew or understood what he or she was doing, and that fed a growing sense of distrust in the discussions. Who was trying to get away with what? Why this approach rather than that? Who wins and who does not?

During the summer the pace of business in Washington slows. Even with the commitment of the House and Senate leadership and the administration, it seemed entirely possible that President Bush would not see his education initiative become law before the end of the year. When he had introduced No Child Left Behind back in January, he had called upon Congress to pass it before the start of the next school year. Now that was an impossibility. Indeed, it seemed it might take another year to get a bill to the president for his signature.

As August approached, and with it the monthlong congressional recess and a presidential retreat to his prairie home in Crawford, Texas, negotiators understood there would be no break for them. August would be the crucial month, the month to make or break an education-reform package that the Congress could then act on upon returning after Labor Day.

The biggest challenge revolved around the issue of accountability. There was general agreement on the broad contours of testing, public school choice and free tutoring or supplemental educational services, reporting of test results, and the need to identify underachieving schools. But the real issue remained to be resolved: how to measure school performance and whether it should be school or student performance that mattered. In addition, what were to be the consequences of failing to get kids where they need to be? And then there was the issue of targeting the achievement gap. How do you design an accountability program that makes it impossible to ignore the gap? These are huge issues, and there were serious differences between the two chambers over them.

The accountability problem was essentially the same one that had so vexed the Senate earlier in the session. More recently, a study by the General Accounting Office suggested that under the prevailing understandings concerning the definition of proficiency and AYP, thousands of schools might be labeled in need of improvement overnight. The negotiators did not want to back away from holding schools accountable, but they did not want a full-scale rebellion coming from educators, parents, and taxpayers who felt their schools were being labeled unfairly. Efforts began to create greater flexibility in the composition of the accountability system. A key concern was that both versions of the bill seemed to call for progress every year, which seemed unrealistic. Yet, neither chamber wanted to yield much ground.

In addition, there was some discussion of shifting the focus of accountability from schools to students. The administration kept pushing for accountability at the school rather than student level, arguing that the schools must be held accountable. Focusing on student achievement might make some sense, it was admitted, but only where state education accountability systems with student-specific data were in place, which was not the case in the vast majority of states. To get at student performance would require a major overhaul of most states' accountability systems, which would take time and money and generate political controversy. Student-specific data was opposed in many places by conservatives wary of government—any government—knowing too much about individuals, particularly kids. Privacy rights advocates would surely grouse at such a scheme, and conservatives in the House and Senate would not stand for it. By measuring school performance, the existing state accountability systems could be employed, most with only modest modification, building upon the accountability regime instituted following the 1994 reauthorization. It was less controversial and something members of Congress were already on the record as supporting.

Some argued that a major shortcoming with the plan advanced by the administration was that it gave no credit to schools that demonstrated improved student performance but fell short of getting kids to proficiency in reading and math. Either they were successful or they were not. In a way, the argument for some sort of growth model made sense. After all, students get credit for improved performance during a semester, do they not? Is it realistic to assert that every child can reach proficiency in reading and math? But the administration would not budge. Proficiency was to be the gold standard—No Child Left Behind—and schools would have to find ways to get students there.

The initial focus on the achievement gap went back to the 1994 reauthorization of the Elementary and Secondary Education Act under President Clinton, the Improving America's Schools Act. That law required states to establish accountability systems based on state academic standards and to test students at least once a year in elementary, middle, and high schools. That law also required states to disaggregate test data according to race, income, gender, and other classifications. But the law did not require states to do anything with this information. In other words, testing and disaggregation were to take place, but what they did with this information was left to states' discretion. This time around, there would be a heavy emphasis on testing with greater frequency and reporting test results for various ethnic, racial, and other learning-related groups. The debate then centered on which groups, how many groups there should be, and how all of this should be counted regarding school performance. The achievement gap between low-income and minority children and their wealthier, white counterparts was well documented, and there was little debate about how to get at that: disaggregating test results by race would do the trick. Rather than coming up with a single average test score for all their students, schools would have to sort scores by race. Without this requirement, the status of minority student performance might be hidden behind a relatively high overall average student score for a school. For years that had been the case. So called good schools with high average test scores kept the relatively lower performing minority scores hidden from view. But how far should disaggregation go? How many groups should be set aside? How should group scores relate to overall school performance? What about students who might fit into multiple categories: low income, minority, non-English speaking, special education?

These were the sorts of issues and details that confronted and confused the large group of staff trying to iron things out during the dog days of August. And they did so in relative isolation, talking among themselves and with a team from the Department of Education but seldom seeking counsel from the large education world beyond. The congressional staff, most of them young, earnest, smart, hardworking, and well educated, had relatively little or no real-world experience in education. This was policy-wonk stuff, hardly blemished by any consideration of how it might eventually play out in schools and school districts. As the summer wore on, the two chambers and two parties, while working closely together and bantering back and forth, seemed to be trying to outdo one another when it came to accountability. Various schemes were put on the table, many so convoluted and complex that they defied description. The number of groups to be identified grew. There were more questions than answers, and tempers at times grew short. Consensus on the big picture had been relatively easy to achieve. But translating that into the specifics was difficult, daunting work.

President Bush spent the month of August at his ranch in Texas. In what became an annual rite, the president would headquarter there and venture out for various reasons to various places or have his aides and members of his administration travel to Texas for meetings. Bush did not like Washington and preferred the isolation of Crawford. The White House Press Corps preferred Washington, even during the withering heat of summer, and that delighted the president, who was no fan of the press.

During August 2001, President Bush made one major policy decision, announcing in a short speech to the nation from his Crawford ranch his position on human stem cell research. Other than that, the month was quiet.

Bush never felt he needed to be the center of attention or on the front page of the papers, in striking contrast to his predecessor.

The disappointing news regarding the lack of resolution on No Child Left Behind did not, however, sit well with Bush and his small team of advisors. His highest domestic priority, the centerpiece of his bipartisan agenda, was coming unglued. La Montagne, Kress, Paige, and Paige's top lieutenants huddled and discussed where things stood. It was simply unacceptable for Congress not to get this done as soon as possible upon the end of the August recess. The administration had put forth the effort needed and upheld its side of the bargain. It was time for the members of the House and Senate to make good on their commitments and get this done. The Hill staff needed a kick in the ass from their bosses!

La Montagne convinced the president that he needed to hit the ground running in early September with a stern lecture to Congress about the need to get No Child Left Behind done as the new school year began. "Congress needs to go back to school too and pass education reform so that not another school year goes by with children left behind." That would be the message delivered by the president, with his secretary of education at his side, at an elementary school, sometime early in September.

September 11, 2001, dawned brilliant, sunny, and clear. It was an early autumn-like day, with a clear blue sky, quite unusual for Washington at that time of year. The president was in Florida for a mixture of politics and business and was preparing to speak at Emma E. Booker Elementary School in Sarasota. After his visit with the children, he would send Congress his message: they needed to go back to school too and get No Child Left Behind done! The message was never sent.

As the president, Paige, and a retinue of aides huddled together before joining the school children, the president's chief of staff, Andy Card, received word that a plane had hit the World Trade Center in New York City. Specifics were not yet available, and the news, while certainly disconcerting, did not seem to warrant any immediate response from the president. Card told Bush that he would let the president know as more information arrived. With that, Bush and Paige joined the kids. The president enjoyed spending time in schools and any chance he had to discuss what he cared so much about: education. It looked to be a pleasant morning, reading to kids and then talking to the press about No Child Left Behind and the need for Congress to get to work. A few minutes into his presentation with the children, Card entered the room from the president's right, leaned over, and whispered into Bush's ear: "A second plane has hit the World Trade Center. The United States is under attack. We need to leave immediately."[6]

No president in the modern age has ever heard those words. The attack at Pearl Harbor, while aimed at U.S. armed forces, was not technically an attack upon the United States. Not since the War of 1812 had there been an assault on U.S. soil. Suddenly, irrevocably, everything changed forever. Bush sat motionless and quiet for moments, trying to take in what he had just been told—trying to control his expression so as not to upset his audience of children and teachers. His aides were already preparing his departure, moving equipment, and readying the caravan to get to Air Force One, in the air, and out of any immediate danger. The president gathered his thoughts and told his audience that something terrible had happened in New York City, that he would have to leave, and that Secretary of Education Rod Paige would complete the program. Minutes later, Air Force One made a steep, sharp takeoff heading who knows where. Nobody yet knew, or could begin to fathom, what was happening to America that day.

From that moment on, the presidency of George W. Bush would be defined by 9/11 and its aftermath. Before then, the president desperately wanted to be known for education, his passion and interest. He wanted to focus on domestic issues, his strength. He wanted to work the two political levers that he understood and knew how to manage, his conservative base and his bipartisan brand of congressional politicking. He had looked to No Child Left Behind to be his signature accomplishment, demonstrating that Republicans and Democrats can work together to benefit every child in America. He truly did think of himself as "a uniter, not a divider," and his approach to education reform would demonstrate that. Up until that moment, George W. Bush was in control of his destiny as president of the United States, as much as any president can be. But with 9/11, that changed. Forever.

The tumult that surrounded the events of 9/11 meant that nothing else mattered for weeks following the attacks. With air traffic halted, it took Paige a few days to get back to Washington and his duties at the department. For days, everyone in official Washington seemed a bit dazed and confused by it all, including President Bush. His initial public response to the attacks, delivered the afternoon of September 11 from an air force base in Louisiana, seemed hesitant and lacked focus and resolve. Later that day, after he returned to the White House and snapped a command to "get Condi," his national security advisor, Condoleezza Rice, his more formal address to the nation from the Oval Office reassured a very concerned country. But it would be months before the nation got its balance back.

The Monday after the attacks, Paige and a small team of his senior managers traveled by rail to visit Ground Zero in New York City. The department had maintained a field office not far from the World Trade Center, and Paige sought to comfort his employees stationed there. He also visited a group of New York City teachers who taught at schools near the attack site. They were real heroes, he told them, real patriots.

On the trip back to Washington, Paige wondered out loud about the chances of getting the deliberations on No Child Left Behind back on track. Congress was understandably preoccupied with what was quickly becoming known as homeland security, and everything else seemed irrelevant, at least for the moment. Paige did not hold out much hope for the passage of the law.

As Washington and the nation began to adjust to life post 9/11, with enormous increases in security and constant reports and updates on perceived or alleged threats, all of the president's attention was on framing the response to the attacks. Within the White House, working groups were created, staffed by senior leadership from all the executive agencies. The idea was to generate and then coordinate a multidimensional response, not only to the terrorism attacks but to the economic, social, emotional, and psychological harm they inflicted at home and around the world. Virtually every agency was engaged in some way or another.

For its part, Congress sought to get back to work, to demonstrate that the attacks would not deter it from doing the people's business. Then, suddenly, its determination was thwarted when anthrax was discovered in a Senate office building. Could it be another terrorist attack, this time employing biological weapons? The Congress was shut down. Medicine was distributed to all on the Hill who wanted it. Offices were vacated. Nothing could get done.

As all this was going on, two conversations took place that helped to move the deliberations surrounding the president's education-reform agenda forward. Meeting with the president at the White House, Kennedy, Gregg, Boehner, and Miller made a commitment to get No Child Left Behind passed before the end of the year. That gave them only a few weeks. It would be their highest domestic priority and receive the same sort of attention the president was also now seeking for his newly proclaimed war on terror.

A second conversation took place at the Department of Education in which Paige told his lieutenants to invite congressional staff to use departmental offices and resources as long and as much as they wanted during this time of trouble and dislocation on the Hill. It was not only a nice gesture on Paige's part but his attempt to forge a true partnership with the Hill in order to achieve the president's goal.

From mid-October forward, the pace of debate and discussion picked up dramatically. The parties could always agree on the focus, leaving the details for later, to be ironed out during implementation. After all, without a law there would be no implementation. All—administration and departmental and congressional staff—agreed that they would be full partners in the implementation process in order to keep deliberations going and to calm any nerves. Suddenly stumbling blocks that had impeded progress for months were cavalierly resolved, and consensus emerged over what had been the most contentious issues only weeks earlier. The House and Senate education leadership were constantly updated on where discussions stood and kept each other engaged throughout this very busy period. The hope was to pass something out of conference before Thanksgiving and then in each chamber before the Christmas break.

It is said that Lyndon Johnson, during that heady time following his election when he came up with the idea of the Great Society, instructed his aides to get him legislation as soon as possible. Do not sweat the small stuff or worry about the details, he is supposed to have argued. All of that can be handled later. He was consumed by the need to get his Great Society programs up and running, recognizing that the mandate the nation had given him would not last long, not with a war raging half a world away. As a result of this strategy, Johnson may have the record for the most legislation introduced by a president to become law. His administration established a host of new federal programs and departments, most of which persist today. Johnson helped create the modern welfare state, building upon the legacy left by his mentor, Franklin Roosevelt. Johnson's critics, of whom there are many, also argue that his hurry-up-and-worry-about-the-details-later approach explains in part why so many of the Great Society programs and policies never really worked.

It would be an overstatement to suggest that the Bush administration and Congress followed Johnson's approach as they sought feverishly to pass No Child Left Behind in the weeks following the 9/11 attacks and the discovery of anthrax on the Hill. But not much of one. The period from the start of the Bush presidency until the terrorist attacks had, after all, been one of long, extended discussion about the president's education-reform agenda. It was during this time that the act's agenda, tone, and broad principles and policies were shaped and agreed upon. Moreover, Bush's proposal built upon already existing law—the Elementary and Secondary Education Act of 1994, or Improving America's Schools Act—and a foundation of federal education law dating back to the 1960s. Bush did not invent the idea of Washington getting engaged in American public education. Still, in order to accomplish what Congress did in the weeks leading up to final passage of the law, many last-minute compromises were made, several tough issues were left unsettled, and concern for unintended consequences was discarded. In the end, Congress passed and sent to the president a monumental piece of legislation over six hundred pages long. President Bush's No Child Left Behind proposal, introduced to the nation only days after he became president, became Public Law 102-110, "An Act to close the achievement gap with accountability, flexibility, and choice, so that no child is left behind." It was signed on January 8, 2002, having passed with just days remaining in the previous year. In an elaborate and symbolic series of events in New Hampshire, Massachusetts, and Ohio, Bush, along with the "Big Four"—Gregg, Kennedy, Boehner, and Miller—and Secretary of Education Rod Paige, celebrated what the president hailed as a fundamental change in the way America goes to school. "As of this hour," the president remarked, "America's schools will be on a new path of reform, a new path of results."

A few days later, at a gathering of education leaders from the states held at Mount Vernon, Paige put his own spin on what the president and Congress had just accomplished and what it was now the responsibility of all present to implement: "This isn't a Republican law or a Democratic law, it's an American law!"

# 4

# Doing It

The day after the elaborate bill-signing road show that heralded the passage of No Child Left Behind, Secretary Rod Paige hosted a meeting at Mount Vernon, George Washington's home overlooking the Potomac River across from Washington DC. It was a gathering of the chief education officers from each of the states. Never before had a secretary of education hosted such a gathering. It was historic. Congressman John Boehner attended; as did Margaret Spellings (La Montagne married Austin-based attorney Robert Spellings in August 2001). Paige had his senior leadership team attend. His chief of staff, John Danielson, had conceived of the idea as a way to establish a working relationship with the state chiefs and Paige's ownership over the implementation of the new law.

Danielson came on board just as the push for No Child Left Behind heated up the previous autumn. A Texan, he had a successful business running for-profit schools for at-risk children. One of those schools was in Houston, where Paige had been superintendent. Danielson had served before in the Department of Education, under Secretary Lamar Alexander. When Paige's first chief of staff left to return to Texas, he had been encouraged to contact Danielson by Spellings and Beth Ann Bryan.

Danielson made it his business to help Paige gain control of the department and reestablish his credentials as secretary of education. Not long after Danielson's arrival, Paige announced a sweeping reorganization that had most of the policy and operational offices reporting to the under secretary and the day-to-day operations of the department under the deputy secretary. Both still reported directly to Paige, and both remained with Paige in the single box at the top of the organization chart that Paige had drawn up when he first arrived. But Danielson sought to move things beyond the organization chart. He sought to build Paige's image and visibility. Visits to offices within the bureaucracy were scheduled. "All-hands" staff meetings were called, during which Paige would moderate a conversation among departmental employees. And Danielson sought to control internal and external communications. Sensing his boss's frustration with the White House and Sandy Kress, Danielson tried to make sure Paige and he had control of the department.

The Mount Vernon meeting was important for more than its history. Paige was determined to reclaim ownership of the president's reform initiative. Now that it was law, he would oversee its implementation. The first step in that implementation was establishing a working relationship with those state policy makers who hold sway over most of what passes for public education in this country. Paige knew that he would have to depend on the various state secretaries of education, superintendents of public instruction, and so forth, in order to make No Child Left Behind a reality in the fifteen thousand school districts in America. By hosting an elaborate dinner at George Washington's plantation estate, Paige hoped to charm his guests. The next day, with a round table discussion focusing on the law and soliciting from each chief his initial views toward it, Paige sought to engage all in a conversation. He wanted to demonstrate that he was interested in hearing from the state leaders and that his department would not "hand down orders from above" but would seek consensus as much as possible.

Delivering remarks after dinner the first evening, Paige combined a sense of the moment and place with an admonition that this new law would indeed become the law of the land. There would be no waivers, no exceptions. Every state, Puerto Rico, and Washington DC would carry out the letter of the law, Paige warned. Boehner and Spellings had sent the same message before dinner. This would not be business as usual.

This was in fact a very important message to send. When George W. Bush arrived in Washington in January 2001, the most recent version of the Elementary and Secondary Education Act—the Improving America's Schools Act—had been reauthorized in 1994 under Bill Clinton. No Child Left Behind built upon many of the provisions of that earlier legislation. But in 2001, fewer than eleven states carried on their books laws, regulations, and policies implementing that earlier law. The Clinton administration's Department of Education had either granted most states waivers regarding many of the law's provisions or negotiated compliance agreements postponing their implementation. In other words, most of American public education remained relatively unaffected by the federal Improving America's Schools Act, and those in Washington charged with implementing that law did not seem to care. Now, seven years later, with a new, more robust federal education law on the books and a president declaring that law his highest domestic priority, the relationship between Washington and the states was about to change. At Mount Vernon, Paige sought to send a clear, unmistakable message: this administration was serious. Each state would have to put in place whatever policies they had failed to implement under the previous statute, then fully implement No Child Left Behind according to regulations the department would publish within the year. There would be no waivers.

The meeting at Mount Vernon was cordial. All agreed it was an atmosphere conducive to productivity and established a firm foundation upon which to build lasting partnerships. As the meeting concluded, Paige invited all to pose for pictures on the veranda of the plantation overlooking the wide Potomac River. He gave each state chief a framed portrait of Washington as a memento of the historic gathering. But the discussions had been superficial and relatively meaningless. The one thing all took away from Mount Vernon was an appreciation for the diverse approaches each state took to public education and federal education policy and how difficult it would be to make No Child Left Behind work in each, given that diversity. There was good will all around, for sure, but it would be tested time and again over the course of the next year and a half.

Paige and Danielson were energized by it all. The implementation of the new law would be their proving ground. While Paige had felt, and had indeed been, marginalized during much of the congressional debate over No Child Left Behind, now was the time for him to take ownership of the law during its most important stage: implementation. He could rationalize to himself that his relative naiveté concerning Washington and politics, along with the strong-arm attitude of the White House, helped to explain the problems with the process early on. But he understood what it takes to run schools, to administer education policy. He could put himself in the shoes of state and local education officials who would have to turn No Child Left Behind into a reality. Margaret Spellings could not. Sandy Kress was back in Texas. This would be Paige's opportunity as secretary of education to demonstrate his unique talents. With Danielson at his side, always looking out for the secretary's interest, Paige felt confident this was his time.

Paige also knew that implementation would be very difficult. In addition to the challenge of overcoming a culture of indifference to federal education law among state leaders, this new law was very, very complex and reached down to the individual school and school district levels unlike any previously enacted statute. Moreover, it was a law that few either in Congress or at the state and local levels really understood or knew much about. Confusion reigned, produced in part by those education interest groups that had opposed the law almost from the beginning. No single such group had supported it. While voicing support for the overall concept of ensuring that all children learn, they had vociferously fought against most of the law's provisions with any real teeth. State boards of education, along with state education chiefs, had decried the federal usurpation of state authority over education, although the Council of Chief State School Officers had not campaigned openly against the law. The two national teachers' unions—the National Education Association and the American Federation of Teachers (AFT)—had opposed much of No Child Left Behind more openly, although the AFT leadership had sought to find some common ground with the Bush administration. The nation's school superintendents, through their national organization, had been very vocal in opposing the bill, recognizing they would be targeted as responsible, fairly or not, when schools were labeled for failing to make adequate yearly progress (AYP).

Added to all this was the challenge of educating people about what the law actually meant—a far more difficult task than most understood. Those reporters who covered national politics had almost no understanding of education as an issue because it rarely, if ever, emerged as a major national concern. They would need an education on education. The state and local media, often covering education politics and policy, were relatively unfamiliar with federal policy as it filters into state and local education policy and administration. They would need an education on education as well. Complicating all of this was the fact that most reporters are lazy and tend to go to the same sources for their stories, and those sources were usually either opposed to No Child Left Behind, confused about it, or ignorant of its provisions. Moreover, the media like to write and report about conflict. From the outset, then, the coverage of the new law would focus on its problems.

Paige understood all of this. He told his team of the countless times he had employed the media to his advantage when superintendent in Houston. He tried to school his colleagues in the need to work the media, in the understanding that perception is reality and that they must create a positive perception concerning No Child Left Behind.

Implementing this law would be enormously difficult. Paige was excited about it.

Rod Paige would say often in the coming months, "It's one thing to pass a law; it's another thing to enforce it." Indeed, transforming a legislative proposal into a statute is just part of the process. Implementing and enforcing its provisions form the necessary next step. And it is not an easy step to take. Most people think that the job is done once Congress acts and the president signs a bill into law. In reality, this leads to a long, complex, bureaucratic process, headed by the executive branch, aimed at translating a law into policies and processes to be followed in its implementation. Here, the bureaucracy has enormous influence in the policy-making process.

The Administrative Procedures Act of 1949, written partly in reaction to the avalanche of legislation that was the New Deal, was Congress's attempt to establish set procedures for how the executive branch shall translate duly enacted statutes into regulations and guidelines for the implementation and enforcement of statues. While it has undergone various transformations since first enacted, the operating principles behind the act have remained unchanged. As the government goes about establishing regulations for the implementation of laws, it is required to follow certain procedures aimed at ensuring that the views of the public, particularly of those most immediately affected by the statutes, are part of the decision-making process that goes into writing regulations. The process is called rulemaking. The Washington bureaucracy goes about it every day, and it is often the most important part of the policy-making process.

Laws are blunt instruments, and no law is perfect. Most consist of vague language and conflicting provisions, embrace nonspecific purposes, and lead to unintended consequences. The purpose behind rulemaking is to give "life to the law" by enacting regulations that clarify the law's meaning and provide direction to those who will be called upon to enforce and implement it. This was particularly important in the case of No Child Left Behind—a long, complex statute with thousands of provisions, hundreds of titles, and a host of vague passages and potentially conflicting language. In some places the law simply instructs the Department of Education to create regulations putting certain policies into effect. In other places it limits the department's discretion in implementation. In others, there is a void—no discernable answer or purpose—which the department is required to fill.

This was understandable—to a point. The law was a reauthorization of earlier statutes dating back to 1965. There was, therefore, both legislative and executive branch history to fall back on. Paige and his team were not starting from scratch. In addition, in the waning days of 2001, as Congress worked hard to complete its task and send an education bill to the president, staff and members agreed to iron out certain details during the rulemaking process. While that process is inherently executive in character, the administration had sent the message that Congress, through its staff, would be a partner in it. But by almost any measure, this was an enormous piece of legislation to translate into regulations that would direct federal, state, and local policy makers.

Most of the provisions followed earlier enactments of the law but contained changes that had to be clarified and adopted through the rulemaking process. For example, Title I, the provision for "improving the academic achievement of the disadvantaged," the original heart of the 1965 Elementary and Secondary Education Act, now took up almost two hundred pages and contained, among many things, the enormously complex and important provisions governing accountability, testing, the identification of schools to determine whether they made AYP, the establishment and delivery of supplemental educational services, English-language instruction, and school-reform strategies, in addition to language dealing with the money authorized to underwrite all these programs and how it was to be distributed. It also contained two new programs that the administration had highlighted as critical to the ultimate success of No Child Left Behind: Reading First and Early Reading First. Title II addressed the status of the nation's teacher corps and contained language outlining the importance of highly qualified teachers in every classroom, what that means, how to accomplish it, how to make sure parents know whether their child's teacher is highly qualified, and what to do when the teacher is not. Title III had new language to govern language instruction for limited-English-proficiency students and immigrant students. The public school–choice provisions were written into Title V. Title VI contained policies to promote greater flexibility for states and local education agencies in the implementation of the law. All of this material would have to be translated into countless pages of rules and regulations, guidance and policy prescriptions before No Child Left Behind could become a reality in the nation's school districts.

But that was only part of the challenge. Congress, frustrated by what it saw as a recalcitrant education bureaucracy under Clinton and a Clinton administration that had demonstrated a casual attitude toward the implementation of the earlier Improving America's Schools Act, included in No Child Left Behind deadlines to be met. The Department of Education had to force all states to comply fully with the earlier law within just a few months of the new law's passage, and regulations implementing it had to be in place within the year. These were unheard of time frames, difficult to achieve under normal conditions and seemingly impossible to meet given the breadth and scope of this new law.

Two approaches to rulemaking were to be followed as the education bureaucracy went about its task. For much of the new law, the department was to abide by well-established procedures for rulemaking. It would write proposed rules, which would be published in the *Federal Register* for public input. After a certain period, the department would collect those responses, address them, and then prepare final rules for publication. This process was to be followed regarding such programs as Reading First and Early Reading First. For the more complex policies relating to standards, testing, and accountability, negotiated rulemaking would take place, which required the department to select a panel of individuals, representing diverse interests—teachers, parents, administrators, state and local policy experts—to engage in deliberations with representatives of the department and reach consensus on draft rules. This was to be done in public meetings, according to a schedule published in the *Federal Register*. Once draft rules were agreed to and published for public consumption and responses, the department would react to the responses and publish draft final rules. Both were long, drawn-out processes, but negotiated rulemaking was the more difficult because it invited direct, extended engagement by those most directly affected by No Child Left Behind.

All of this began to unfold in an atmosphere that combined a sense of accomplishment with a sense of mission, but with no small degree of mistrust mixed in. The passage of No Child Left Behind was a milestone, a major accomplishment for a still-new president against the background of a new kind of war. After the Mount Vernon meeting, some of Paige's key aides had been invited to the White House for individual pictures with President Bush. Congratulations and gratitude were extended all around. Paige followed up with several high-level meetings with department staff who would be critical to the rulemaking and implementation effort. He would be personally and directly involved. On Capitol Hill, however, there was anxiety. Staff, primarily Republican staff, harbored serious doubts about the competence of the department to discharge its duties efficiently and responsibly. They worried that Paige and his team, rather than taking charge, would let career bureaucrats run the process and thereby permit the sort of bureaucratic mindset to develop that had undermined the implementation of earlier versions of the law. And they wanted to be full players in the rulemaking and implementation process, as promised during the waning hours of the legislative process. Hill staff, primarily those who worked directly with John Boehner and Judd Gregg, would be relentless in their attempt to influence, and even direct, the flow of business within the Department of Education. A period of considerable bipartisan consensus building and harmony was about to give way to bickering, taunting, quarreling, and quibbling, as Republicans on the Hill and within the administration started turning on one another.

❧

The office within the department with the primary responsibility for managing the day-to-day processes of rulemaking was the Office of Elementary and Secondary Education. The assistant secretary of that office, Susan Neuman, a very highly regarded scholar of early childhood education and reading, had been recruited by Spellings and Beth Ann Bryan and was among their favorite hires. She knew her stuff, did not suffer fools gladly, had little patience for the bureaucratic process, and could be trusted, Spellings and Bryan felt, as a loyal soldier. However, she had little understanding of the Department of Education and the rules and procedures that govern rulemaking. Her knowledge of Congress and the ways of Capitol Hill was rudimentary, stemming primarily from what she may have picked up in classes and the media. Both Spellings and Bryan understood all that and did not care. They hoped to employ her expertise to guide the process toward outcomes they favored, particularly in reading, and have others on Paige's team deal with the world beyond.

It became pretty apparent early in the process that Neuman would not be managed so easily. As she assembled her staff, she drilled and grilled them on her management style. No one was to speak with others in the department about the policies and processes being pursued in her office without going through her first. That extended to all types of communication: e-mail, phone, and person to person. Should someone from the executive team—the under or deputy secretary or the secretary himself— reach out to one of them, they were to report to Neuman, who would handle it. Her insistence upon this was unwavering and quite obviously caused strain within her organization. It was also, quite simply, both an impossible and an illogical management mentality. Neuman and her staff worked for the secretary of education and reported directly to him through the office of the under secretary. If the under secretary or his chief of staff wanted to talk with someone on Neuman's staff, he needed to be able to do so without having either to seek Neuman's permission or to speak directly to Neuman herself.

Neuman's management style reflected her character and background. She was immensely insecure in her new position, aware of her weaknesses and vulnerabilities. Yet, she possessed at the same time the arrogance of an academic. These two personality traits led her to seek to control all operations under her office. Rather than reach out for support and counsel as someone new and unsure of her new job, she sought to shut out any external influence that might reveal her shortcomings. Her arrogance convinced her she was right, even as her insecurity caused her to seek to control everything for fear that some mistake might be made. All of this took its toll on those closest to her. It was an untenable working environment.

Something else caused Neuman to seek to keep a lid on much of what her office did. She was working closely with Bryan and, through her, with Spellings at the White House, as well as with Reid Lyon at the National Institutes of Health. All four had a deep background and expertise in reading and the science of reading instruction. President Bush often referred to Lyon as the nation's "reading czar." They had set ideas regarding what really works regarding reading instruction, and now, with the passage of No Child Left Behind, and with it Reading First and Early Reading First, the opportunity and the money to put their ideas into practice. They could not afford to have this chance muddied by bureaucrats or politicians who might care too much about either process or interest groups. And so, as the point person in the department, Neuman sought to insulate herself from her superiors there and relied upon cover and protection from Bryan and Spellings. This would come back to haunt her and, eventually, to destroy the administration's reading initiatives.

At the same time Neuman was getting her head around her responsibilities, Paige, prodded by Danielson, began to market the president's new education plan. All were stunned by the level of misinformation out there about No Child Left Behind and convinced that a massive public relations campaign would have to be waged. The problem was that the U.S. Department of Education was ill equipped to wage such a campaign and had never done so before. Many agencies in the government engage in extensive public-affairs campaigns to inform citizens of services available. Health and Human Resources, for example, spends million of dollars annually on such campaigns regarding such things as Medicare, Medicaid, and prescription-drug programs. But this was uncharted territory for the Department of Education. Still, with so many of the new law's opponents well organized and well funded and already fully engaged in a grassroots campaign to undermine No Child Left Behind, Paige felt it was imperative that he mount a counteroffensive.

What Paige wanted was a war room similar to those set up during presidential campaigns: a central place within the department to coordinate and implement a public relations strategy for No Child Left Behind. He wanted a team of people assigned to the room to monitor what was being said and written about the law around the country. He wanted to be able to dispatch to anywhere in the nation someone from the department who could respond to and correct any false statements. He wanted the ability to determine where the arguments and opposition were coming from and to counter them immediately. He wanted to demonstrate to the White House and his allies on the Hill that he was fully engaged in a campaign to convince America of the wisdom of No Child Left Behind.

He badly needed to be able to do that. For as the spring of 2002 approached, it was becoming quite evident that the law was a source of massive resistance, fundamental confusion, and growing resentment, some from surprising areas. When the law was passed by Congress, both chambers and parties heralded it as a major accomplishment. But even as the rules and regulations to implement the law were just being developed in Washington, resentment was building, especially among those school districts long considered strong and possessing good reputations. Places like Fairfax, Virginia, and Upper Merion, Pennsylvania, publicly worried that the law would make them look less successful than they were, clouding their reputations for being among the nation's best and leading parents and taxpayers to question district leadership.

They had reason to worry. At the time No Child Left Behind emerged, most of the nation's better school districts could point to consistently high average test scores on state and national tests as one of the many indicators of their success in educating students. The time was long past when districts could make their case by relying primarily upon graduation rates

and college-admissions figures. The standards-and-accountability movement that commenced in the 1990s had made test scores the coin of the
realm now. Good districts hailed good scores as evidence of success. Poorly
performing districts shrugged their shoulders and sought to downplay poor
test scores. But No Child Left Behind would add a new wrinkle to things.
Even while the details had yet to be worked out, it was beyond question
that districts would now have to disaggregate test scores. This meant, for
example, that the scores for low-income or minority or special education
students would have to be separated out from the overall average student
scores in an attempt to uncover any existing achievement gaps among
groups of students within a school and school district. This would in all
likelihood expose heretofore hidden weakness among some of the nation's
most highly regarded school districts. High overall average scores could
hide lower average scores among certain student subgroups. Indeed, in
many districts it was common practice either not to test or to discourage
the testing of certain students generally considered to be poor test perform-
ers, such as special education students and non-English-proficient students.
Neither the number of groups to be disaggregated nor how schools and
districts were to go about doing that had been determined, but there was
no mistaking the fact that this would become a fact of life. Leaders among
the nation's more highly regarded districts feared their reputations might
be tarnished unfairly.

Ironically, of course, many of these districts are among the posh suburbs
of the nation's major cities and are often Republican strongholds. It had not
taken long for superintendents in such places to let their representatives in
Congress know of their dissatisfaction and the pending possible harm to
their reputations. Among the nation's urban areas, where most felt the new
law might do the most good, there was anxiety too. Here school and political
leadership felt they had been singled out by the law. It was already difficult
enough to succeed in places like Philadelphia, Los Angeles, and Chicago,
given the myriad of challenges such districts face. The new law would make
success even more difficult. The cities had more diverse student populations,
hence more possible subgroups to disaggregate, making it more difficult to
succeed overall. The cities had more special education students, as a percentage of the overall student body, and more students who were not proficient
in English. The new law, it seemed, was stacked against urban schools. The
more subgroups within a school or district, the more difficult it would be
to make AYP, since each subgroup would have to improve each year. More
homogenous schools and districts would have an easier time. The nation's
urban centers, largely Democratic strongholds, were therefore not shy about
letting their representatives in Congress know of their concerns as well.

Soon members on both sides of the aisle were hearing complaints about
No Child Left Behind, even though the rules and regulations that would

inform the implementation of the law had yet to be written. This led to growing and widespread concern on the Hill that the administration and the department had to be actively engaged in countering many of these doubts. After all, the mid-term elections were looming in the fall of 2002. Members who voted for No Child Left Behind had to be able to explain their vote to constituents, among them school personnel who held out high anxiety about the law. Paige understood all of this and wanted desperately to fight and win the public relations battle.

Gradually, the war room took shape. It was designed to resemble the room established in response to 9/11 in the Old Executive Office Building, the Eisenhower Office Building next to the White House. Just as that office sought to monitor events worldwide and prepare responses when necessary, so would Paige's war room. It looked the part, with computers, maps, charts, and publications strewn throughout. But the department could not monitor fifteen thousand school districts; it was not even prepared to monitor fifty states, Puerto Rico, and the District of Columbia. It became painfully obvious early on in the implementation of this new law that the department was not equipped or prepared to enforce federal policy in education; it had never had to before. The challenge confronting Paige was far more profound that anyone, including the secretary, had realized. But that did not diminish others' belief that the job had to be done and that Paige must do it.

The true nature of the public relations and political challenge confronting those who supported No Child Left Behind became much more obvious during a meeting held in the Eisenhower Office Building in the early summer of 2002. At that meeting were Paige's top aides, GOP staff from the House and Senate, Barry Jackson from the White House political shop, and David Dunn from Margaret Spellings's office. The purpose of the meeting was to discuss the upcoming congressional elections and how to employ No Child Left Behind to the advantage of Republican candidates. Arguing that it was a major triumph for the president and his party, most argued the GOP should exploit the new law by hosting various events at public schools just as the new school year got underway, then playing off those events during the campaign. But those in attendance from the department knew all too well that educators were at best lukewarm, if not downright hostile, to the law, and staging pro–No Child Left Behind events at neighborhood schools would not produce positive press. "I hate to throw cold water on this, but your superintendents and teachers don't like this law. You need to understand that. This isn't something they feel like celebrating," one of Paige's aides commented. The Hill staff were silenced for the moment. "You might think about going to local business groups—Jaycees, chambers of commerce. They recognize the importance of accountability and good schools. But I would stay away from schools, at least initially."[1]

The fact that GOP staff and campaign professionals failed to understand how No Child Left Behind was playing out among the nation's schools was, on the one hand, perplexing. Did they really think superintendents, principals, and teachers want to be held accountable? And even if some did, they scoffed at the idea of standardized tests being the tool to measure student performance. Did campaign staff not understand what Congress had done by passing No Child Left Behind? On the other hand, given the fact that most of those who worked on the legislation knew next to nothing about how schools work and instead relied upon earlier renditions of the Elementary and Secondary Education Act, it should come as no surprise that they did not understand the wrath that they might encounter from the education establishment. And given the fact that many in both the House and the Senate who supported the law probably did so out of loyalty either to the president or to their political party's leadership, having little firm knowledge of what the law really said, it is entirely predictable that they might not understand that a major legislative accomplishment aimed at improving America's schools might be seen as anathema by those schools.

As the meeting broke up, the true scope of the political challenge was beginning to take shape. The focus would have to be on turning public opinion—not necessarily educators' opinions—in favor of No Child Left Behind. This would become a major concern for the White House, the department, and the GOP congressional campaign committees going forward. It would have to be a coordinated effort, emphasizing certain themes and ideas, focusing on a positive image, or "brand," for the law, and telling the important story about how the Republican Party and GOP members in Congress were working hard to improve public education. The staff in the GOP campaign offices got to work immediately. The department, by now bogged down by the heavy lifting of writing the rules and regulations to steer implementation of the law, and lacking the talent, resources, and experience to mount a major campaign, continued to struggle to get its bearings. Within a few days of the meeting, the congressional Republicans had prepared a press kit with a CD on No Child Left Behind and presented it to Spellings. Impressed with what she saw, she called Paige and asked where the department's response to the challenge was. There wasn't one—yet.

But the department was making progress on rulemaking. Negotiations over the standards, testing, and accountability provisions continued through the summer and were producing begrudging consensus. The issues still entailed how to count the various subgroups for purposes of AYP and how to deal with students who might belong in more than one group. Testing non-English-language students and special education students continued to generate discord as well. How to fold existing state testing and accountability regimes into the No Child Left Behind provisions was becoming a major stumbling block. After all, every state already had in place some sort of accountability system before No Child Left Behind arrived. The degree to which those systems could be coordinated with the new mandates of the federal law would depend on the specifics in each state. Here the politics could get as dicey as the policies. For more than a decade, governors and state education leaders had been busy erecting sometimes very complex testing and accountability systems, often investing a lot of money and political capital. They would not appreciate having to dismantle those systems or to change them substantially in order to accommodate federal law. Moreover, the president and Congress had hailed the flexibility of No Child Left Behind. The true measure of that flexibility would now be tested.

Virtually every state watched the negotiations with interest, but two stood out. The Bush administration had hailed North Carolina as an example of a strong accountability state. Yet, ironically, the way negotiations were going, it appeared North Carolina would have to make extensive changes to its system to comply with the new law. Florida, under Gov. Jeb Bush, the president's brother, had earned a national reputation for education reform and its extensive accountability program. But it was at odds with the direction in which negotiations with No Child Left Behind were heading. This could present problems in a number of obvious ways.

The issue of federalism—granting states as much flexibility and deference as possible—concerned Paige and his team a great deal. In the end, they would have to rely upon the good will of governors and state education chiefs to make the promise of No Child Left Behind a reality. Forcing state policy makers to abandon what they had spent years constructing surely would not create the sort of good will Paige knew he needed. Time and again during the rulemaking negotiations, Paige and his aides would go to Spellings and lobby for as much flexibility as possible. She seemed unmoved by their efforts. The law, in truth, offered little room to maneuver in its testing and accountability provisions, and Spellings was leery of state efforts in this area anyway. Urged on by Bryan and Neuman, she scoffed at those state leaders who claimed they had strong accountability systems in place. The regulations, as they began to take shape, would hold out the hope to state policy makers that states might be able to find some common ground between what they already had in place and what No Child Left Behind expected. But that hope would prove hollow.

❦

While all of this was playing out during the summer of 2002, Paige was also busy pulling together his budget projections to present to Spellings and the White House Office of Management and Budget (OMB). The budget process is never-ending in Washington. No sooner is one budget put to bed than the next has to be prepared. Ostensibly, the federal government's fiscal year begins on October 1 and ends on September 30. But seldom does the process itself adhere to that calendar. Presidents deliver their budgets to Congress in February each year. Congress, according to design, massages the president's requests and passes a budget for the president to sign. The budget itself usually reflects a coming to terms between the executive and legislative branches of government and is, in many ways, a roadmap of the two branches' politics and priorities. Members of the president's administration, cabinet officers, subcabinet officers, and so forth, appear before the budget and appropriations committees of both the House and Senate to defend the president's budget request and respond to members' questions. It is truly the heart of the political process in the nation's capital.

With regard to education, money matters. When No Child Left Behind passed, it included language that authorized Congress to spend a certain amount each year to underwrite the various provisions of the law. For Title I, for example, Congress had authority to set aside, over the first five years that the law was in effect, upwards of $70 billion for grants to local education agencies just under Title I's programs for improving the academic achievement of disadvantaged students. Similar projections were written into the law for the other programs it embraced.

But in the congressional budget process, there is an important distinction between how much Congress might authorize to be spent on something and how much Congress actually appropriates for that purpose. Seldom do the two match. There are good reasons for this. The committees that oversee the policy-making process in each chamber—the Senate Committee on Health, Education, Labor, and Pensions and the House Education and Workforce Committee, in this instance—attempt to arrive at some consensus concerning how much Congress might be willing to spend on legislation that it passes. These are authorizations, therefore targets established by the legislation. Often the authorized amount is very high, usually to get members on board to support the bill by enabling them to go home to voters and say they supported adequate funding for policies they voted to adopt. But as each budget is assembled, the appropriations committees look at both the authorization amount contained in legislation and how much money is available at the time, reflecting fiscal realities and political needs. For this reason, the actual amount Congress appropriates for something is often lower than the amount authorized for that same purpose.

When No Child Left Behind was passed, there was not much talk of money. The president had asked Congress in his first budget for sizable increases in education spending, primarily in Title I and special education, reflecting his priorities and in an effort to get his education proposals enacted. And surely, Bush's willingness to open his pocketbook contributed to the bipartisan support for his proposals, a strategy he had employed while governor of Texas as well. His succeeding education budgets likewise contained substantive increases in education spending. But the amounts authorized for No Child Left Behind exceeded Bush's actual budget requests, leading his critics to argue that he was not backing up his priorities with enough money. This became a political issue, at least among congressional Democrats, almost immediately. Both Ted Kennedy and George Miller argued time and again that the president was not living up to his promise to "fully fund" his highest domestic priority. As Paige prepared the next budget, he began to hear this refrain not only from Congress but from educators around the country. Even the considerable increases both he and the president would send to Congress were criticized as underfunding No Child Left Behind. Paige would hear this chorus throughout his tenure as secretary. And no matter how much he tried to rebut it, it was a chorus that resounded time and again in the media.

Money was only the most visible issue confronting the administration as the early implementation of the education-reform law got underway. Before any regulations were final, everyone recognized that testing would become a growth industry in American education. The nation's major test providers, firms such as Pierson, McGraw-Hill, and Houghton-Mifflin, for example, had long been supplying states and school districts with standardized tests to satisfy a number of objectives. But with No Child Left Behind, testing would take on increased significance, and every child in grades three through eight would be tested annually in math and reading at least. There was considerable concern, both within the Bush administration and among the test companies, about their capacity to shoulder such a heavy demand. As it was, there had already been more than a few incidents of breakdowns and mischief in the administration of tests among the states. With so much riding on testing, it was critical that the testing companies be able to demonstrate both the capacity to meet the demands of No Child Left Behind and the ability to ensure the integrity of the process.

Paige and his senior aides agreed to meet with leaders of the nation's test companies to get a sense of their thinking. Gathered around the secretary's conference room on the seventh floor of the Department of Education, executives listened as Paige explained his concerns and asked whether they were baseless. He also let it be known that he felt the new law created a huge market for the services these executives had to offer and that they would need to step up vigorously to meet its demands. All gathered at the table agreed they could handle the challenge, while also admitting that some capacity building would have to take place. And they offered the observation that some federal funds to assist in making that capacity building possible would be very helpful. At that, Paige turned to his aides with a look of disbelief. Here were the representatives of some of the nation's largest textbook publishers and test providers being given a huge new market for their products and asking for a handout from the government. Absurd,

Paige thought. He adjourned the meeting abruptly and thanked all for coming, remarking that he was encouraged by what he heard. He then walked into his office and admitted to his staff his wonder that such large, successful, and wealthy companies still had the chutzpah to seek a handout.

Still another concern from the outset centered on two new and potentially very important aspects of the law that were both controversial and, in Paige's opinion, essential to the success of No Child Left Behind. The provisions for public school choice and free tutoring had emerged during the congressional deliberations as substitutes for vouchers in response to the need to help students stuck in struggling schools. The law stated that kids in such schools—schools not making AYP two or more years in a row—should be allowed to attend another public school of their choice and have access to free tutoring. The provisions were wildly popular with conservatives and not too offensive to liberals, and on the surface, they made sense to many. But now it was time to implement them, and that was proving difficult.

The school-choice option had shortcomings from the get-go. The law did not require interdistrict school choice, only intradistrict choice. Thus, a child could choose another school within the same school district. Going outside the district was not denied. States had the authority, as always, to promote interdistrict school choice, and some already did. But that would remain a state and local prerogative. The problem with all of this was that in many, if not most, troubled school districts, few, if any, schools would in all likelihood be able to make AYP. Hence, students would not be able to choose a successful school and escape a failing one. And in the event that such a school did indeed exist within a failing district, the chances were that it was already at or above capacity. But even here there was a problem, for it would be up to districts and states to determine just what constituted capacity for purposes of school choice. So, a school with some empty seats might be defined as at capacity merely because school administrators liked to maintain lower student-teacher ratios. Then there was the problem of schools and parents not wanting to allow children from failing schools to attend their successful school, fearing these students might lower test scores and drag the school down. Any way you slice it, the school-choice option seemed to have the potential to break down completely—to become no option at all. This concerned Paige greatly.

The tutoring provisions seemed to hold great promise. But here the problem was how to make sure quality programs were provided, how to keep districts from trying to limit outside providers, and how to determine the impact the services might have on student and school performance. On the surface, the concept made great sense. Kids stuck in failing schools should be able to access quality tutoring underwritten by federal taxpayer dollars. Paige and his staff felt there should be as few restrictions as possible regarding the provision of tutoring services. But they recognized there would have to be some. They also knew that districts would want to provide the services in order to be able to tap into the federal dollars that would underwrite them. This made no sense to Paige. Why should a district that failed to get the job done in the first place be allowed to provide tutoring and get paid for it? The debate went on as the rulemaking process proceeded.

Gradually some consensus on tutoring services emerged, however. It was tentatively agreed that states would decide who qualified to provide them. They were to seek as wide and diverse a mix of providers as possible: nonprofit and for-profit, community and faith-based organizations, and so forth. But providers would have to demonstrate, to the satisfaction of the states, their bona fides to provide such tutoring services. Schools and school districts failing to make AYP would not be eligible to provide the services, although teachers employed by such districts could. A hotly contested issue surrounded whether providers had to employ only certified, highly qualified teachers. Paige's team argued they should not be so limited. Surely there were men and women qualified to tutor kids who did not possess teaching certificates, for example, college faculty and graduate students. The decision would be reached later.

By late summer, every state not in compliance with the 1994 Improving America's Schools Act had reached an agreement with the department to get into compliance. That, in and of itself, was no small accomplishment. Drafts of regulations and guidance covering much of the new law were winding their way through the department, the White House, and the clearance process at OMB and were being circulated among staff on the Hill. The goal was to complete the process in the fall. But at almost every turn, GOP staff on the Hill took issue with the drafts they saw. There were testy confrontations with department leadership both in person and over the phone, with accusations hurled back and forth. Hill staff saw the proposed regulations as way too bureaucratic and reflecting the influence of the education establishment. Staff felt too much was being conceded to state and local decision makers, which would undermine the entire reform effort. After all, it was at the state and local levels that American education was failing. Paige's team adamantly disagreed, arguing the law was overly prescriptive, making it difficult to write regulations other than those drafted. They took offense at the accusation that they were bending to the education establishment, "the Blob." And they found it stunning that their most vocal critics were Republicans on the Hill!

The loudest of these critics was Sally Lovejoy, an aide to Congressman Boehner, who was fiercely loyal to her boss, deeply skeptical of Paige and his team, and very vocal about her concerns. Picking up the phone, she would call Margaret Spellings to vent, leading Spellings to call the department to vent. Lovejoy and Spellings enjoyed a unique relationship because their bosses had a unique relationship. And Lovejoy employed it to go around the department and undermine its credibility at every step. She took great pleasure in screaming at lower-level staff at the department, knowing Spellings would echo her concerns to higher-ups there. All the while, as the relationship among the three—the White House, the department, and the Hill—began to buckle under the strain, Paige felt more and more at pains to try to establish his authority. In his eyes, the Hill should deal with the department, and the department should deal with the White House. Lovejoy and her colleagues were hurting the department by violating appropriate procedures and making him look bad. And Paige did not feel comfortable knowing some of his most senior staff were engaged in extended conversations with both the Hill and the White House without his permission. This violated his chain of command and his desire to make sure communication within and from the department was managed properly. Time and again he lectured his top aides, complaining that they should not talk to the White House or the Hill without going through his office. Danielson echoed the secretary's concerns, more than once traveling down the hall to monitor what was going on and who was talking to whom. Gradually, an aura of mistrust began to gather within the department at the very highest levels. The concern about control within the department became an obsession. Sometimes it seemed no one trusted anyone.

There was more than enough evidence to suggest this general mistrust was well deserved. It was becoming almost impossible to get straight answers about the progress of the rulemaking process and the implementation of the president's reading programs from Susan Neuman. Initially, Paige and his lieutenants gave Neuman room to maneuver. After all, she was the nationally recognized expert on the subject. But as time went by, it became more and more difficult to get information from her office. There were reports of run-ins with lawyers in the office of the general counsel. Neuman would want them to provide her with what she needed by way of legal advice and chaffed when they did not. There were rumors that she would instruct her staff to do what she wanted, even if that was at odds with what the lawyers told her. On more than one occasion, one of Paige's top aides, when visiting the Office of Elementary and Secondary Education, would find her huddled in her small conference room with Beth Ann Bryan and David Dunn of the White House. This would encourage speculation on Paige's part that Neuman was doing her own thing, in conjunction with White House instructions, either delivered directly by Dunn or through Bryan. Paige's aides repeatedly told the secretary that they were unable to manage Neuman, that she was not willing to give them the information they needed to do their jobs or to tell Paige what he wanted to know. When Paige confronted her about this, which happened frequently, Neuman would become defensive, saying that she had a difficult time working with some of Paige's people and then going out of her way to be gracious and informative. The problem was that there was no way to confirm the accuracy of the information she was providing.

Susan Neuman was under a great amount of pressure to produce. On her shoulders stood the success of the rulemaking process and much of the implementation of No Child Left Behind. The president's two reading programs, very visible and very important to the White House, were in her care. Staff on the Hill watched her every move and hounded her and her staff for updates on every aspect of implementation. As her superiors at the department sought to understand where things stood, she began to look upon them as intruders rather than allies and colleagues. She grew in her apparent paranoia. Her staff would meet secretly from time to time with some of Paige's leadership team. Often in tears, they would tell of difficult working conditions, an assistant secretary obsessed with control and chain of command, and an almost tyrannical management style. They would invariably end such sessions with pleas that they be kept confidential, fearing retribution should Neuman learn that they were talking to others.

On top of all of the pressure surrounding the efforts to write and publish regulations and guidance for No Child Left Behind, as well as to get programs underway, Neuman and Paige were being pressed to find some way to demonstrate tangible evidence that No Child Left Behind was already beginning to make a difference. Rulemaking was essential, surely, but few beyond the Beltway knew or cared much about that bureaucratic process. Visible evidence was needed that this time federal education policy was being implemented and felt at the state and local levels.

One response to the White House's pressure was to hit the road. Paige, Neuman, and much of the senior leadership team traveled extensively, trying to call attention to No Child Left Behind. Frequently, their travels coincided with opportunities to present checks for grants, often in congressional districts where important elections were at stake. Neuman hosted events aimed at highlighting reading. Others attended programs aimed at focusing on school choice and supplemental educational services. The goal, always, was to generate good news about No Child Left Behind. There were visits to local editorial boards and conference calls with writers who covered local and state education beats. It was an unprecedented attempt to get a positive message out. And it did very little good. The pressure from the White House and the Hill continued to mount.

As autumn approached, the administration wanted a trophy to hang on the wall, something that would make national news about No Child Left Behind. The regulations would be made public no later than November, and they contained provisions requiring states to submit draft accountability plans to the department by the end of January 2003. The anniversary of the bill signing was approaching. The goal became to stage some White

House event, with the participation of the president, to commemorate the first anniversary of the signing of the law and the progress made during the year. January 8, 2003, became a target date. It became imperative that the department be able to deliver a positive message for the White House and congressional Republicans on that day.

The climate of pressure, distrust, and confusion had boiled over into a confrontation in the secretary's conference room in late summer. Margaret Spellings asked the team overseeing the regulatory process to meet with her, Sally Lovejoy, and a delegation from the Hill. The draft of the regulations was almost complete, and she wanted all to gather for an informal sign off. Instead, a screaming match ensued, with Lovejoy complaining that the draft regulations were completely unacceptable. Spellings sided with Lovejoy, even though she had purportedly read the draft and provided little reaction to department staff. This angered Paige's people, who disliked the idea of someone from the administration siding with the Hill against them. Heated recriminations were thrown about. There were threats of resignations. It was very ugly. As the meeting broke up, Spellings remained behind to calm feelings among department staff and to seek some way to move things forward.

Eventually things did progress, but the meeting left a bitter taste in everyone's mouth, poisoning an already difficult relationship all around. Paige himself knew little or nothing about the confrontation and the feuding among the White House, the department, and the Hill. His closest personal aide, Susan Sclafani, had attended the meeting; she had been very engaged in the regulatory process and felt it had been going well. In Lovejoy's eyes, however, Sclafani was just another member of "the Blob," not to be trusted. Indeed, so was Paige for that matter. And Lovejoy detested Susan Neuman. Her criticisms of the draft regulations grew as much from her distrust of those overseeing the process as it did from the language in the draft itself. But Paige had little knowledge of any of this. His only concern was getting things out before the end of the year, preferably before the end of November. That would be in line with Hill and White House expectations and permit his team to work for some sort of visible event to coincide with the anniversary of the bill signing.

Despite all the drama, the regulations were published as Thanksgiving arrived. While they would not be final for some time yet, the general expectation was that there would be few changes since they were the product of a rough consensus achieved through negotiations. During December, Neuman and Paige's top aides were given the job of pulling together some sort of event to highlight the accomplishments of the year and to demonstrate that No Child Left Behind was already having an effect in America's schools. The accomplishments of the year were not trivial, but they concerned the work of the bureaucracy primarily and were hardly the stuff of the news, even within the Beltway. And it was silly to argue that the new law was somehow winding its way into the nation's public schools in any real sense. Surely, there was talk, all kinds of reporting, and no small amount of conjecture about the impact it would have. But its real effect would only begin to be felt in the coming year, as implementation took hold. Still, politics, as Paige often quipped, is about perception as much as anything else, and the White House wanted to create the perception that things were moving along at a fast pace.

In addition to preparing for some sort of event in January, Neuman was trying to get the first slate of grants out for Early Reading First, a pre-K through grade three reading program, to be administered through a competitive grant process. This would be as much a true signal of the coming impact of No Child Left Behind as anything else.

⚮

The gentle dance that would have to take place with the states during the implementation of No Child Left Behind commenced in earnest in November 2002. Everything hinged upon getting state leaders to buy into the law. For years, most had all but ignored federal education law, while taking in billions of dollars in federal education money. The administration was hellbent on making sure things were different this time. Paige was consumed by that mission. Still, he had few enforcement mechanisms at his disposal. The secretary always retained the ability to penalize states for failing to comply with federal law by withholding federal funds. Indeed, the new law contained language instructing the secretary to do just that, whereas previous versions had merely given him the authority. This was Congress's way of sending the message that it was fed up with the department's lackadaisical enforcement in the past. Moreover, in the history of the Elementary and Secondary Education Act, going back to 1965, no state had ever seen any of its federal dollars withheld.

But Paige did not want to employ that tactic if he did not have to. He knew any attempt to withhold funds would be met with fierce resistance from state officials and Congress, even though Congress now insisted it be done. Moreover, he saw it as a very limited enforcement device. It would be one thing to punish one or two states, but should a number of states seek to challenge the law, Paige knew his hands were tied. The problem then was how to convince state leaders to undergo close scrutiny by federal officials, change existing education policies and practices, spend resources to meet federal mandates, and take on the politics of education within their communities. How do you get someone to do something he does not want to do, to spend time and money he does not want to spend and claims he does not have enough of, and to risk incurring the wrath of constituents, when you have no real ability to force him to do it? This is the conundrum Paige confronted.

Public policy, in essence, is all about getting people either to do things they normally would not do or not to do things they might want to do. Here, then, was a textbook case of public policy to be played out on a national stage. Paige and his lieutenants hatched a plan laid during the writing of the regulations that were to guide implementation. As each state moved to draft an acceptable accountability plan, state officials would complete a workbook developed at the department. Because each state had a unique approach to education policy generally and to accountability specifically, each workbook would also be unique, serving as a guide to the law's implementation for that state. Someone or some group within the department would be assigned to each state, working with its education leaders to complete the workbook. In addition, a panel of "peers" selected by the department would review each plan in order to provide an independent voice to verify compliance. The workbooks become a blueprint for No Child Left Behind compliance within each state. Once a book was completed to the satisfaction of officials in Washington, a state's plan for implementing No Child Left Behind would be approved.

This approach had a bit of both desperation and genius. The desperation was obvious: enforcement depended on the willingness of state leaders to do what the law required. But the workbook approach, if it worked, meant state leaders would gradually buy into the law and acquire some ownership of it within their state. They also would work closely with the U.S. Department of Education in a cooperative rather adversarial relationship. Disagreements would be ironed out. The goal would be to work together to achieve mutually satisfactory results. Washington would hold the upper hand, surely. Paige held tight to the "no-waiver" pledge first committed to at Mount Vernon months earlier. But he would seek to charm the states rather than bully them. He instructed his chief aide in charge of this phase of implementation, the under secretary, to begin meeting with state education officials from each state.

Together, Paige, Danielson, and Spellings hatched a plan. They wanted to announce the first states to come into compliance with No Child Left Behind on the first anniversary of the bill becoming law, January 8, 2003, well ahead of the January 31 deadline. This would indeed be newsworthy. It would be unprecedented in federal education policy, demonstrate real movement in implementing the law, and create, they hoped, a sense of momentum that might drive other states to get in line. The problem became finding states willing to come forward, make the changes needed, and step up. Moreover, they could not be just any states: it would be important to have both Republican and Democratic—red and blue—states. This would have to be seen as a legitimate accomplishment for the administration.

As November bled into December, Neuman focused on two tasks: finding promising states for a January 8 event and releasing the first round of grants under the Early Reading First program. The great challenge with the first project was finding someone at the state level willing to step forward. There was a general reluctance among state chiefs to be out front on No Child Left Behind. All held out the hope that the administration would find greater flexibility than it had so far and grant states greater deference going forward—this in spite of Paige's constant protestations to the contrary. But over the months, as the regulations had evolved and conversations among departmental and state leadership had gone forward, it seemed that perhaps a few individuals at the state level might be coaxed into moving forward. The focus fell almost immediately upon two politically important states that seemed within reach: Ohio and Massachusetts. The obvious political significance was the fact that these were Boehner's and Kennedy's home states. But the education leadership in both, Susan Zelman in Ohio and David Driscoll in Massachusetts, had worked well with Neuman and her staff during the preliminary discussions on their state accountability plans. Both seemed willing to seek common ground with the department on how their existing accountability systems might be revised to fit under the provisions of No Child Left Behind. Driscoll was already considered a leader among his colleagues, having chaired the Council of Chief State School Officers, and had a national reputation for the education reforms he had advanced in his state. Though less well-known, Zelman understood the state and national politics involved. Neuman and her team, along with David Dunn from the White House, began courting them both in earnest as the holidays approached. At the same time, the education chief in Colorado, Bill Maloney, a good friend of one of Paige's senior aides, was approached, and Beth Ann Bryan began quiet negotiations with Richard Mills in New York. Indiana's education commissioner, Suellen Reed, eager to cement her credentials both in the state and nationally, seemed approachable. Throughout December, then, these five worked with a very small cadre within the department to complete their workbooks and reconcile their states' education policies with those prescribed under No Child Left Behind.

Between Christmas and the New Year, real progress was made, and it appeared that all five leaders would be able to make the case that they had plans in place to bring their states into compliance with the law. Obviously, these would only be plans; strategies to achieve real compliance would follow. They would need to go back to their state boards of education, and in some instances to their state legislatures, to actually enact the changes needed to achieve full compliance. And there were no guarantees that any of that would happen. Still, being able to announce that five important states were well on their way was politically significant and would help create some momentum for other states to follow. The fact that each of the state chiefs had been told of the possibility of participating in an event at the White House with the president certainly made negotiations a bit easier, although in keeping with administration policy, no commitments were ever made.

As the date approached and all returned from the holidays, Paige became more and more agitated. He had been kept informed of the states involved and where things stood. But he knew none of the details, and he liked to know details. Neuman had met with him infrequently, and getting information out of her had been like pulling teeth. Paige's top aide, who had overall responsibility for the implementation of the law and oversight of Neuman, had not been very forthcoming either. Finally, a few days before the proposed White House event and only hours before he was to meet with the president to brief him on where things stood, Paige began a quiet panic. With his aides and Danielson in his office, he demanded to know more of the details and chastised his aide for not getting him what he needed. "I am getting ready to go in to see the president, and I don't really know what's going on. Do you understand?"

His aide looked at him and said with resignation and frustration, "Secretary Paige, neither do I."

"But you're in charge of this; it's your responsibility."

"I can't get the information I need from Neuman. She refuses to work with me or my folks. She won't tell me what I need to know so I can tell you."

Suddenly Paige got it. Summoning Danielson, he admitted there was a serious problem. He wanted Neuman in his office immediately. She arrived a bit wide-eyed and anxious. After trying to explain where things stood and to relieve the secretary of his concerns, she handed Paige two papers that she felt would be the primary focus of the discussion with the president. In order for these states' plans to be approved, Paige and the president would have to allow them to put off most of the serious work of making academic progress until well into the future. The law required adequate progress each year but permitted states to compute their progress in three-year averages. Each of these five states wanted to report only minimal progress during the first several years with the promise of greater growth in achievement, toward the goal of universal proficiency, in the out years. They wanted to be able to delay the serious work for a few years, no doubt in the hope that by then the law would have changed. Neuman and her team said this would be a necessary condition for almost any state to sign on. Paige worried it would easily be seen as an attempt to put off the heavy lifting the law required.

The second document provided a brief assessment of how things might look going forward if the law and regulations were put into place, given where America's schools were. It suggested that within a few years, perhaps a majority of the nation's schools would be labeled as inadequate. This was the direction the law seemed to be taking things. It might even be worse. It was important for Paige to understand this and to make sure the president did as well. Did the administration really want to be in the position in a few short years of saying most of America's schools were failing?

Paige had already seen both papers. What had frustrated him was their lack of context and his knowing that the president had received them the evening before and quite understandably might want to question Paige about them. Now he had some of the background he needed. He studied them for a while, discussed them with his aides, and prepared for his meeting with the president.

That afternoon, Paige and his aide, the under secretary, traveled to the White House. In the reception room of the West Wing, they were met by Spellings and Dunn. The purpose of the meeting was to brief the president on where things stood for January 8 and get his sign-off on the two issues discussed in the papers Paige had been studying. As they left the reception room heading to the Oval Office, they were joined by a retinue of White House staff, along with the vice president.

There is a gentle choreography that goes into meetings with the president in the Oval Office. People are expected to sit in certain places. The president sits in a chair with his back to the fireplace, facing the room, looking out toward his massive desk and the South Lawn beyond. When in attendance, the vice president sits next to the president in a similar position. Two sofas flank the room, set apart by a coffee table and paralleling the Seal of the Presidency embroidered on the magnificent rug that occupies the middle of the room. On this day, Rod Paige was to sit on the sofa to the president's right, Spellings, Dunn, and the under secretary on the sofa to his left. Others, among them White House Chief of Staff Andy Card, as well as members of the president's speechwriting team, policy shop, and press and communications team, assembled. Also in attendance was Karl Rove. The January 8 event was as much about politics as policy, after all.

As all took their places, Spellings began to explain the purpose of the meeting, after some gentle banter back and forth among the president and all in attendance. He shot some digs at Rove and Spellings before focusing on the upcoming event. "Where's Texas?" Bush quipped. Spellings and Dunn blushed a bit and told the president Texas was not quite up to the job at this point.

Before Spellings could bring up the two primary issues for discussion, Bush pulled out the chart explaining the time line for states to get all students to proficiency and the steep hill they would need to climb a few years down the road. He was aware that critics could read this as an attempt to put off the tough business until later but seemed unfazed. "I have no problem with this," Bush snapped. With that the first issue was resolved.

Both Paige and his aide then brought up the issue of a large number of schools not making AYP. They wanted to make sure the president understood the potential liabilities involved in telling the American people that a majority of their schools were not getting the job done. Again, the president seemed matter-of-fact in his response. "If that's what the data tells us, if that's where the numbers take us, so be it. Dealing with the fallout isn't my problem, it's his," he laughed, pointing to Rove, hovering toward the back of the Oval Office. It was Bush's casual way of saying, let the numbers play out, and let Rove deal with how the politics play out.

It was a brief session. As it ended, Bush asked how "Rod" was doing, gave Spellings a peck on the cheek, and joshed with aides about the day's news. It was, in all, a nonevent. The president had come to the meeting understanding the concerns, prepared to resolve them, and ready to move on.

Three days later, as promised, President Bush hosted the representatives of five states at a short ceremony in the East Wing, congratulating them on their accomplishments and sending the message that his education law was indeed beginning to make a difference. The event was widely covered by the media, and as Paige, his aides, and the state leaders returned to the Department of Education for a brief ceremony and reception, all were excited. Paige was particularly pleased, both because of what his team had accomplished and because the president seemed so happy.

In attendance at the East Wing on that day had been several staff from the department, among them many who had toiled so hard to get the five states ready for compliance. Also in attendance was Susan Neuman. As the president spoke, she beamed with pride. Within hours she would no longer be employed by the Department of Education; nor would she be a member of the Bush administration.

⟨∞⟩

The story of the nation's assistant secretary for elementary and secondary education resigning her position on the same day she witnessed an important milestone on her watch is one of incompetence touched with arrogance. Only hours after the White House event, Neuman was sequestered with Brian Jones, the department's chief lawyer, responding to his inquiries about the decision making that had gone into the planned distribution of grants under the administration's Early Reading First program. He needed her to respond to some troubling aspects, and Neuman became agitated, angry, and very emotional. It was unpleasant business.

Early Reading First was one of the two high-visibility reading programs introduced by No Child Left Behind. It and Reading First were created to change the way the federal government underwrote reading instruction in this country. During the presidential campaign, Governor Bush had repeated over and over again the mantra that education policy should be based on sound research. The most obvious problem with that argument, however, was that relatively little sound scientific research existed on what works in education. What was available focused on reading. For a generation, research conducted at the National Institutes of Health, primarily under the direction of Reid Lyon, had established the essential components of sound reading instruction. With Reading First and Early Reading First, the administration wanted to apply those principles through federal grants to states and schools.

Reading First, according to No Child Left Behind, was to replace the reading program that had existed under earlier versions of the Elementary and Secondary Education Act. It was to be a formula grant to the states, but with a twist. Formula grants are awarded to states according to criteria usually established by statute. States get a share of the total available and spend the money to advance the purposes of the grant, usually with some guidance from the federal government. Under Reading First, this was to continue. However, to receive its allocation of money, each state would have to apply, and that application would have to be approved by the department. It was the first time a formula grant—considered an entitlement by the states— would require an application. And the reasoning behind this was to force states to agree to spend the money to support reading instruction that embraced the principles established by the National Institutes of Health. The administration wanted to change the way Americans are taught to read, and this program was to be the primary tool for accomplishing this.

Early Reading First was a competitive grant that states, school districts, schools, and early-learning programs could seek. Under competitive grants, applications are supposed to be reviewed by an independent panel of department-selected experts, who rank them according to criteria established by the department. The panel's recommendations are then sent to the office within the department overseeing the program for final review and sign-off before grants are awarded to the winning recipients. The purpose of having a panel of experts is to insulate the grant process from politics, inappropriate influence, and potential conflicts of interest. A way of involving expertise from the field in shaping public policy, it is also a long-standing practice in most government agencies.

While grants under Reading First were still months off, Neuman had sought to expedite the Early Reading First program in order to get the first slate of grants out to winning recipients before 2002 ended. Working closely with Beth Ann Bryan and Reid Lyon, she assembled her panel of experts, many of whom were well established in the reading research and instruction community and some of whom were close to either Neuman or Bryan or both. It was a panel, in other words, that both felt confident would choose only those applicants who would fulfill the research and instruction principles they embraced. They did not want administration money going to tired, untested reading programs that might have local and state support but were not getting the job done, in their minds. They wanted to make good on President Bush's policy of giving taxpayer dollars only to proven policies.

In December, the panel had completed its task and forwarded its list of recommendations to Neuman. Because in such cases these are recommendations, department officials retain the authority to make adjustments to the list. Officials' ability to exercise such discretion is important, however. Each administration seeks to put its imprimatur on the management of public policy, which usually means overseeing, and often overriding, the decisions of career civil servants within the agencies. The competitive grant process is run by such career employees, and there are always risks of their controlling the agenda and the outcomes. For this reason, Neuman and Bryan wanted to be actively engaged in picking the panel of experts and shaping the final slate of grant recipients.

When the final slate arrived at Neuman's desk, she made some adjustments to the panel's recommendations, moving some of the applicants receiving lower scores up higher on the list. They would now be awarded grants, despite the panel's not recommending them as recipients. Following procedure, toward late December, she sent the final list for departmental authorization. She asked for expedited clearance, which meant she wanted all those offices that needed to sign off on things to do so as quickly as possible. This would have been a problem in most instances, given the notorious pace of the bureaucracy, but this was also a new program and therefore entailed a higher level of scrutiny. And the holidays were approaching, with office receptions and staff taking some leave. Neuman pressed hard, however, and was getting her way.

Just before Christmas, the slate of potential award recipients arrived in the office of legislative affairs and that of the under secretary. Again, this was procedure. The legislative office would want to know where the award recipients were located to determine which members of Congress might be affected. The under secretary's office would be the last hurdle in the clearance process, since that was the office Neuman supposedly reported to. As the slate arrived, Neuman pressed staff in both places for a quick turnaround before the holiday. This raised some suspicions since there was no apparent need to rush. A closer look revealed that the list of finalists differed from that the panel of experts had recommended. Further study revealed that some of those slated to receive awards used curriculum materials written by Susan Neuman during her career as an educator, before she came to the department. This set off some alarms, and the department's lawyers were contacted. It appeared Neuman had adjusted the slate to award grants to individuals or organization that employed materials she had written. The question became whether she had done this deliberately and would benefit from the action she had taken; was there a conflict of interest?

As Brian Jones and his staff in the general counsel's office studied the situation, two things became almost immediately apparent: the slate had been adjusted, for sure, and those moved up the list were those who used Neuman's materials. She had to have known this. In addition, others had agreed to the change, among them Beth Ann Bryan. Again, there was nothing inherently suspect about rearranging the slate. The lawyers were concerned, however, that some of the recipients had a relationship with Neuman through the materials she had written. There was no real concern that Neuman stood to benefit financially directly from the decisions that had been made. When she joined the department, she agreed to forgo any income she might derive from the sale or use of her curriculum materials while employed by the government. But she did stand to gain once she left the government. In other words, her decision could benefit her directly later, and this was a problem.

The clearance process was halted as staff looked into the issues. Neuman was told that the holiday had slowed things up. As the apparent potential conflict of interest became more obvious—potential because the awards had not yet been made—Jones notified Paige of his concerns. He also contacted the Office of White House Counsel. There the reaction was swift and harsh: they felt the conflict was real, intentional, and demanded immediate action, potentially criminal charges. Jones convinced them to slow down, arguing that Neuman was no criminal and that the problems stemmed as much from her incompetence and naiveté as anything else. Upon being briefed about the situation, Paige felt Neuman needed to be confronted and, should her explanation prove unsatisfactory, dismissed.

That confrontation took place on January 8, just after the White House event. Neuman argued that Jones and others were reading too much into things, that she did not stand to benefit from what she had done and all were being unreasonable. She argued that some in the department did not like her and wanted her out, while others had known what she was doing and signed off on it. Jones was compassionate as Neuman broke down, but he was unrelenting in his assertion that her actions were wrong and had the potential to cause the secretary and the administration embarrassment or worse. After a long, difficult discussion, she agreed to resign immediately. By January 9, Susan Neuman was in the private sector. No public explanation was given for her abrupt departure other than her formal letter of resignation, accepted by Paige with a formal note of thanks on his part for a job well done.

With this, Paige finally began to grasp, as did others, the full effect of Neuman's tenure at the department. The event was a symptom of her larger management shortcomings—problems that would have hampered implementation of No Child Left Behind going forward. Her departure offered Paige an opportunity once again to gain a stronger hold on the management of the law and the department. Within days, Spellings, who had been surprised and stunned by the allegations against Neuman, asked the under secretary to fill the void on an acting basis. Implementation of No Child Left Behind would have to go on without a full-time assistant secretary to oversee it.

c∞∞

The excitement surrounding the January 8 White House event quickly dissipated. Neuman's sudden departure left people questioning what had happened. Paige and his team remained silent, only adding to the apparent mystery. On the Hill, staff reacted with a combination of relief and concern. There was no love lost there for Neuman, but with the challenge of implementation getting into high gear, the lack of an assistant secretary to oversee things was troubling. Even more troubling was the growing discontent over the law among educators and members of Congress.

Within the department, Paige and his team started a concerted effort to build on the momentum generated by the five states signing on to No Child Left Behind. He had instructed his top aide to meet in Washington DC with delegations from each state to discuss implementation issues and how best to move forward together as a team. These meetings, usually consisting of two- to four-hour sessions with key staff from the U.S. Department of Education and their counterparts from the states, consumed most of the days between mid-January and early spring. Taking place in the conference room of the under secretary, the conversations were unfailingly cordial, generating considerable good will and contributing to the sense of partnership Paige deemed essential to the ultimate success of No Child Left Behind. Each state was assigned a contact within the department, someone who would work with that state's designated team to complete the state's workbook and establish a strategy for bringing it into compliance with the law. These networks of relationships, with ongoing conversations, helped to ease the early tensions surrounding its implementation. Gradually a sense of trust and even collegiality began to emerge, at least among many of the state leaders and the department.

Even collegiality, however, may not be enough to get people to do what they are reluctant to do. Even the most willing state leadership confronted the challenges of convincing state and local education leaders to go along with changes to established state policies. And some among the states adamantly refused to play ball. Nebraska's brusque commissioner of education, William Christianson, was vocal in his disregard for No Child Left Behind and his unwillingness to change established state policy. Kentucky commissioner Gene Whilhoit, often credited with overseeing dramatic education reform within his state, was not interested in departing from the reform strategies he was pursuing in order to comply with No Child Left Behind. Louisiana's state education board was equally adamant about maintaining its accountability system rather than bending to the mandates of No Child Left Behind.

Each of the meetings with each of the states had begun with the same commentary coming from state leaders. Each expressed support for the goals of the new law and appreciation for the invitation to come to Washington to discuss concerns and ideas. All proclaimed the virtues of the accountability system established within their states and how, if left to their own devices, they would be able achieve the purposes behind No Child Left Behind. Each left these sessions, no doubt, more comfortable than when they arrived but less convinced that their state's existing system would survive completely intact. They were right.

Even with the apparent good will generated by the department, it became obvious that some external pressure would have to be applied to get the states to move beyond conversation and to act. This pressure would come in the shape of another deadline that states would have to meet in order to comply with the new law. This strategy had already worked once. In order to get the original five states on board, and to get the other states moving toward compliance, the department had set the date of January 31, 2003, for submission of draft plans for accountability under No Child Left Behind. All the states met that deadline, an accomplishment much ballyhooed by Paige, even though it was really an empty gesture on the part of most. Most had merely sent along what they were already doing as placeholders for the discussions that were to ensue in the under secretary's office. But another deadline seemed necessary in order to move things beyond discussions. Following a look at the calendar, it was decided the deadline for final approval of the states' accountability plans would be June 8, five months after the first five states had been approved. If a deadline had worked the first time, the thinking was one might do the trick again. At the same time, the idea of another White House event as incentive to push things along was hatched as well.

Everything hinged on getting the states to adhere to the dictates of the law—something they neither wanted to do nor had been forced to do by earlier administrations implementing earlier versions of the Elementary and Secondary Education Act. At any step in the elaborate process of discussions, negotiations, and bargaining between the department and the states, it was very possible that things would break down, that the state leadership, with the help and support of its congressional delegation, might simply refuse to go along with what was being asked of it and call the department's bluff. Department officials were painfully aware of this, knowing that if merely a handful of states stood firm in their opposition to the new law, they had almost no leverage to force compliance. This realization, no doubt, had led prior administrations to get whatever compliance they could from states. Forcing the issue might bring down the entire federal-education-policy house of cards. It was simply that simple.

As February stretched into March and April, days were consumed with state discussions and negotiations. At the end of each day, a team would gather in the under secretary's office to review progress, compare notes, and seek solace. Each state had to be dealt with on its own terms. Each state plan would reflect the discreet negotiations with the state. As those negotiations continued, stated leaders compared notes and sought to find concessions their colleagues may have won. Department staff stood firm, asserting the uniqueness of each state. Over countless hours and in often heated conversations, state and federal teams sought to settle differences. As progress was made, mild celebrations were held in the department. When a state finally acquiesced to departmental demands, a pin was stuck on a huge map of the United States hanging in the reception area in the under secretary's office—an official tote board of progress in getting state accountability plans approved. The map became something of an attraction within the department. Paige would often stroll down to gaze at it and see where things stood.

With spring it seemed progress was being made. But getting all fifty states, plus Washington DC and Puerto Rico, on board did not look promising. Negotiations, if anything, were getting more difficult. Certain states, like Virginia, were digging in their heels and calling upon members of the congressional delegation to seek concessions from Paige and his team. A governor or member of the House or Senate visited the secretary on more than one occasion, eager to engage him in a discussion that might find greater receptivity on Paige's part for state discretion.

As all of this was going on, two events took place that, in the end, would help to spur implementation forward. Two states, Georgia and Minnesota, were found to be in violation of compliance agreements they had reached with the department. These agreements had been made to bring those states in line with the earlier version of No Child Left Behind: the Improving America's Schools Act. Moreover, they had been negotiated by state officials no longer in place. In Georgia, a Republican governor and state education chief had been elected since the agreements had been made. A similar situation existed in Minnesota. Here was a test of the department's enforcement authority and attitude. If it looked away, as previous administrations had done, it risked sending the message that other states might be able to get off the hook without penalty. If it sought to enforce the law by withholding federal dollars, which it had the authority to do, it ran the risk that both states' congressional delegations and governors would raise hell and force the administration to back down, exposing the empty threat of enforcement and endangering the entire implementation of No Child Left Behind. Federal education dollars had never been withheld from a state for failure to comply with federal education law.

Paige, when presented with the issue, was convinced of the need to stand firm. Spellings was less strident, recognizing the dicey politics of it all. Behind the scenes, conversations were taking place between the under secretary's office and the state chiefs in Georgia and Minnesota. Both chiefs recognized the problems they faced; neither disagreed with the finding that her state was out of compliance. The department, they were told, was not interested in making a big deal out this; there would be no chest-thumping about enforcing the law. But it had no choice, the chiefs were told. In Georgia's case, close to $1 million in state Title I administrative funds would be withheld. For Minnesota, guilty of a lesser offense, the penalty would approximate half that amount. These dollars usually went to underwriting the implementation of federal policy at the state level; the money did not go to schools and children but instead was absorbed by the state education bureaucracy. Both state leaders begrudgingly admitted their fault and accepted the department's decision. Indeed, on a conference call with Georgia's congressional delegation, organized by the department to inform members of the decision, they expressed gratitude for the department's willingness to work with the state and to keep things low key. After the call, those from the department who had participated looked at each other in amazement: here were members of Congress thanking them for the way the department had acted when deciding to withhold money from their state.

The department kept its promise, and its action was not publicized. Official correspondence between the department and the states, letters that were public documents, memorialized the decision. But no publicity was generated by either side. Word of the department's enforcement did get out. State education leaders, through their tight network and professional association, learned quickly about what had happened. The Department of Education in the Bush administration had done something no previous department or presidential administration had ever done. That surely helped to move negotiations on state accountability plans forward. Absent any bravado from Paige or his team, but with a sense of his holding firm and living up to his promise first articulated at Mount Vernon, those charged with implementing No Child Left Behind seemed a step closer to getting that job done.

cᢁᣑ

As the strategy had worked, a White House event was planned for June 10, 2003. If the department managed to get enough states in line by that date, established by the artificial deadline of June 8, a Sunday five months after the one-year anniversary of the signing of No Child Left Behind into law, then the president would host the states at the White House. Word went out to the states still negotiating with the department. Again, no promises were made, but preparations got underway. Paige kept a vigil on the map down the hall from his offices. There were daily briefings in the under secretary's office by those most directly engaged in discussions with the remaining states. Phone calls and conversations went on well into the evenings and on weekends. It was a frantic scramble to get all the states on board. Utah kept holding off—conservative, very Republican Utah. Virginia did not like being told what to do by the feds, and its former governor and current U.S. senator, George Allen, did not mind letting Paige and the White House know how much he resented the whole process. Kentucky remained distant and hardly interested in discussing things. But those were the few remaining holdouts. The White House political shop joined hands with the intergovernmental shop to put pressure on states where it might work. A Republican state like Utah or Virginia would be loath to embarrass the president by not getting on board. They wanted to be at the White House, didn't they? Promises were made about politics and policy in order to get the recalcitrant states in line.

As morning broke on June 10, every state but one had submitted an accountability workbook approved by the department. These were only plans. Real compliance remained months away as states would have to make good on the plans in place. Still, this was unprecedented in national education history and worthy of some recognition. The weekend before, the go-ahead for the White House event had been given. Representatives from the states had begun arriving over the weekend. Atop the roof of the Hay Adams Hotel, overlooking the White House, a reception and lunch would be held for them and the departmental staff who had driven the process. From there, all would proceed to the Rose Garden, where Bush and Paige would hail a seminal accomplishment in the implementation of No Child Left Behind. Only one state was a holdout: Kentucky.

As the luncheon began and state representatives chatted with one another and their federal counterparts, last-minute negotiations with Kentucky continued over the phone. Those gathered at the Hay Adams varied widely in their embrace of the new law. Most had been brought to this place begrudgingly. They did not look forward to the tests yet to come—putting the plans into action—and resented having to bend to federal will. But they respected Paige and acknowledged the good-faith effort he and his team had made over the months. On this day they would celebrate.

Just as the large delegation began to make its way to the White House, word came that the last holdout was on board. Now the president could announce all fifty states had plans in place.

At a little after two o'clock that afternoon, Bush and Paige stepped out into the Rose Garden to a standing ovation from a large, excited crowd. Among those in attendance were education officials from the states, Washington DC, and Puerto Rico, members of Congress, and department staff. John Boehner was there, still stunned that all fifty states had signed on. Judd Gregg of the Senate was there. The various staff from the Hill who had harassed departmental staff so much during the forgoing months were in attendance. Bush stepped to the microphone and declared, "The era of low expectations and low standards is ending; a time of great hopes and proven results is arriving. And together, we are keeping a pledge: Every child in America will learn and no child will be left behind."

Later that day, during a reception at the Department of Education, Rod Paige continued the celebration. "This is not an end," he commented, "it's a beginning." He was right, of course. With the approval of the state accountability plans, the real work had indeed just begun. Now each state would have to bring those plans to life, convincing state and local education officials, and in some cases governors and state legislators, of the wisdom of going forward. And federal officials would have to devote energy and resources to putting out the brushfires that would flare up time and again as the real work of putting No Child Left Behind into practice began in earnest.

The pattern of state and local action in response to No Child Left Behind became familiar quickly. As state officials began to see the full implications of their accountability designs—how many schools would become labeled for not making AYP—they would seek, time and again, to revise those plans in an effort to limit the fallout from the law. Local education leaders, as though singing in a chorus, repeated their mantras about how unfair the law was—how it labeled schools and kids and punished them even when they worked hard and experienced some success. Within hours, it seemed, of the sign-off on state plans, the response from Democrats on the Hill was all about money. They told constituents who complained about No Child Left Behind that the Bush administration was underfunding the law. They told the leaders of the education establishment that the Bush administration was not living up to its promise to fund the law adequately. As time went by, the complaints grew legion: it required teaching to the tests and narrowing the curriculum; it was punitive and one size fits all. State leaders complained that the law's mandate to test all students in grades three through eight was not only unrealistic but cruel; special education and limited-English-proficiency students could not, and should not, be expected to take the same tests as their counterparts. The administration, recognizing this, would bring forth policies aimed at alleviating some of the stress created by this issue, and those policies were universally criticized as unhelpful. Each time a state came forward seeking some relief from this or that provision, Paige would go the Spellings and argue the case. In each instance the response was, "No, hold the ground."

Among the districts, particularly among superintendents, the criticism was withering. The requirements for highly qualified teachers were totally unrealistic. The labeling of schools undermined morale and made it all but impossible to achieve real improvement. The school-choice provisions were totally absurd; there were no choices in urban settings, and in rural ones they were impractical. The requirements for free tutoring robbed needy schools of money that they should keep to help students. The tutoring providers were unproven and trying to entice kids and their families with free giveaways for enrolling in their programs. The department's guidance was vague, confused, and wholly out of touch with what really goes on in schools. The idea of labeling a school as failing either because fewer than 95 percent of its students took the tests on any given day or because special education students did not make AYP targets was ludicrous.

Paige continued to press the issue, however. As unrelenting as the criticism was, he was no less unrelenting in his defense of the law and its implementation. He traipsed back and forth about the country, countering the growing chorus of naysayers with his ongoing refrains about leaving no child behind, and every child can learn, and testing tells us who knows what and where the weaknesses in the curriculum are. In countless media interviews, his optimism was undiminished. He labeled the critics the "coalition of the whining," after the president's oft-repeated slogan about the alliance he had formed to fight the war on terror: the coalition of the willing.

In a response to the criticism, the administration produced ongoing increases in federal dollars for education—record increases well above those the Clinton administration had offered and certainly surpassing anything supported by previous Republican administrations. But they got no credit for them. Indeed, the Democrats and critics merely continued to assert that the administration was underfunding the law.

Time and again, governors complained to the department about how the law was undermining their own education strategies and agendas. Republicans and Democrats alike seemed united in their criticisms. Gov. Jeb Bush of Florida, who had by this time established a national reputation for education reform, took the department on directly and put the administration in the awkward position of pitting brother against brother. According to the governor, he confronted the confusing fact that schools rated A under his education-improvement plan were getting failing marks under No Child Left Behind. He wanted that corrected; it was not. Other governors found themselves in similar predicaments. Most had run as "education governors" and brought forth various education reform proposals. Now, with increasing numbers of schools failing to make AYP in their states, they had to defend themselves against critics who argued they had failed to live up to their promises.

In a few states, real grassroots rebellions began. In New Hampshire, at that time about as conservative and Republican a state as any, school boards began talking about opting out of the law and turning down federal dollars. The state legislature held hearings and debated resolutions calling for the state to do likewise. In Utah, a Republican state legislature did the same thing, as did the GOP in Virginia. In each instance, someone from the department was dispatched to patch things up, usually by promising to find solutions to the problems cited by state officials. Occasionally the White House would send someone in to appeal to Republican loyalty to the president. Once in a while, someone from Karl Rove's shop would place a strategic phone call in an attempt to quell discontent within the party ranks.

All this, of course, had a cumulative and growing effect on the law's authors and supporters on the Hill. They heard only the criticisms. Support for the law seemed absent. To their minds, neither Paige nor the White House was doing anything to counter the growing negative chorus about No Child Left Behind. They saw it as a totally unacceptable situation, and they wanted something done about it. Paige and his senior team were summoned to the Hill and met with Boehner and Gregg. Accompanied by Barry Jackson, they sat and listened for forty-five minutes as Boehner and Gregg chastised them for their inadequate efforts. The two congressional leaders saw implementation going poorly and absolutely nothing being done to counter the critics. And their own colleagues in the House and Senate were beginning to complain more and more as they heard from their constituents. They wanted something done immediately. Another election would soon be upon everyone after all. This president had run, and won, on No Child Left Behind. Now it appeared he could lose because of it, and the GOP could lose control of Congress.

Much of the situation was exacerbated during the 2004 winter meeting of the National Governors Association. Gathered in the East Room of the White House for a morning discussion with President Bush, the governors were hearing from some of the president's cabinet about various administration initiatives. Paige was there to tout No Child Left Behind and respond to any concerns the governors might have. During the question-and-answer session, he was asked about the teachers' unions: "Aren't they the real problem with getting things done in education and the ones complaining about No Child Left Behind?" The questioner, the governor of Alaska, had posed the question as a softball for the secretary, whom he had come to know and respect during Paige's recent visit to his state. Paige, assuming correctly that there were no media in the room, responded with his usual bluntness. "I think the teachers' union is a terrorist organization," he said, and then explained how the unions try to undermine every reform initiative introduced. The comment was meant as something of a joke. But it fell flat. Worse than that, there was audible gasp as many in the room reacted to Paige's misguided words. Gov. Jeb Bush of Florida held his head in his hands and shook it back and forth. Others laughed nervously. Paige, for his part, tried to recover with additional commentary. After the session, while waiting for the president to appear, he leaned over to his aide and commented that he had probably gone too far with that terrorism quip. He had.

Within hours it was the lead story on the television. While the media were not in the room when Paige spoke, someone had given the story to reporters, who ran with it. The department press office, tipped off about what had happened, was ready with a response: the secretary was "clearly joking." The White House quickly distanced itself from the secretary. Paige's press office issued a statement from the secretary, regretting his "inappropriate choice of words" and seeking to distinguish teachers from the union: "Our nation's teachers . . . are the real soldiers of democracy, whereas the NEA's high-priced Washington lobbyists have made no secret that they will fight against bringing real, rock-solid improvements in the way we educate all our children regardless of skin color, accent or where they live."

The statement fell on deaf ears. NEA president Reg Weaver responded that it was "morally repugnant to equate those who teach America's children with terrorists." Democratic Party chairman Terry McAuliffe called Paige's words "hate speech" that the president and the Republican Party should renounce. "It is a revolting attack on America's teachers to suggest that it is an act of terrorism to disagree with President Bush and to be outspoken advocates for students and teachers." Citing a list of blunders and inadequacies on the part of Paige, the *New York Times* editorialized that his terrorist comment "had finally exhausted his credibility and disqualified him as a spokesman for national education policy." Editorials in papers across the country called for Paige to resign or the president to fire him. Though he offered a series of apologies, it seemed the secretary's credibility was completely gone, just as the presidential campaign was about to begin.

Unbeknownst to the media during all of this, things had continued to go downhill the day after Paige uttered his gaff. Paige had been scheduled to meet with Senate and some House Democrats on the education committees who had felt frozen out of discussions on the implementation of No Child Left Behind for months. They had a point. The Republicans had not held any oversight hearings in either chamber, trying to limit the Democrats' ability to get their criticisms of the Bush administration on the record. But the pressure on Paige had increased, and he agreed, on the advice of his legislative assistant, Karen Johnson, and with the White House's concurrence, to meet behind closed doors with select Democrats.

As Paige and his aides arrived for the meeting, everyone seemed cordial, albeit the secretary's "terrorist organization" comment of the day before surely hung in the air. Greeted by Senator Kennedy, Paige was assured this would be an informal, off-the-record session, and no one was interested in beating up on him. With that, all took their seats, and the screaming began. Kennedy, pounding his fist on the table, demanded an apology from Paige for his outrageous comments of the previous day. Paige offered one up, reluctantly. Senator Christopher Dodd of Connecticut wanted to know why the law's highly qualified teacher provisions did not apply to providers of supplemental education services. Paige demurred to his aide. Senator Hillary Clinton expressed her outrage about the Bush administration's failure to "live up to its commitment" to fully fund No Child Left Behind. One by one, those in attendance reeled off their gripes and lectured and hectored the secretary and his aides about their implementation of the law. Paige was given little chance to respond. In truth, no response was necessary or expected. What the Democrats had not been permitted to do in committee, they had been determined to do in this session: vent their frustrations.

When it was over, Paige looked at his aides and laughed. He understood political theater when he saw it. He did not take it personally, but he did not like having to put up with it, and he really did not like having to apologize for his remark about the teachers' unions. In truth, he did feel they were akin to a terrorist organization in the way they maintained control of the public education monopoly, stifling reform and innovation. And he did not like having to ask the forgiveness of those in the education establishment, the Democratic Party, and the media who had, from day one, been a thorn in his side. As far as he was concerned, he had been in their sights from his first day in office, and nothing he might say or do would garner any support from them.

Over time, as is usually the case, the firestorm that erupted over Paige's comments dissipated. He would survive the calls for his resignation or dismissal. But he had injured himself in the eyes of the White House and his allies on the Hill. He was now seen as something of a liability that required close oversight and management by the administration, especially as the 2004 campaign approached. With this in mind, it was decided that a special unit would be installed at the department to help manage the media, press, and travel that would increase during 2004. The White House wanted a politically savvy team in place to coordinate all events with the White House and, informally and indirectly, with the presidential campaign, as well as to decide Paige's schedule, and that of his senior aides, with an eye to maximizing any political dividends.

Barry Jackson, Karl Rove's deputy, was dispatched to inform Paige of the White House's decision. Paige bristled at the idea of being micromanaged and particularly at having to accept the White House's assigning someone to determine where he would go, what he would say, and so forth. He had worked hard to assemble the team he had in place. For Paige, bringing in someone new was akin to having a virus enter the body. But his protests were in vain. Spellings was adamant, as were Boehner and Gregg. The stakes were too high, and too many mistakes had been made, too many gaffs. And so, Emily Lampkin, a bright, energetic, woman who was both politically and media savvy, was assigned to head a team she would assemble to manage the next rendition of the war room. For the remainder of Paige's tenure as secretary of education, Lampkin and her team would shape much of the public face of the Department of Education. Paige would protest, encouraged by his relatively new chief of staff, Anne Radice. (John Danielson had resigned in summer 2004. Spellings had grown tired of the ongoing tension between her office and Paige's and felt Danielson had contributed to it. Moreover, she was being pressured by some on the Hill to remove Danielson as he was seen as part of the problem surrounding Paige's relations with the media.) Both Paige and Radice would assert time and again that they were in charge and that all senior managers were to look to them for direction and leadership. Paige looked to his deputy and other close aides to enforce his assertion of managerial control. And they tried. But the White House, through the war room, decided who went where, when, and why. In essence, the war room told Paige and his team what to do, where to go, and what to say. Spellings, Boehner, and Gregg had confidence in Lampkin and had lost faith in Paige.

Having a political team within the department was, at best, flirting with illegality. Everyone understood that a president might be expected to campaign for reelection based on his record and that the members of his administration might be called on frequently to act as spokespersons for the president and that record. But Washington has laws in place to limit administrations' ability to exploit for political advantage the executive branch. Sharp distinctions are made between official government business and political activity, and employees, from the top down, are briefed on those distinctions and how to manage them. With the war room, those distinctions were blurred as staff were sent to competitive congressional districts to deliver checks, and Paige and his senior assistants were dispatched to create positive media buzz for friendly members of Congress, governors, and GOP supporters. This was hardly anything new: the Clinton Department of Education had made a reputation for reaping political capital for the president. But with Lampkin and the war room, the Bush administration's efforts were transparent to a fault. It was brazen politics. And they got away with it.

Education played almost no role in the 2004 election. While President Bush attempted time and again with a number of education-related campaign events to get the media to pay attention to his No Child Left Behind accomplishments, the war in Iraq and the war on terror overshadowed every other issue. To everyone's relief, nothing the Department of Education did caused any hiccups. Paige and his team worked hard throughout the campaign to ensure two things: No Child Left Behind would not hurt the president's reelection chances, and the department would not become the source of any bad news during the campaign. Both missions were accomplished.

The day after the election, Bush's supporters and members of his administration gathered in the pavilion of the Ronald Reagan Building in Washington DC to welcome the reelected chief executive. As Bush and his family walked onto the platform, there in the front of the crowd stood Paige and other members of the cabinet, along with a number of the president's closest advisors. Bush lavished praise on Karl Rove, the "architect" of the campaign victory. He spoke briefly about this being his last campaign. With tears welling in his daughters' eyes, he talked about going back to Texas after his time in office was over. Then, to the cheers of admirers and supporters, the First Family walked off stage. Within days, some who had cheered most loudly for their president would learn they were not to be a part of his second administration.

# 5

## Legacy?

As George W. Bush's first term drew to a close, he could point to precious few domestic-policy accomplishments. The war on terror and the war in Iraq, two distinct but related commitments, dwarfed anything else the president might hope to point to as a product of his leadership. He had delivered on the promise to his base of tax cuts early in his tenure, even while some on his economic team had counseled caution. But other than that, the crush of international events had consumed him. No Child Left Behind was his single, signature domestic-policy victory. And it was the one he had always cared the most about.

President Bush did not come upon his interest in education casually. Rather, it had become a passion while he prepared to run for governor of Texas. As governor, he embraced education reform with a genuine fervor, achieving substantive change, and the state saw education improvements because of his leadership. For George Bush, education was deeply rooted in his "compassionate conservative" philosophy. It was linked to his deepest political instincts as well. When he decided to run for president, there was no question that education would be a high priority in his campaign, even though it was a very low priority in national politics and government. Bush changed that, perhaps forever.

As Bush's second term approached its end and another presidential campaign began, the prominence of federal education policy generally, and No Child Left Behind specifically, became subject to question. The impact of No Child Left Behind was being felt, surely. It remained very controversial, largely dismissed as bad policy by most educators and bad politics by a majority of both parties. Yet, it was in place and functioning in every state, with schools posting adequate yearly progress results and regularly reporting state scores on No Child Left Behind tests, the National Assessment of Educational Progress (NAEP), and other indicators. It seemed that account-ability in public education was fully ensconced in America, whether or not No Child Left Behind remained the fundamental federal education law it became in 2002.

That became the primary concern for Secretary of Education Margaret Spellings and the Bush administration throughout the remainder of Bush's tenure. The law was supposed to be reauthorized in 2007, but the combi-nation of competing priorities within the Congress, a Democratic majority in both chambers for the first time during Bush's tenure, ongoing disputes over funding the war and about the education package, and unrelenting criticisms of the law by education advocates prevented any consensus for reauthorization. This, in and of itself, was not all that unusual. Typically, education statues are seldom reauthorized on time. Indeed, during 2007, Congress was still squabbling over reauthorizing the Higher Education Act, which had been set to expire two years earlier. It had been extended through the budget process with no changes, which is what happened to No Child Left Behind as well, its status left unchanged until Congress and the administration could come to some agreement over its future.

Spellings could not move toward resolution in either chamber, despite courting the law's most visible advocate, Senator Ted Kennedy of Mas-sachusetts. Writing editorials and even making joint appearances with the senator had not generated enough good will to create any traction on the reauthorization process. House Education and Workforce Committee chair-man George Miller, himself a prime sponsor of the original law and a firm advocate for its renewal, had offered some draft language for his colleagues and the White House to consider. But it was seen as "squishy" on account-ability and as moving away from some of the major tenants of education reform embraced by the president. Nor did it attract much support within either party in the House. So, 2007 ended with a general malaise of spirit regarding the law's reauthorization, even as the president and his secretary of education vowed to make it a high priority in the new year.

The new year, of course, brought a presidential election. The chances of any substantive progress being made on any legislation are dramatically diminished during a presidential campaign cycle. With no incumbent or sitting vice president running, 2008 would prove to be an especially volatile election year with a number of serious contenders in both parties. But throughout the caucus and primary season leading up to the parties' conventions and then the November election, education was barely a blip on the political radar screen.[1] There were reasons for this. Both parties were divided on the issue. At the grassroots level, opposition to No Child Left Behind remained high among both Republicans and Democrats. But leaders in both parties had at one time been the primary advocates for it.

Republican contenders for the nomination tried to evade discussing one of their president's most valued accomplishments. Democrats were a bit more outspoken in their criticisms, trying to court traditional Democratic supporters like the teachers' unions. But they were hesitant to condemn too harshly a program Ted Kennedy, a Democratic Party icon, had helped to author and remained deeply committed to. Loyalty and respect for Kennedy took on added significance when the senator was diagnosed with brain cancer. And so, except for a few speeches delivered during the summer of 2008, education generally, and No Child Left Behind specifically, were almost completely ignored by the two parties' nominees: Senators Barack Obama and John McCain.

President Bush had entered his final year in office surrounded by unfavorable poll numbers, with presidential contenders either openly hostile to or politely distancing themselves from him, stuck in an unpopular conflict overseas with an economy rapidly approaching a recession. On January 7, 2008, he traveled to Chicago to encourage reauthorization of No Child Left Behind, admitting that it needed some changes but resolute in his commitment to its basic premises. But on January 8, the sixth anniversary of the signing of the legislation, a date the president and his secretary of education had celebrated annually, no celebration occurred. There was, in any event, little reason to celebrate and every reason to be concerned about the law's future.

Putting aside the politics of No Child Left Behind—and that is difficult to do—the question remains, Has No Child Left Behind changed education in America? Has President George W. Bush's education-reform initiative turned the generation-long decline in American education around? Does the Bush initiative move American education in the direction needed to ensure its students and schools are globally competitive?

Even after President Bush has left office and the Obama administration has entered, it remains too early to answer such questions. But it is not too early to draw some preliminary conclusions and to consider where things stand and where they are going.

Surely, accountability has become the watchword in American education. If nothing else, President Bush deserves great credit for forcing America to pay attention to results in education. It is difficult to overstate the significance of this. Up until No Child Left Behind, the focus at the local, state, and federal levels had always been on spending. More than a generation of litigation among the states produced a myriad of funding formulas aimed at moving toward equity in public school finance. The argument was eloquent in it simplicity, albeit simplistic in its significance: equal per-pupil spending will move the country toward true equality in education.

Low-income communities need additional money so their schools can perform at a level approaching that of schools in more affluent communities. Spending matters. More spending matters more. Focus on adequate and equitable resources, and a rising tide will lift all boats.

As George Bush entered office, spending on public education was increasing at dramatic rates. Bush contributed to these increases with the largest boosts in federal aid to education in history.[2] But he coupled those increases with the accountability demands set forth in No Child Left Behind. Spending would be tied to results; results would drive everything. For the first time in the entire history of American education, student achievement became the bottom line. For the first time as a matter of national policy, superintendents and teachers, school boards and state policy makers had to find ways to explain poor performance and develop strategies to turn around failing schools. As a nation, Americans before No Child Left Behind tended to do two things when confronted with failing schools: throw more money at them, and close their eyes to the problems they present. Because of President Bush, the nation can no longer close its eyes to the problems confronting its education system.

To be sure, Americans' attitude toward public education had been changing before Bush introduced No Child Left Behind. Indeed, it can be argued that Bush might not have seen his education agenda become a reality had it not been for the work going on among the states during the decade before he came to office. Standards-based reform and testing-and-accountability movements were well underway by 2000, driven by state and local education leaders and complimented by Bill Clinton's 1994 Improving America's Schools agenda. Still, Bush made the issue a national preoccupation—no a small accomplishment considering the small fraction of total education spending that comes from Washington and the pressing national and international issues that competed for attention.

The focus on results and accountability also represents an important shift in education policy away from a traditional emphasis on seat time. For years, public education has been all about class schedules that revolve around so many hours of class instruction. That continues of course. But with No Child Left Behind, the real issue became not how long a student sits in a class but how much a student learns. Rather than the process, it is about results—a subtle but important difference in education policy and a focus that may yet prove transformative.

In addition to a focus on results, Bush's agenda brought to the nation's attention the travesty of the achievement gap. For years, educators had known about the performance gap between minority and low-income students and their wealthier and white peers. A poorly kept secret, it was most obvious among the nation's urban school systems, but it was hardly confined to the cities. The irony of all of this, of course, is that such a gap might exist given the preoccupation with equitable spending and the focus on desegregation in American education that began more than fifty years earlier. One might rightly wonder how so much money, litigation, and hard work could yield, years later, schools that are in fact very segregated and a culture that has come to expect and accept the idea that whole populations of young people will not achieve at appropriate levels.

Bush brought the achievement gap out from behind the curtain with his very memorable exhortation to end the "soft bigotry of low expectations," and suddenly America had to confront the ugly truth that American public education was not serving the very kids it was created to benefit. Indeed, it can be argued that public education is contributing to rather than remedying the problem. For the achievement gap is biggest in those places where some of the highest per-pupil spending takes places. High per-pupil spending and an ongoing achievement gap can be found in major urban centers where public education was originally seen as the ticket to the American dream. Public education's animating purpose has always been to act as the great American equalizer: with a good education provided at taxpayer expense, poor children from all walks of life and immigrant children new to this country should be able to rise above their situations and grab a piece of the American dream. Now, it turns out, in school systems across the country, poor, minority, and non-English-speaking children are stuck in schools that more often than not keep them in their place. Public education, at least for these kids, has undermined their chances of success. Stuck in schools that do not work, these children seldom get a good education and seldom rise above their challenging conditions, which more often than not those schools perpetuate. It is as if the purpose of public education has been turned on its head; it tends to perpetuate, if not worsen, social inequalities rather than ameliorate them.

No Child Left Behind, with its testing requirements and mandates to disaggregate achievement data by various socioeconomic indicators, has exposed the achievement gap not only in this nation's urban centers but in schools in the wealthy suburbs that often ring those centers. For years, white flight from urban areas has created rings of suburban school districts that often have developed sterling reputations, even as they have contributed to the de facto segregation that has come to haunt American education. Even with the early accountability movement, these schools could boast of high average test scores, bolstering their reputations for academic achievement. But with disaggregation, the achievement gap is no longer hidden in the averages. Given that the number of minority, low-income, and non-English-speaking children may make up a smaller percentage of the students at these schools, the fact has been unmasked that they, much as their urban counterparts, experience the achievement gap. As a result, many "outstanding" schools are not making adequate yearly progress. And this has punctured the image of those schools and school districts, leading some to question just how outstanding they are and others to argue that the measures being used are unfair and paint an unjust portrait of their schools. All of this is surely up for debate.[3] And much of that debate will color the No Child Left Behind reauthorization discussion. But the existence of the achievement gap is beyond debate. And George Bush and No Child Left Behind deserve credit for framing the discussion about what to do about it.

It is something of a mystery, given all of this, that the achievement gap has not generated greater outrage. There have been pockets, surely. But given how extensive and deeply entrenched the gap is and how obviously it runs counter to the very ideals the country stands for, one might have expected a grassroots or popular reaction to this fundamental failure of American education.[4] Instead, blame has come to rest on a lack of adequate resources, coupled with the breakdown of the social fabric in so many of our cities and minority communities. These kids are difficult to educate. They require more money, more time, and more support. The standard response remains the standard response. But the fact remains that the progress on narrowing the achievement gap has become an integral part of how the nation measures performance in education. And that can only be a positive development.

President Bush deserves some credit, too, for getting Americans to pay more attention to reading and math. These are the two gateway disciplines of education, essential tools for more advanced learning. No Child Left Behind quite rightly, then, focused accountability in these disciplines, from an early age, and that has led more Americans to pay more attention to them. Bush successfully overrode the education establishment's fixation with the reading wars—phonics versus whole language—and forced his "scientifically based" education policies on public education. Reading First and Early Reading First were implemented with a feverish devotion to read-ing instruction backed by years of solid research. Much to the chagrin of many beneficiaries of government largesse under earlier reading initiatives, the administration's dogged determination meant money would only go to programs that worked. There were problems with this approach. Some in the administration were too committed, too driven, and too strident, and that undermined the programs' success. The Department of Education's inspector general found significant problems and perhaps criminal conduct in the administration of the Reading First program, and the Government Accounting Office issued a very critical study of it. Hearings were held on Capitol Hill with Chairman Miller referring to those who oversaw the ad-ministration of Reading First as criminals. In reality, of course, Reading First was caught up in a political debate fueled by those who resented being cut out of federal reading funds. But the administration's conduct provided its enemies with what they needed, and Congress gutted the program, even while many in public education praised it. In spite of all this, reading instruction has been moved in the right direction under Bush's watch, and student achievement is up.

The same thing cannot be said for math instruction and student achievement, primarily because the science of math instruction has not been adequately developed. But the administration's emphasis on math in the elementary and middle school years has helped it to reclaim a centrality in the education curriculum that has been missing.

Other advances during the Bush years should not go unnoticed and may, with time, yield substantial educational dividends. The advent of supplemental educational services—which the policy's most ardent supporters referred to as "free tutoring"—underwritten by federal taxpayer dollars was a sea change in federal education policy. Under attack before the ink was dry on No Child Left Behind, free tutoring has potentially enormous popular appeal and represents the first time federal education policy has encouraged competition for the provision of educational services. It also created a huge new education industry and market that might lead to more extensive opportunities down the road. Despite this, however, neither actual demand for nor enrollment in supplemental educational service programs has ever reached the potential foreseen by its advocates, primarily because the program is administered by state and local officials keen to keep federal money in their public schools. These officials have been less than eager to inform parents of the opportunity for free tutoring for the children, and they have gone out of their way to make it difficult for providers of tutoring services to offer them in school districts. Local school officials have seen supplemental educational services as a drain on their resources, requiring them to set aside a portion of the federal funds to underwrite the program. Moreover, as conceived by its creators, the program was designed to limit the degree to which poorly performing schools could themselves provide the services and to encourage active participation by nonpublic schools and even for-profit providers. Therefore, the local public school leadership only begrudgingly implemented the tutoring provisions, and participation rates never reached the potential envisioned.[5]

The school-choice provisions of the law have had even less of an impact than the tutoring provisions. The original idea was to make it possible for children attending schools that consistently perform poorly to choose another, better-performing public school. It was a compromise, for the Bush administration had wanted a more robust school-choice option that would have included nonpublic schools as well. From the outset of the implementation of No Child Left Behind, the school-choice provisions were a nonstarter. Even as officials at the Department of Education sought to make it difficult for school districts to erect obstacles to the implementation of choice, district officials found ways to effectively eliminate the choice opportunity. In many districts, real choices were not available because no schools eligible to receive students existed, because of either enrollment or academic concerns. But even where some choices might exist, district officials were reluctant to make the opportunities available to families. And interestingly, many families chose not to take advantage of school choice even when it was available to them, preferring to keep their child in the current underperforming school out of a sense of loyalty to that school or a desire to limit the disruption to their child's routine. School choice therefore never really became an important component of No Child Left Behind. In actuality, it never really existed. Early into Bush's second term, efforts were made to make tutoring services available on a wider basis by allowing districts to substitute those services for school choice. This had the effect of killing what little school choice there was while not really expanding the tutoring program since district officials opposed that too. In the end, school choice was a hollow hope under No Child Left Behind, offering almost no real opportunity for families and children and posing no real threat to public schools.

The issue of teacher quality, interestingly, gained greater traction under No Child Left Behind, even while most states evaded the law's requirement for a highly qualified teacher in every classroom. But there is something intuitively appealing about the argument that teachers need to know what they teach and parents should know whether their children's teachers have that knowledge. The great problem with the law's highly qualified teacher provisions is that they are unenforceable. Washington has virtually no leverage to ensure states and school districts develop and implement policies that ensure a qualified teacher is in every classroom. And Washington has no way to gauge whether America's teachers are qualified. The highly qualified teacher provisions, the product primarily of Congressman Miller's insistence that teacher quality be addressed in No Child Left Behind, reflect Washington policy making at its worst. The problem is not with the concept; the nation indeed needs to insist that its professional teacher corps is professional. But it is impossible for Washington to accomplish this. Washington does not hire teachers. Washington does not certify teachers, evaluate them, or compensate them. All of that is the product of state education policy and administration.

Consider the provision in No Child Left Behind mandating that states work with school districts to make sure the most qualified teachers are where they are needed most—in the poorest performing schools. Again, there is nothing wrong with the concept. It makes very good sense. The problem is that teacher school assignment is almost universally a local issue. No state gets engaged in the process, so how can a state carry out the mandate of the law? Moreover, in many states, teacher school assignments are covered by local teacher union collective bargaining contracts, which cannot be overridden or discarded in the name of No Child Left Behind. As a result of all of this, another noble intention of the law goes unfulfilled.

The law sought to ensure that states would only permit individuals with proper certification into classrooms and that certification would ensure teachers had subject mastery in the disciplines they teach. This is a more significant step than one might think. States certify teachers, and certification or licensure requirements differ among states. But everywhere it is a bureaucratic process, overseen by state bureaucrats. And in almost every state, certification does not really ensure mastery of the subject matter to be taught. Indeed, certification typically is more of a threshold requirement—the minimum knowledge one must possess to enter the profession. As a result, many math teachers in America's schools were not math majors, or perhaps not even math minors, in college. In many places, high schools history teachers are hired for their coaching skills and enter the classroom as a value-added proposition. No Child Left Behind sought to address this ongoing problem.[6]

But it did not, and it could not. States developed elaborate strategies to align their teacher-certification processes with the law's highly qualified teacher provisions, but they really only massaged existing policies. Moreover, given the teacher shortage in some disciplines, the unique challenges surrounding special education (where teachers do not get certified in a discipline but in special education), and the various approaches to teacher credentialing for elementary and middle schools, most states argued for waivers or exceptions to some of the law's teacher provisions. And then there are the issues surrounding how states enforce, or do not enforce, their own laws and regulations governing teacher certification. Most states turn the other way on the issue, deferring to local decision makers, in recognition of the challenge some districts confront in finding qualified men and women for their classrooms. The Bush Department of Education could do little, if anything, about most of this. They knew it and uttered frequent incantations about the need for highly qualified teachers in America's classrooms, but that was about the extent to which they sought to further the law's objectives regarding the issue.

No Child Left Behind is replete with provisions similar to those intended to govern teacher quality. For example, the law mandates that every state must come up with a definition of "persistently dangerous schools" and then publish annually a list of all such schools within the state. Students enrolled in such schools are then supposed to be able to transfer to another public school of their choice that is not supposedly "persistently dangerous." The states have been quite creative in their definitions of such schools, which vary so wildly that the phrase "persistently dangerous" is bereft of any real meaning. But there is a greater folly to this again noble enterprise. It is one thing to tell a parent her child is enrolled in a school that is not performing adequately. It is altogether something else to tell a parent her child goes to a school that is dangerous. The former is inadequate; the latter is potentially life threatening. States and districts have every incentive to develop strategies to limit their liability under the safe-schools provisions of the law, or they could very well have a grassroots rebellion on their hands in some places. Because of this, and because there is no adequate way for the U.S. Department of Education to do anything about it, most states have defined persistently dangerous schools in such a way as to eliminate the problem completely. In the 2003–2004 school year, only thirty-eight schools in four states were identified as persistently dangerous according state definitions. In the 2007–2008 school year, the number of states admitting to having persistently dangerous schools had dropped to three and the number of schools to twenty-six. California, for example, would have you believe it has no dangerous schools; neither does New York or Illinois. Yet, by its own reckoning, South Dakota has two.[7]

Both the teacher-quality and safe-schools provisions illustrate a fundamental problem with Bush education law: it relies on state and local policy makers, administrators, and educators for the enactment of policies mandated by the law, the implementation of those policies, and the production of all the data necessary to the administration of the law. States have to generate academic standards, define what proficiency and adequate yearly progress mean, decide which subgroups within a school will be disaggregated, determine what constitutes a highly qualified teacher and a "persistently dangerous school," and virtually every other important provision of the law. They must also collect and produce the data supporting all of the law's accountability provisions. And Washington has to rely on the states to do all of that and on the integrity of the data they collect. This leads to a complex and confused array of definitions that vary among the states. Proficiency in Massachusetts might vary wildly from proficiency in Virginia. And since there exists no external way to determine the validity of the data coming from the states, Washington is left having to trust the states and school districts to do the right thing and produce accurate, timely, and usable data. There are two real problems with this, in addition to those already reported. First, most state departments of education do not have the capacity—the resources, people, or processes in place—to collect such a mountain of data. They have never had to do so before, and with No Child Left Behind that mountain became even higher than it had been. The states continue to have problems generating the data consistently and reliably and in a timely fashion. But the second problem is more pernicious. There is no incentive for a state to do the right thing and come up with policies and data that tell the truth about the quality of public education within its borders. Indeed, No Child Left Behind carries disincentives for states to do the right thing (hence the problems surrounding the safe-schools provisions). And the evidence suggests that state and local political and education officials are gaming the system in an attempt to look good to their constituents. A general dumbing down of the standards-and-accountability systems is taking place. No Child Left Behind, aimed at raising expectations and performance in America's schools, is having the opposite effect as states are engaged in a "race to the bottom" rather than to the top.

In light of this, it is truly ironic that from its inception critics have seen Bush's education initiative as undermining state sovereignty. Surely No Child Left Behind represents a major increase in the federal government's role in public education, but at its heart the law relies on state and local decision makers to be both willing and able to give substance to and implement its many mandates. This is hardly unfamiliar territory in Washington politics. For most of the modern era of American government, Washington has authored policy requiring states to do this or that and held out financial carrots to get them to go along. But this has not quite been the case with education policy. Surely, policies enlarging the federal role have been enacted, and federal funds have been conditioned upon states' abiding by those policies. But Washington has also been shy about forcing states to comply with education laws and regulations. No Child Left Behind can be seen as merely the latest extension of a years-old process: more laws and more regulations accompanied by more money. But this time, conservative critics see it as going too far. And since those charged with implementing the law pushed hard to make sure that this time around federal education policy did indeed become the law of the land, those critics found allies in school districts all over America who rebelled against testing, against standards and accountability, and against being labeled as unsuccessful. It did not really matter that they were state standards, state-defined accountability systems, and state definitions of proficiency and adequate yearly progress.

By and large, state education leaders have done little to dissuade the public from thinking federal education bureaucrats are gradually taking over their schools. They resented, from the beginning, Washington's more energetic approach to public education, even while acknowledging the nation's schools were not getting the job done. State education leaders, already engaged in the standards-and-accountability movement, resisted pressure to shape their policies to reflect No Child Left Behind's rules. Ultimately they did so, but often while pointing a rueful finger at Washington and telling local school officials they had to do what they had to do because "Washington is making us do it." At the local level, superintendents would tell their employees and parents, "The state is making us do this because Washington is making the state do this." And so, over time, the idea that Washington was trampling on state sovereignty became something of a self-fulfilling prophecy. It no longer counted that states were deciding most of what mattered under No Child Left Behind and being given boatloads of money to do it. A gun was being held to their heads, and there was not enough money anyway.

As No Child Left Behind played out, the portrayal of the Washington bureaucracy as trying to run America's schools became the received truth, providing the law's critics, from every political persuasion, the ammunition they needed to fight back. All the while, those responsible for public education in this country, state and local education leaders and policy makers, began devising strategies to get around the more challenging aspects of the law. During the first round of state negotiations with federal education officials over the accountability plans, state officials sought to soften the potential blow No Child Left Behind might deliver by devising statistical arguments to limit the effect disaggregation might have upon their schools. They would run all sorts of models, determine which would have the least negative impact, and pitch the idea to the feds. Having no way to determine either the statistical validity of what they were being told or the integrity of the data they were given, officials in Washington usually found ways to sign off on state plans, urged on by higher ups eager to see the president's plan take effect. In what became an annual ritual, state leaders would look to Washington each year to allow them to revise their accountability systems. And, over time, Washington, first under Secretary of Education Rod Paige, and then, more willingly, under Secretary Spellings, granted broad flexibility and discretion to states and larger school districts. Initially, as Bush's policy advisor, Spellings had instructed Paige that there should be no flexibility, no waivers. But as secretary she embraced a very different position, often going out of her way to accommodate state requests.

Surely Spellings did this to avert a full-scale rebellion against the law, one that had been brewing since the passage of No Child Left Behind, primarily in more conservative and Republican states and school districts. She also sought to tamp down the criticisms coming from the education establishment, which was growing more and more antagonistic about the law. Never supportive, the establishment had sought to soften its image as an opponent of No Child Left Behind when it became obvious Bush would get a bill from Congress. The unions, superintendents, and school boards did not want to be seen as stubborn adversaries of education reform. But by the time Spellings became education secretary, the criticisms were coming from almost every quarter, and hoping to keep the law in place and looking to its reauthorization, she needed to find ways to counter them. She did so by announcing new policies governing accountability and students in special education. She softened the department's position on supplemental services, allowing poorly performing districts to access funds and deliver the services themselves. She announced a plan to permit states to request authority to embrace alternatives to the No Child Left Behind accountability regime. Spellings was trying to keep the law from collapsing as its opponents piled on, but her softer strategy did not satisfy the critics or ensure the law's reauthorization. It did, however, make it easier for state and local officials to soften the impact of No Child Left Behind by redefining, sometimes frequently, just what constitutes proficiency in reading and math. In the end, Spellings's strategy worked. The law was not reauthorized during her tenure, but nor was it discarded. At the same time, its original potential impact was surely affected. That was the price that had to be paid to ensure President Bush's legacy remained in place.

The willingness of federal officials to grant greater discretion to state leaders, coupled with the fact that they had no way to determine the integrity of the information those leaders provided them, allowed states to respond to the pressure of No Child Left Behind testing by lowering state standards. This, in turn, had the effect of making it appear to parents, teachers, and taxpayers that schools and students were improving when, in reality, they were not. Going forward, such gaming of the system has the potential to make a mockery of accountability in education generally, for accountability in education requires that there be ways for the public to determine, with accuracy, how well their schools and kids are doing. When public officials redefine the meaning of such things as proficiency and grade-level achievement—when they lower the proficiency cut score on a test so that more students will achieve it—they destroy the very foundation of a school accountability system. Because of the way state and local education officials are responding to No Child Left Behind, the law may in the end undermine the very idea of accountability in education even while its primary purpose was to promote it.

Research has corroborated this "race to the bottom." Comparisons of results on state tests used for No Child Left Behind purposes with state scores on recent NAEP tests provide additional evidence of the degree to which states seem to be reporting greater improvements in student achievement than really exist. In Texas, for example, the home of Bush and both his education secretaries, the disparity between state exam results and NAEP scores has grown since the early 1990s. The Texas state exam has been made very easy to pass, with students needing to answer only twenty-one of sixty questions correctly to pass the mathematics section of the accountability exam. A score below 50 percent appears to be good enough to pass in Texas. As a result of this sort of gaming of the system, a review of two hundred Dallas-area elementary schools, ranked by their performance on the state's fourth-grade math exam, reveals the lowest math passing rate to be approaching 95 percent—not surprising, given what passes for passing in Texas.

Similar things are happening in other states. In Arizona the eighth-grade passing score on the state's reading test was 73 percent in 2003 but had fallen to 59 percent by 2005. By lowering the passing score, Arizona increased the percentage of Hispanic students passing its tests and thereby kept more schools off the No Child Left Behind needs-improvement list. Indeed, the state could brag that the percentage of Hispanic students passing its reading test jumped from 11 percent to 46 percent in a single year—a stunning accomplishment, albeit a hollow one.[8]

Most reports coming from the National Center for Education Statistics say that almost every state in the nation reports higher percentages of students proficient or above in both math and science state assessments than on NAEP tests. This is due, in part, to the way NAEP defines proficiency and the fact that NAEP is not a true assessment but a sample test. However, the evidence is clear that most states do not expect as much from their students as NAEP suggests they should. If NAEP is truly "the nation's report card," as it is so often described, then the nation is not measuring up, regardless of what states are reporting.

Aside from the problems associated with the standards-and-accountability provisions of No Child Left Behind, there are real problems with how schools are identified under the law. As the law is written, schools are the measure of achievement rather than the students in those schools. No Child Left Behind identifies schools as not making adequate yearly progress when students or student subgroups do not score as proficient or above over periods of years. The actual targets are set by the states with approval from Washington. Progress—more students scoring as proficient or above each year, over a three-year average—is supposed to drive school improvement. Schools that do not continue to improve are identified as needing improvement and, over time, must offer students opportunities for academic support and initiate strategies for reform. Schools also must make sure that at least 95 percent of their students take the assessments when they are administered, or they will be designated as not having adequately improved. There are obvious problems with this approach; indeed, they were debated as the bill was considered in Congress. Some argued then that student achievement should matter, of course, but expecting all students to achieve proficiency was unrealistic and the focus should be on improvement over time rather than getting all students on grade level. A real problem with the compromise Congress produced, however, is that it compares different cohorts of students to one another over time—for instance, this year's crop of third graders with last year's and next year's. It makes more sense to track the achievement of students as they progress through the school, grade by grade.

At the time, however, there were real challenges to establishing such an accountability system. Most states did not have sophisticated student-based accountability systems in place, making it impossible to follow student achievement over time. Moreover, such student-specific systems remain very controversial due to concerns over privacy and confidentiality. A school-based system aimed at all students achieving at grade level emerged as the most realistic approach. Secretary of Education Spellings's recognition of the problems with this approach to accountability and her willingness to embrace one that looks at student achievement over time reflects the administration's attempt to adjust the law to fit circumstances. Spellings even allowed a number of states to proceed with such an accountability system, exercising authority some felt she did not have. Almost everyone engaged in the debate tacitly recognizes that the existing statute has real flaws when it comes to accountability.

The gap between the promise of No Child Left Behind and the reality of how it has played out across the country is hardly the fault of the Department of Education, however. Both Paige and Spellings mounted vigorous campaigns to educate the American people about the law. Both traveled greatly, met with education leaders at every level of government, and sought to combine a get-tough approach to implementation with a recognition that the fate of implementation rested by and large with the very people who resisted the law the most. The Bush administration made a good-faith effort to turn the country's schools around. But the education establishment at all levels strongly opposed the president's education policies, seeing them as a threat to public schools and a drain on school district budgets. Others saw them as a threat to state sovereignty. Still others could see the writing on the wall and acted to soften the impact of the law by redefining it away through clever manipulation of data.

When President Bush first outlined his ideas for No Child Left Behind, he asserted that it would be premised on four principles: accountability, flexibility, choices for parents, and scientifically based policy. By almost any measure, well into the law's implementation, it has fallen short in terms of each of these principles. The accountability provisions are being undermined at the state and local levels, with something of an education shell game taking place, even as Washington is rethinking what accountability should look like. The flexibility for the states, sorely limited by the law's prescriptive nature, was promoted by Spellings, even though she tested the limits of her authority as secretary. For many at the state level, the flexibility Spellings offered seemed hollow. And yet, because of how it was written, in that it gives the states the authority to determine much of what school accountability might look like, the law has provided the loophole that many state and local administrators have manipulated in order to look good to their constituents. The school-choice and tutoring provisions have fallen dramatically short of what their proponents had hoped for, and political controversies have undermined the two policies arguably grounded in solid research, Reading First and Early Reading First. Bush's signature domestic accomplishment is in trouble.

But to say No Child Left Behind has fallen short of its hopes and expectations is not to say it is a failure—far from it. The law has had a profound impact on American education, having helped to change the way Americans think of public schooling. The fact that it has not achieved all that its most ardent advocates sought can be traced, in part, to the fact that it aimed to accomplish so much: to leave no child behind. It can be traced to flaws in the law as well, surely. And it can be traced to how the law has been received and implemented—in Washington and in the statehouses and schoolhouses across America.

*Some believe . . .*   ∞

On January 20, 2009, the junior senator from Illinois, Barack Hussein Obama, became president of the United States. After a historic election culminating a long campaign, record crowds greeted inauguration day in Washington DC, eager to witness real history. A man of color with an attractive wife and two young children was becoming the nation's chief executive. The media touted the parallels to John F. Kennedy. Obama's approval ratings not only soared, but those of his predecessor, George W. Bush, were the lowest of any president completing a second term in office. And the numbers for the Congress—a Democratic Congress to match a Democratic administration—were just as bad. But the new president enjoyed unparalleled popularity as he assumed office.

President Obama arrived in Washington with the city and government confronting the most serious economic challenge since the Great Depression. Bush had devoted much of his last year in office to trying to calm capital markets and the banking and mortgage finance and housing sectors as they experienced record-breaking defaults and a credit crisis loomed large. Lehman Brothers, a Wall Street fixture, was gone, and other firms had to be propped up with huge government-financed plans. The nation's largest insurance firm, AIG, almost collapsed from the weight of its toxic investments, and Washington had to bail it out. The nation's Big Three automobile manufacturers came to the nation's capital asking for help in order to remain afloat and stave off bankruptcy. (Ford was able to persist without a loan from the federal government; both Chrysler and General Motors received loans and underwent reorganization.) It was an economic crisis of epic proportions, creating a recession and national credit crisis seemingly greater than anyone had seen. Around the world, other economies were caught in the debcale and thus looked to the United States as the primary contributor to their economic problems.

Into this swirling maelstrom arrived a young, relatively inexperienced new president. He had acted quickly to surround himself with an economic team to develop strategies to move the country forward. He asked of Congress, and received, a stimulus package approaching a trillion dollars. It passed both houses quickly, with Republicans by and large in lockstep opposition to it and many Democrats voting for a bill they really had not had a chance to read or understand. The bad economic news continued well into the president's first months in office, threatening to overwhelm anything and everything else he might want to pursue. But Obama did not let that happen.

During the campaign, even as the economy began its tumble, Obama had embraced a comprehensive and bold agenda to tackle ongoing issues: health-care reform, banking and economic reform, energy independence, an end to the war in Iraq, and education reform. Most observers felt he would have to back away from some of his program, at least temporarily, until the economic crisis had passed. But in a series of speeches and forums, President Obama continued to press his agenda.

The president's point man on education was to be his secretary of education, Arne Duncan, a longtime acquaintance and basketball buddy of Obama's and a much heralded reform-minded superintendent of the Chicago public schools. As superintendent, he gained a national reputation for helping to move the city's troubled school system in a better direction. He championed accountability, charter schools, and the closing of schools that do not work. He was credited with having the skill to work with the teachers' unions as well as the reform advocates. When Obama picked him to lead the Department of Education, the media heaped almost universal praise on Duncan. His confirmation hearings were a cakewalk, with Senator and former education secretary Lamar Alexander calling him the best cabinet nominee chosen by the new president.

Duncan's selection came as no surprise, although the media speculated that there had been a struggle within the nascent Obama administration over who the new secretary of education would be. Some felt Obama might choose someone more directly appealing to the education establishment that had helped get him elected. In reality, there was never much debate over the president's choice. More importantly, Obama did not select anyone on his White House staff to oversee policy efforts in education like he did with health care, energy, the economy, and the environment. Obama named "czars" within his White House to help supervise and coordinate a number of his major policy initiatives. But there would be no education czar. Education would be handled by Duncan and the president, two men who knew, trusted, and liked each other.

Duncan brought a fresh energy to the secretary's job that was evident from the moment he arrived in Washington. He spoke often and eloquently about the need to improve the schools. He touched on familiar themes—accountability for results, high standards and expectations, quality teachers—echoing much of the education rhetoric that had so dominated the Bush years. But Duncan made the words sound less threatening to the education establishment. The teachers' unions, long hostile to much of Bush's agenda and angered by the Bush administration's style, saw Duncan as an ally, someone willing to work with, not against, them to achieve change. Surely they were anxious when Obama and Duncan spoke about merit-based compensation for teachers. But early on, the concept remained somewhat vague—vague enough to allow the unions and the new administration time to check one another out on the issue.

Duncan did not waste much time getting to the apparent and by now well-documented "race to the bottom" among the states. Seeing it for what it was, he argued there needed to be a "race to the top" and initially outlined two strategies to get there: national standards and a big pot of money to encourage the states to move in the right direction.

The idea of national academic standards had been bandied about since the mid-1980s. Typically, the subject attracts the attention of education-policy wonks but fails to gain much political traction. There was a brief flirtation with the notion of implementing national standards after President George H. W. Bush assembled the nation's governors in Charlottesville, Virginia, for a national education summit. But when then chairman of the National Endowment for the Humanities Lynn Cheney and others in Washington ridiculed draft national history standards, any momentum behind the movement died. (Cheney had helped to underwrite the draft standards through a grant from the endowment, ironically.) But Duncan brought increased interest to the topic through his willingness to broach it as the nation's secretary of education. He did not call directly for national standards; rather, in numerous speeches not long after assuming office, he discussed the need for greater clarity and consistency in education accountability. He talked about the problems inherent in a federal education system in which each state has its own set of standards and defines proficiency in its own way, and he spoke frankly about the issue of states adjusting their accountability systems to look better, that is, altering passing scores in order to ensure more schools made adequate yearly progress. He suggested that a single set of standards for the nation's schools might ameliorate these problems. He was short on details—for example, who would establish the standards and administer the national accountability system—but merely by his raising it, the issue seemed to gain some credibility.

Duncan may have been moved to speak about the idea because of a curious development that had transpired before the new administration took office. In the fall of 2006, the conservative Hoover Institution at Stanford University published a forum on national standards in the journal *Education Next*. The argument for national standards was made by the Thomas B. Fordham Foundation's Checker Finn, a prolific pundit on education and a former education official under President Ronald Reagan. Supportive of Bush's No Child Left Behind early on, Finn had more recently been critical of the law and its inconsistencies. National standards, according to Finn, might finally provide the leverage to achieve much of what No Child Left Behind had been created to accomplish.[9] With this, the idea seemed to gather some casual momentum. Then, during the 2009 winter meeting of the National Governors Association, the governors passed a resolution offering provisional support for the concept of national standards, which they referred to as "Common Core State Standards," an idea that had until then seemed at odds with how the governors had always approached education policy. The Council of Chief State School Officers formed an alliance with the governors on the issue. With this, it became much more politically palatable for Secretary Duncan to advance the idea and to make sure it was a part of any discussions that might surround the eventual reauthorization of No Child Left Behind. The politics of national standards had changed rather dramatically since that law's 2001 passage.

But Duncan's real weapon to advance an education agenda was money. Reacting to the deepening economic crisis he confronted upon entering office, President Obama had prevailed upon Congress to enact a broad and very expensive economic-stimulus package aimed at injecting money into the economy to create jobs and galvanize the economy. It was a very controversial and complex piece of legislation, managed legislatively by Speaker of the House Nancy Pelosi and Senate Majority Leader Harry Reid, that few in Congress took the time to read or understand. Representing the first real assertion of Democratic majority power since the November election, it passed along party lines. No Republicans in the House of Representatives voted for it; only three GOP senators did.

At a price tag of around $1 trillion, the stimulus package was a staggering statement about how bad the economy was. Money was directed at about every sector of government and society. In education, the package included over $100 billion as a "one-time" investment aimed "to stimulate the economy and improve education." Four principles were to guide the stimulus education investments: spend quickly to save and create jobs, ensure transparency and accountability, invest thoughtfully, and advance effective reforms.[10] Funds were to go to statewide data-collection systems, to programs aimed at improving teacher effectiveness, and to assigning the best teachers where the need is greatest. Money was to be targeted at turning around poorly performing schools and advancing college and work-ready standards. These policies were much in line with the sort the previous administration had sought to advance under No Child Left Behind. Indeed, as the president spoke about the education economic-stimulus package, he employed rhetoric that President Bush would have been comfortable using, although he seldom mentioned Bush's signature education initiative by name. On the surface, then, the economic-stimulus package for education, officially the American Reinvestment and Recovery Act, offered the new Obama administration a chance to advance serious education reform through the timely deployment of a huge amount of money.

But a closer look at the package revealed that most of the money was tied to existing funding streams already in the Elementary and Secondary Education Act. That is, there were dramatic increases in Title I and special education funding, for example, with no strings attached to ensure real education reforms were implemented with those funds. Indeed, almost all the existing funding streams saw huge increases. In addition, a major portion of the stimulus money went to something called "state stabilization," money that governors applied for and received in return for promises to advance the education-reform principles espoused by the Obama administration. The stimulus package called for assurances that state and local education policy makers would advance the reform agenda contained in the package. But the package, and its accompanying spending guidelines, fell short of actually requiring recipients to enact reforms. For the recipients of these monies, state and local education agencies, it was a lifesaving infusion of cash, helping to limit layoffs and program cuts that might otherwise have to take place. Critics of the Obama administration and advocates of serious education reform saw the stimulus as a desperate attempt to give more money to a system that seemed to devour it and the waste of a chance to tie real reform to that money. It was also seen as a massive infusion of federal taxpayer dollars that would greatly increase the national debt future generations would have to manage.

The money was to be allocated over a two-year period and, according to administration and congressional advocates, would not continue beyond that. But critics argued the new spending levels created a new public education baseline to which future federal education budgets would be tied. In either case, it represented a major increase in funding and influence in American education coming from Washington.

Included in the stimulus package was a major increase in the amount of discretionary money available to the secretary of education. Traditionally, Congress has been reluctant to give the education secretary money to spend at his or her discretion. Indeed, often in the past, while pots of money have been allocated for the secretary's discretion, the actual distribution of that money has been earmarked by Congress. In other words, Congress narrowly proscribed the education secretary's discretion. The stimulus package, however, gave Secretary Duncan a whopping $4.3 billion to spend as he saw fit. Labeling it his "Race to the Top Fund," Duncan announced he would only finance a limited number of state reform efforts aimed at ending the accountability games the states had been playing in their "race to the bottom." Indeed, he would seek to advance a more national accountability-and-standards framework, with the help of governors willing to advance that framework and eager for the money. The money represented a major statement by Congress and the Obama administration of faith in Secretary Duncan. No other member of the president's cabinet received a similar vote of confidence.

Duncan's Race to the Top Fund sought to advance four key principles that, in truth, were rooted in George W. Bush's No Child Left Behind. In order to be considered for the funds, states would need to adopt internationally benchmarked standards and assessments, outline policies aimed at recruiting and rewarding effective teachers and principals, build data systems to measure student success and inform teachers and principals about how to improve their practices, and develop strategies for turning around low-performing schools. These were the basic education-reform themes emerging from the Obama administration, themes that seemed to take up where the Bush administration had left off.

All of this new money offered President Obama and his secretary of education the opportunity to stimulate real reform in American education, and that may yet take place. On the surface, however, it seemed primarily to be a vehicle for getting more money into a tired, underperforming system while advancing the rhetoric of reform. Time would tell whether any real change would occur.

In early March at a meeting of the Hispanic Chamber of Commerce, President Obama delivered his first major education address. Coming on the heels of the economic-stimulus package, the speech seemed to embrace much of the rhetoric and education policy of the previous administration while suggesting the need for new thinking regarding charter schools and teacher success. Obama spoke of lifting state caps on the number of charter schools permitted in states and of measuring the effectiveness of teachers rather than dwelling on how they are trained, certified, and assigned. The rhetoric went from "highly qualified teachers" to "teacher effectiveness" and "teacher competence." He spoke of the need for true transparency and accountability and talked about universal pre-K for kids and the ideal of everyone going on to some sort of postsecondary education. He offered, in language strangely familiar to those who had advanced George W. Bush's education efforts, four "pillars" on which he based education reform. He spoke of the centrality of improving education to the future of the nation and its ability to compete globally. The speech was well received. It was really nothing new.

As the stimulus package gradually made its way to the states, there was genuine concern about just how much "stimulus" it was generating. Unemployment increased during the first quarter of the year, suggesting that the package was not creating many new jobs. In education, it seemed money was being spent to stop teacher and staff layoffs, not to create new positions. Gradually, the Obama administration's rhetoric shifted a bit to reflect the realities of the situation. Now the stimulus package was about creating and saving jobs.

The secretary's Race to the Top Fund, even before any states had sought or been targeted for monies, did seem to be having an effect. As the Department of Education gradually developed guidelines for how the funds might be used and what conditions states would have to meet in order to be considered for the money, it became apparent that the $4.3 billion represented an opportunity to create real incentives for states to enact education-reform policies embraced by the administration. Obama and Duncan let it be known that any state that capped the number of charter schools it allowed or had laws in place that made it difficult to authorize charter schools would be ineligible for Race to the Top money. This represented a major shift in thinking for the Democratic Party. For years, the Democrats had been somewhat muted in their support for the concept of charter schools, reflecting the party's desire to maintain a strong partnership with the teachers' unions, which have always been wary of charters. Now, under Obama and Duncan's direction, charter schools were to be embraced and encouraged with policy, politics, and money.

Race to the Top would also promote the important policy of relating teacher effectiveness to student achievement. An idea euphemistically referred to as "merit pay" had been tossed about during the 2008 campaign by both candidates, but neither had given the concept much substance, and the teachers' unions had been restrained in their comments about the issue. With Race to the Top, Duncan moved closer to promoting some sort of merit-pay system. No state would qualify for Race to the Top funds if it had on its books laws or regulations that forbade tying teacher compensation to student performance. Duncan's initial goal was not to establish compensation-performance plans but to make sure they were at least a possibility among the states. But his agenda was really much bolder: states that embraced strategies aimed at tying at least some aspects of teacher compensation to student achievement would have the advantage when it came time to distribute Race to the Top money.

The effect of Duncan's strategy was felt almost immediately. Legislators in California, for example, where tying teacher pay to student achievement was outlawed, argued the policy needed to be changed so that the state, suffering from a huge financial crisis, might qualify for Race to the Top monies. Other states started seeking to adjust their education policies to reflect the Obama administration's preferences, lifting caps on charters and trying to work around any policies that could be seen as forbidding the consideration of student performance as a factor in deciding how much teachers get paid.

As the summer of 2009 stretched out, it became apparent that Obama and Duncan might get considerable leverage with the money they and the Congress were willing to spend on education. The economic-stimulus package generated goodwill at the state and local levels, even if it did not create many new jobs. The Race to the Top Fund seemed to be encouraging education-reform opportunities that had been stalled for years. Given the price tag of the secretary's discretionary fund, about $4.3 billion, and the amount of money America's taxpayers spend on K–12 education annually, approaching $800 billion, it seemed like a potentially pretty successful investment. But the way things transpired going forward would decide everything.

As August descended upon Washington and most in Congress returned to their states and districts to field tough questions about the proposed health-care reforms, the reality of Obama and Duncan's education efforts seemed to dawn finally on the leadership of the teachers' unions. Commenting on the proposed regulations that would accompany Race to the Top, the National Education Association (NEA) argued the administration embraced a "narrow agenda" centered too much on charter schools and a "top-down approach" to reform. The NEA cited No Child Left Behind and painted Race to the Top as "another layer of federal mandates that have little or no research base of success and that usurp state and local governments' responsibilities for public education." And the union chided the Obama administration for apparently having decided that "charter schools are the only answer to what ails America's public schools."[11]

The NEA's criticisms of Race to the Top were predictable and reflected a pattern that the union had followed during the eight years of the Bush administration. They merely represented more in the ongoing tension between the education establishment and those seeking to reform things. That the union was attacking a Democratic administration, however, did add a greater sting to the criticisms. On top of all this, however, President Obama and his secretary of education would see the start of another school year under trying circumstances. By August, the economy was showing some signs of improvement, but Obama's initially very high approval rating had plummeted, and public opposition seemed to be growing to some of his major reform ideas. The enormous good will that had greeted him upon his entering office had dissipated, which would make it all the more difficult to enact the sorts of reforms he sought. Moreover, the American people seemed to have grown tired of and disappointed with the way Washington had handled education reform. A Gallop poll published in late August reported that "Americans doubt the effectiveness of No Child Left Behind." Indeed, those claiming to be very familiar with the law were the most critical of it, saying it had made things worse rather than better.[12] It seemed the education establishment and the American people were wary, at best, about Washington weighing in again on public education. No Child Left Behind helped to make it easier for Obama and Duncan to talk of education reforms that were quite controversial only a few years earlier. But it would also make it difficult for the president and his secretary of education to transform their reform ideas into reality.

The long, drawn-out debate in Congress over President Obama's health-care-reform proposals consumed the remainder of 2009. Time and again, the president, Speaker Pelosi, and Senate Majority Leader Reid tried to cobble together enough votes to pass the sweeping reform proposals; time and again they fell short. Just before the Christmas holidays, the House passed a version of the health care bill. The Senate passed its version early in the new year. But getting both chambers to agree on common language seemed an unrealistic goal. Besides, no one was sure the votes would be there to pass another health-care-reform package. On top of this, a special election to fill the term of the late senator Ted Kennedy (a lifelong advocate of health-care reform) had sent a relatively unknown Republican state legislator to Washington. Having a Republican fill Kennedy's shoes was shocking enough, but this also meant the Democrats in the Senate no longer had the supermajority needed to pass controversial legislation. And the Republican victory in heavily Democratic Massachusetts had come on the heels of Republican gubernatorial victories in Virginia and New Jersey, two states Obama had carried convincingly the previous year. Republicans heralded the victories as signs of voter discontent with Obama and his health-care plan. Democrats grew even warier of having to vote on such a controversial agenda.

After much maneuvering and intense and sometimes heated debate, with large numbers of Americans getting engaged at the grassroots level and parliamentary moves aimed at limiting the political fallout that might accompany the vote, Congress passed, and the president signed, a health-care-reform bill. As he did, his standing in the polls and that of congressional Democrats had hit all time lows.

While all of this was taking place, Secretary Duncan went about the business of advancing his education agenda through his Race to the Top policy. States were to compete for the money, and a panel of individuals would judge the education-reform proposals they submitted and rank each state. Duncan would choose the winning states based on those recommendations. This was unique and somewhat extraordinary: a national competition among states for a large amount of money that would underwrite important education reforms. For months, teams in all but a handful of states spent hours pulling together their applications. In most states, efforts were made to seek buy-in from local education agencies and teachers organizations. The competition attracted a lot of media attention, almost all of it positive. As the deadline for submitting proposals approached, state and national media seemed unusually interested in how the competition would play out.

In early March, Duncan announced the finalists in the first round of the Race to the Top competition. Of the District of Columbia and the forty states submitting applications, sixteen finalists were invited to interview with the panel of judges who would recommend the winners to Duncan. In the end, just two states, Delaware and Tennessee, were chosen to receive funds. In a statement the department explained that Delaware and Tennessee were chosen because their applications emphasized what the Obama administration was hoping to promote in education reform. Both states were dedicated to promoting standards and assessments to ensure student success in college and the workplace. Both were committed to building data systems that could measure student growth and success and help improve instruction. Both emphasized recruiting, developing, rewarding, and retaining effective teachers and principals and aimed to turn around low-performing schools. Delaware was to receive $100 million and Tennessee $500 million. That left $3.4 billion in Race to the Top funds that could be awarded during a second round of the competition to be completed in June.[13] The winners were surprising to many. States touted for their education reforms and given favorable press regarding their Race to the Top applications did not make the cut.

Two things stood out about the Race to the Top competition. From the time Duncan announced the initiative through the application process and up until the winners were chosen, the press coverage was almost universally favorable. There was speculation about what role, if any, politics might play in the process. And some groused that this was another example of Washington getting overly engaged in state and local politics and policies. But there was an almost total absence of any criticism of the fact that a single member of the president's cabinet was deciding who would receive a very large amount of money and why and how that money was to be spent. Nothing similar had ever happened before, and that did not seem to matter. In addition, once the winners were chosen, there was only a little grousing from the states that did not receive awards. Most merely announced their intention to compete in round two. The press coverage noted that both Tennessee's and Delaware's applications combined important reform strategies with buy in from state and local educators, including the teachers' unions. Critics carped that Duncan placed too much emphasis on such buy in and wondered how much real reform might be accomplished in the end. That will be determined in the months and years to come.

During his first year in office, Obama was almost totally absorbed in issues relating to the economy and health-care reform. He spoke often about education, however, and his secretary of education was a very visible advocate for what he called real reform. By the spring of 2010, reform that seemed all but impossible only a few years earlier appeared like it might indeed be achievable.

Many of the reform ideas the Obama administration sought to promote were rooted in policies and proposals that can be found in No Child Left Behind. And many of the ideas found in Bush's education initiative took up where earlier presidents' education initiatives left off. As is so often the case, education policy making in Washington has been the product of a long, extended process in which one set of policies has been erected on top of others already in place. Those policies then create the foundation upon which the next set will be built. Should the Obama administration achieve its goals for education reform, that success will be due in part to the foundation laid by George W. Bush's accomplishments. Should Obama succeed, both he and his secretary of education will deserve great credit, but President Bush and his education secretaries will deserve some credit as well.

# 6

# A Leap of the Imagination

Early in Barack Obama's presidency, the talk of reforming American education echoed conversations started by George W. Bush and earlier presidents. Whether or not the talk will lead to real reform for the nation's schools will be determined in the months and years left in an Obama administration. But if history is any indication, it is doubtful that the sort of transformative change needed in American education will take place anytime in the near future.

The No Child Left Behind Act and the ideas President Obama is proposing embrace a few basic assumptions, the first and foremost being that the existing public school system will remain in place. No Child Left Behind imposes an accountability regime on the nation's school districts. It has almost no effect on the governance or financing of American K–12 public education, except for the increases in federal spending directed at education. In addition, while the law influences policy, curriculum, and spending decisions at the local level, it embraces the structure and function of public education. It takes for granted that the system of elementary, middle, and high schools will continue in place, and its testing provisions reinforce this idea. The same can be said of the proposals brought forth by Obama and Arne Duncan; even if they are completely enacted and implemented, the overall structure, governance, and finance of American public education will remain pretty much unaltered with incremental changes along the margins. But although these might be important and effective incremental changes, much more is needed.

Embracing the structure or architecture of the status quo, while seeking to challenge it at the same time, sells the nation short. Americans should be asking more of education than ever before. But the reform ideas that have dominated the national dialogue seem to encourage the American people to settle for something slightly better than what we have instead of encouraging new thinking in order to consider what we might be able to create. Surely the calls for better school and student achievement are important, as is the attention to results, accountability, and teacher quality and competence. But whether the nation can get to where it needs to be with the existing education system, even with the reforms envisioned by President Obama in place, is open to question. After all, our educational system remains wedded to an agricultural calendar and an industrial model, when we live in a digital age. Ours is a system born early in the previous century that remains firmly ensconced in the thinking of that era. Most importantly, even should the promise of No Child Left Behind be fully realized—something most would argue is all but impossible—American K–12 education would not produce young men and women equipped with the knowledge they need to compete successfully in a global marketplace. The status quo simply cannot provide America and America's students with what is required, even with No Child Left Behind. And the reforms promoted by Obama will not get America where it needs to go either.

The next generation of Americans will need a "next-generation" American education in order to succeed globally. This system of education should be organized around and promote what American education should be about: every student achieving at the highest levels and receiving an education that reflects and promotes freedom, opportunity, equality, responsibility, ownership, and hope. It is the sort of education reflects the principles of the nation every bit as much as it provides the quality of learning needed to ensure those principles are nourished in a world in which they are challenged daily.

First things first: it is important to distinguish education and learning from schooling. No Child Left Behind is about schooling, as are President Obama's reform ideas. Virtually every education-reform effort of the last twenty years has really been aimed at schooling reform rather than education reform. A focus on schooling considers what goes on within the school system, including existing structures, institutions, processes, and procedures. This is the gist of No Child Left Behind. Education, on the other hand, begins the moment a child is born (some research suggest it actually begins before a child is born, in the womb) and goes on for a lifetime. In order to produce the next generation of American education, it is critical to distinguish between education and schooling and to focus on the former while challenging the assumptions of the latter.

The ongoing debate over pre-K education exemplifies both the importance of the distinction and the problem with many contemporary policy debates surrounding it. While the data are mixed, most agree that a child who enters kindergarten prepared to learn has an advantage over those who do not. The early years are critical to success in schooling. Moreover, far too many young people enter school without the preparation necessary for early success. The response, predictably, is to create some sort of universal preschool so that the neediest children can compete successfully with their peers. The problem, however, is that most preschool proposals call for strapping some sort of program onto the existing public school structure and system. In this sort of approach, K–12 becomes Pre-K–12, with additional public funding needed—sometimes quite a bit of additional public funding. The argument goes that early childhood education will help ensure that every child enters kindergarten ready to succeed. But merely adding additional time, money, exposure, and instruction to the existing system hardly ensures success. Indeed, if the existing system is less than successful currently, why should we expect better results by adding more to it?

Those seeking to coordinate public elementary and secondary education with postsecondary education are mounting a similar argument, one that is both superficially appealing and simplistic. In an age of academic standards and accountability, it should be possible to wed K–12 education to postsecondary education so that we have a "seamless" K–16 system. Academic standards for high school students should reflect the expectations of colleges and universities. Postsecondary admissions policies should then reflect existing high school academic standards so that students can enter college knowing what to expect and possessing the skills and knowledge to succeed.

Again, however, this approach merely builds on, rather than altering, the status quo. To embrace a K–16 public education system merely embraces, and even extends, the poorly performing status quo. In such a system, colleges and universities might have the effect of increasing high school standards, but the greater likelihood is that postsecondary standards will slip in order that graduating high school seniors may be enrolled. Indeed, that already seems to be the case. Remedial and "developmental" courses are growing dramatically on the nation's college campuses. The retention rate for college freshmen is abysmal in some places. The six-year graduation rate—the government does not even bother to collect data on the four-year graduation rate—hovers just south of 50 percent, and on some campuses it is nearly in the single digits. There is room to question whether higher education is really still higher education even today. Is it realistic to expect that a seamless K–16 system—let alone a seamless PreK–16 system—will move the nation beyond the mediocrity of the existing system? The last thing we want to do is drag what is left of higher education down with K–12.

Instead of adding reforms on top of the existing public schooling structure, we need to totally rethink that structure—and education in America generally. Virtually every other social institution in the country has undergone profound and fundamental change in the last two decades or so.

Banking and finance today hardly resemble the business of just a few years ago. The same can be said of insurance, health care, transportation, communications, and the media. We live in an age in which is it literally possible to be anywhere, anytime, all the time. But public education—schooling—has resisted such profound change.

Think about it. If the men who created this republic, the Founders, were to reappear magically, they would be stunned by the way the world works. But if they entered the classroom in any public school in America, they could take comfort in the fact that there nothing has changed all that much in two hundred plus years, with students seated at their desks, the teacher in the front of the room; things are pretty much as they left them. Oh, there are some differences: America embraces education for all, rather than for the privileged few; there is greater access to every level of education; computers are now ubiquitous in America's schools, and there have been some wonderful innovations in education technology. But by and large, that technology is being employed within, and in support of, the existing public schooling framework—a framework almost perfectly constructed to protect itself from fundamental change. It is this framework that must be disassembled, and a new understanding of education in America must be embraced and assembled in its place.

What might the next generation of education in America look like? As already noted, first and foremost it must get beyond schooling in order to focus on education. It should ensure that every student receives an education that reflects the needs of society and the interests, talents, abilities, and ambition of the student. Every student should have his own "education plan," worked out by the student with his or her family and educators. The next generation of American education should be driven by the needs and desires of students and families rather than the interests of the public schooling system. Just as importantly, a system of education—or a non-system—built upon the six fundamental American principles of freedom, opportunity, equality, responsibility, ownership, and hope will look very different from the current system and potentially make good on the promise of leaving no child behind.

Before considering what the contours of such a different approach to education might look like, let us consider the degree to which the current system of public education in America reflects and promotes the principles that America stands for.

On a very superficial level, the current public education system is a pretty much one-size-fits-all system. That is, each state runs public schools in pretty much the same fashion. Each has school districts run by school boards, which oversee the public schools. The selection and powers of these boards may differ among the states, but the system's overall architecture is pretty much the same. Again, the number of districts in each state varies, as do their size and the number of schools they comprise. But the architecture is the same. Finally, each state maintains elementary, middle, and high schools.

The way states pay for public education does vary, but for each, public education is a big business and usually the single-largest recipient of state and local funding. It is a high priority among the states. How funds are distributed among districts and schools varies among the states as well. Most employ some sort of distribution formula that seeks to get at adequacy and equity in some fashion.

States are responsible for the overall governance of public education. When local school officials complain about "unfunded mandates," they are usually referring to mandates emanating from the state capital. Or they may be referring to "mandates" created by local collective bargaining agreements worked out by school district officials and teachers' unions. It is not unusual to see local districts locked well into the future into budgets that leave very little room for discretionary or special spending. Nor is it unusual to see school district budgets in which personnel-related expenditures consume upwards of 80 percent of the spending.

Regulations and legislation governing such things as school days, the school year, curricula, and teacher credentials—the everyday issues that consume the attention of the public school community—are issued by the states. The No Child Left Behind Act actually did little to change this education landscape, except to require states to test more frequently, identify schools not making adequate yearly progress, and disaggregate data. How it complies with the federal law is pretty much up to each state. The law told states they had to do certain things—ensure every classroom had a "highly qualified teacher," for example—but it left it to the states to decide how to go about accomplishing them.

This system of public education has been in place for generations. And it is one that in essence tells parents, "This is public education, this is the school your child is supposed to attend, and this is what we do, how we do it, when we do it." Parents are supposed to accept whatever the school district in which they reside tells them about educating their children. The overall concern would seem to be managing the district. The concerns of families and children would seem secondary—something of an afterthought.

But to better understand how the current system works (or does not) and the degree to which it might reflect American principles and values, it is important to visit a school and see what happens in the classroom. So let us visit an inner-city public elementary school. It could be in almost any medium or large city in America. As we walk into a fourth-grade classroom, we are struck immediately by the energy in the room. These are energetic kids. They are mostly minority children, mostly from low-income families. The room is crowded—overcrowded—with thirty students, too many for a single fourth-grade class, but that is the rule in big cities rather than the exception. The room emanates happiness. There are books everywhere, posters on the walls, drawings by the students, various work spaces set aside for activities, and lots of color. It is a happy place, and the kids seem, for the most part, happy.

At the front of the room is the teacher. She is also a minority. She has full certification to teach elementary school, something of a rarity in many urban settings, where securing fully credentialed staff can be very difficult. She has some help from aides, not all that rare in public schools these days. The teacher is a veteran and loves her job; she loves her "kids," and they love her. It is the type of setting that brings a smile to the face.

But let us take a closer look. Beneath the energy, excitement, and optimism of this fourth-grade classroom in a big city lies the fact that most kids in the room are not at grade level in either reading or math. Indeed, most are far below grade level. In fact, of the thirty students in this classroom, twenty-six cannot read. They entered fourth grade unable to read proficiently and, in all likelihood, will go on to fifth grade unable to read at grade level. Math scores are comparable, perhaps worse. But this is a happy place. The children are smiling. Their teacher is smiling. The students love their teacher. The teacher loves her kids.

When the teacher is asked about the class, the school, how things are going, she glows with enthusiasm. She talks about how well the school year is going, the progress her students are making. She could always use more resources, more parental involvement, more time, but on the whole, she feels good about things. "Things are going well," she says, "particularly considering these kids, who they are, where they come from." This is her way of saying one cannot expect too much from her students, given their background, given who they are. She does not begin to realize what she is saying that she is practicing the "soft bigotry of low expectations" spoken of so frequently by President Bush as he campaigned for No Child Left Behind.

At a very fundamental level, these children are not getting the education they deserve and that America has promised.

While this classroom scene may seem an exaggeration, data from the National Assessment of Educational Progress and student scores on state tests suggest it is not at all. In some of this nation's inner-city elementary schools, upward of 60 to 70 percent of fourth graders are well below grade average in reading and math. And the practice in far too many inner-city elementary schools is to promote these children to the next grade. Indeed, they will fall farther behind each year. Many will drop out of school, in large part from frustration. In far too many inner-city high schools, therefore, class size is in reality not an issue because relatively few students make it all the way from elementary to high school.

It is a disturbing picture. Obviously, public education is not accomplishing its primary purpose: educating. Not for these kids in this school. The data are compelling. And the system with the overall responsibility for educating these children spends large sums of money on a per-pupil basis—upwards of $8,000. The argument is that it takes more money to educate children from minority, low-income, non-English-speaking families. It is difficult to teach kids who come from single-parent homes, or no homes at all. All of this is certainly true. But teaching these kids is exactly what we expect of public education in America. This is why our children are required to go to school. Public education exists in America to educate our children, even those who are difficult to educate. This is why Americans are willing to pay more for public education every year. The problem, of course, is that it is not working. Not for these kids in this school in this city. And not for far too many kids in too many schools in this country.

Putting aside, for the moment, the most obvious concern—are the children being educated—consider the way the system is structured. Consider how the system is at odds with those very principles that underwrite much of what the nation is supposed to be all about. The children and their families were assigned to this school. The district makes the decisions regarding who goes to school where. The families have no freedom in this matter but are subject to the processes and bureaucracies in place. If the families were wealthier or had connections, they might be able to make some alternative choices. Freedom in education in America, it seems, can be purchased; it is available to those who have the resources and can afford it.

But there is a deeper loss of freedom here as well. Children who do not get the education they need and the education promised to them will live lives less free than others. Ignorance limits freedom. Ignorance threatens freedom—for a child, for a nation.

The parents and children in this school have precious few opportunities to consider regarding education. Not only is the school chosen for them, but so is the teacher, the curriculum, the length of the school year and school day, and the activities and support services that might be available. Opportunity in education, it would seem, is decided by the system. This is to say, of course, that on the whole, in public education in America, there is not much opportunity. Opportunity defined by others is opportunity denied.

But there is yet an even deeper loss here as well. Children who fail to get the education they need and promised to them will have fewer opportunities as adults. They will experience closed doors. They will make less money, commit more crimes, serve more time in jail, marry younger and more times, have more children and fail to care for them adequately, and thus give birth to yet another generation of young people who fail to get the education they need and promised to them. And so the cycle will repeat itself. The system will persist. Ignorance limits opportunities for children and adults. Ignorance limits opportunities for a nation.

And what about equality? How does the current system advance equality? Certainly one of the major arguments for mass public education in this country was the promotion of equality. Education erases the inequalities that exist in America. Education levels the playing field. Or, does it? Obviously not—not at this school and not at far too many schools in this country.

The data tell us, and has for years, that low-income, minority students consistently experience an achievement gap compared to their white counterparts. This has been going on for generations. And for generations, America has closed its eyes to this equality problem. That is not to say that equality has not been a subject of discussion in American education. Indeed, it has been something of an obsession among education policy makers and pundits. But the obsession has generated little progress.

The nation first stared down the education inequality problem in 1954, when the Supreme Court issued its landmark decision in *Brown v. Board of Education.* In perhaps the single most significant decision of the last half of the twentieth century, the Court held that the "separate but equal" doctrine is inherently unequal and struck down state-sanctioned segregated schools. The decision ushered in a generation of civil rights advances and controversies that changed America forever. Education after the *Brown* decision strove to move away from segregation and sought true equality. School districts were redrawn, students were bussed, and judges started running schools. The nation became embroiled in controversy as it attempted to confront the principle of equality in education. It still is.

A second generation sought to deal with the equality issue by focusing not only on who goes to school where but on how much is spent, on a per-student basis, on education. Here the principle of equality was transformed into a simple, if simplistic, formulation: equal per-student expenditures is what equality in education is all about. Virtually every state in the nation found itself subjected to lawsuits regarding the distribution of state education funds. Equity lawsuits became the fundamental vehicle to achieve equality in education. Many states were forced to change their funding formulas to accommodate the equity issue. Those suits continue.

Yet, more than fifty years after *Brown* initiated the civil rights revolution, the achievement gap provides compelling evidence that equality in education remains more promise than reality. There is a reason for this. For generations, efforts to advance equality in American education have focused on the wrong issues. Ending segregation was a necessary first step, surely. But making sure schools are integrated does not ensure all students are being educated. Making sure per-pupil spending is equal does not ensure equality in student achievement. And that should be the goal regarding equality in education. Student achievement and school performance should matter, not how much money is spent or who goes to school with whom and where. This is not to say that money does not matter or that de facto segregated schools are okay. It is to say that all the money and all the race-based public policy in the world do not matter if minority students continue to fall victim to an achievement gap.

And so, what about equality of education at this inner-city school? In a way, there is equality here. Just about all the students are failing. They all reflect the achievement gap when compared to white students in the city's and the nation's schools. And while the law has forbidden de jure segregation for generations, this inner-city school is overwhelmingly minority; most urban school districts are. And per-student spending is higher at this poorly performing school than at many better performing schools in the state.

Equality in education cannot become a reality as long as we expect less from minority, low-income, non-English-speaking students than we do from their wealthier, white counterparts. It cannot become a reality as long as we practice the "soft bigotry of low expectations." Surely achieving equality will require more than expecting more from our most at-risk kids, but it can never be achieved by expecting less.

There is a deeper equality problem at this school though. Because these students are not at grade level in reading and math and, in all likelihood, will leave fourth grade underachieving, then fifth grade, and so on, they may never be able to participate fully in the American dream. While perhaps not victims of state-imposed discrimination, they will in all likelihood suffer the discrimination that comes with being uneducated or undereducated. They will not have equal opportunity in life—due not to a lack of concern or caring or public policy or litigation but to a misguided sense of what equality in education should be about.

Surely accountability has become the watchword for No Child Left Behind. The law represents the flowering of a decade of education accountability-reform efforts among the states. Whatever else may become part of the popular impression of No Child Left Behind, accountability seems permanently etched into the public education landscape. Or is it? What can be said of accountability in this inner-city school, for its teachers and students?

If accountability in education is about teachers being dedicated to their profession and their students, then this teacher in this school is the poster child for accountability. If it is about caring for students and creating an environment conducive to learning, then kudos go to this teacher and this school. If accountability is about children building a positive self-image, developing socially, and having positive interactions with others, then this school measures up. But if accountability is about the efficient and responsible expenditure of taxpayer dollars on educating children, then there are real problems here. If it is about making sure instruction yields student learning, then this school does not measure up. If accountability is about making sure children learn, that teachers teach and schools succeed, then this school is failing.

It cannot be argued that a school in which the great majority of students consistently perform below grade level over time is getting the job done—no matter how difficult that job may be. For generations, the remedy given to help such ailing schools has been more money. The public has been supportive and willing, contributing more each year, primarily to help troubled schools. But the troubles have not gone away; the schools continue to underperform, and the students continue to fall farther behind. Because true accountability has been absent in much of public education for so long, it has been all but impossible to determine where there are educational successes and failures. It has been difficult to determine what works and what does not in education and teaching. It has been impossible to determine the amount of education that takes place for each public dollar invested in public schools.

Until relatively recently, accountability in public education has been the product of impression and reputation. People know good schools when they see them, and everyone knows about the bad schools; it is the same with teachers. Student achievement has been determined by teachers, the ultimate arbiters of whether a child is learning to read, write, and calculate. Parents have come to rely and depend upon their children's teachers, therefore. They have come to rely upon principals and superintendents, and their words have been the currency of accountability. Parents and taxpayers have relied upon and trusted teachers and principals and superintendents. That has been the architecture of accountability in American public education.

At this school, the words and actions of the teacher and her principal and their superintendent might indicate that things are going well—"particularly considering these kids, who they are, where they come from." But, of course, this is not the case. It is not that the teacher, principal, and superintendent do not work hard enough or care enough. If hard work and compassion were the touchstones of accountability in education, America's public education system would be world-class, and the kids in this school would be superachievers. But accountability is about results, not effort. It is about results, not spending. It is about results, not caring.

Accountability in education has to be about more than a teacher's assessment of a student's progress. It has to be about more than a principal's assessment of a teacher's effectiveness. It has to be about more than a superintendent's evaluation of a principal's effectiveness or a school board's assessment of a superintendent's effectiveness. Accountability in education should be about whether learning is taking place, how much, and how well. It should be about dollars yielding learning. That is, after all, why we have teachers and principals and superintendents and schools.

At this inner-city school, there is no accountability as long as a hard-working, well-meaning, and dedicated teacher, principal, superintendent, and school board accept unacceptable student performance.

And what about the parents? If accountability begins at home, then surely there are problems here. The children in this inner-city school come from troubled, broken families or no families at all. They are victims as children every bit as much as they are victims as students. Surely some level of accountability must be placed upon the parents, families, and extended families of these children. Surely their poor performance is due, in large part, to the world in which they are growing up. Surely these children are doing pretty well when one considers that world.

But public education is supposed to educate every child in America, regardless of the world he or she grows up in. The task may be made more difficult by parents, families, and communities that do not care—but that is essentially irrelevant. Public education takes each child on his or her own terms, the system is supposed to teach that child, and that child is supposed to learn. Children are supposed to learn, in part, so they will not be held captive by those parents, families, and communities that do not care; this is part of the promise of American public education. But in this inner-city school, that promise goes unfulfilled as teachers, principals, administrators, school board members, parents, families, and communities are not held accountable.

But a deeper sense of accountability is at stake here as well. Young children who do not get an education confront serious challenges as adults. They lack the skills, knowledge, and ability to make responsible, informed decisions. And so they get into trouble—personal, legal, moral trouble. Or they simply disengage, wandering aimlessly through life, contributing little, depending on others or on the state. Accountability begins with self-government—governing one's self. And an uneducated or undereducated person has a very difficult time exercising responsible self-government. The children at this inner-city school—where everyone cares, means well, works hard, and "loves these kids"—run the risk of becoming men and women who will not know how to govern themselves, how to hold themselves accountable for their decisions and actions. And so they will become accountable to others. They will become the responsibility of others.

In education, accountability must merge with a fuller sense of responsibility. Accountability focuses on academic achievement and results. Responsibility focuses on doing what needs to be done to foster achievement and results. Paying attention to test scores can only get us so far. Those engaged in the work of educating young people must accept a greater sense of responsibility for their welfare and future. And as they get older, students must learn to accept a greater sense of responsibility as well. In its fullest sense, education is the responsibility of all Americans. How we live up to that responsibility will determine how well our nation lives up to its potential.

What takes place in this inner-city school seems so at odds with what America has always talked about regarding its schools, students, and families. America's image of its schools seems almost indelibly printed in the public imagination, even though that image departs radically from reality. The image is of children attending neighborhood schools with teachers they and their parents know. The image is of parents as partners in their children's education, attending Parent-Teacher Association meetings and volunteering at school. The image is of local schools that are the heart of neighborhoods and communities. The reality is often quite different. Children often attend school far from home; parents often know little about what goes on there, and some could care less. Those who do try to become partners in their children's education far too often run up against recalcitrant bureaucrats or mind-numbing processes that discourage their interests. The school may even be in the neighborhood. But it is not "of" the neighborhood. It may be the local public school, but for many it is more akin to a government school located nearby. In some places it is as though the public has given up ownership of its public schools—if, indeed, they ever really owned them. In far too many places, the public school is simply a place parents send their children to learn. It is not a welcoming place. And it is not working.

When President Bush started his second term in office, he spoke frequently of America as an "ownership society." This was to be a major theme of his second-term agenda. Much of that agenda broke down, as a combination of natural disasters, administrative incompetence, and the war in Iraq led to plummeting polls and increased partisan bickering. Moreover, Bush's emphasis on home ownership may have helped to produce the mortgage and finance crisis that erupted toward the end of his presidency. But surely Bush was right to assert that America is very much an ownership society. A greater percentage of Americans today own their homes than ever before in the nation's history, and a far greater percentage are home owners than in any other nation. Americans own automobiles, and computers, and corporations and companies. It is very much a part the American character to aspire to own as much as possible so as to be able to control one's own destiny. The idea is woven into the very fabric of the American ethos, and it shapes how Americans view their lot in life.

Consider the effect home ownership has on a person. Beyond the obvious tax and financial advantages, home ownership brings a sense of responsibility with it—a personal stake in the maintenance of one's property and domicile. The nation was taught a lesson about the power of home ownership during the 1960s as urban policy sought to manage the huge influx of relatively poor, rural black Americans into the cities of the north.

Huge housing projects were built in places like Chicago, Detroit, and New York City. These sprawling complexes of hundred of apartments were constructed to provide shelter for those on welfare or with low incomes. After a relatively short period, however, the projects became infamous for crime, violence, and rapid disrepair. Surely there were many explanations for the problems that plagued the projects, but at base one problem was that those who lived in the projects had no real stake in their upkeep and future. The tenants considered themselves temporary residents. They hoped to move on to become home owners in their own right. The fact that most did not and became more or less permanent residents of the projects speaks to the social and economic disruptions that clouded urban centers at the time. The point is that for those stuck in them, the housing projects provided shelter, not a home. They were a place to stay, not a place to build a future. These residents had little personally vested in the projects, and so the projects gradually fell apart from neglect, as much as anything else.

Public schools are not housing projects. But surely one reason public schools are not working in this country can be traced to the lack of ownership many parents, neighborhoods, and communities feel they have of their schools. This lack of public ownership of public education has evolved gradually over time.

At root, public schools were once robust evidence of a community's commitment to its children and its future. Once established, a community would make providing an education for its children a high priority. And a community's public schools were centers of activity as well as education. The community took pride in its school and took care of it. Over time, however, the local community public school gave way to the public school district. Numbers and economics shifted the focus from individual schools to networks of schools in districts. The managerial and financial demands shifted the focus from the local school to a system of public schools. And as this happened, the way many Americans identified with their local schools began to change. As finance and governance in schooling began to overshadow education, and as more and more responsibilities and expectations were placed upon the system, managing the system came to take priority over providing education. Local schools were seen as operating units within the larger institutional framework. Deciding who would attend what school became the product of often elaborate attendance formulas that looked at such things as residency, bus routes, race, income, and building occupancy. Gradually the requirements of maintaining the system outstripped its original purpose: educating children.

All of this took place against a larger backdrop of social change in America. The civil and women's rights revolutions of the 1960s, 1970s, and beyond changed the social fabric of the country and led to fundamentally new approaches to marriage and family, employment, culture, and education.

America went through transformations, but American public education did not. And so the relationship many Americans had with their schools changed. That sense of ownership in the local school—of having a stake in it and what took place there—gradually weakened, and in some places it disappeared entirely. Americans looked upon schools as places their children went to get educated. Taxpayers looked upon them as necessary expenditures. They became government schools rather than public schools. Teachers, still highly regarded by their students' parents, became organized public employees. The system of public education gradually acquired a life of its own, and parents, families, and entire communities seemed to be governed by the decisions of the system rather than vice versa. It was as though the idea of public education had been turned on its head. Rather than communities creating and running schools for their children and families, the public school system decided what educational opportunities would be made available to them. Americans no longer own their schools; the school system owns them. For if ownership means anything, it means the owner has the authority to make decisions concerning that which he owns. With public education, that authority has been transferred to the system.

There are, of course, institutional mechanisms in place that should ensure the public actually retains ownership of its schools and school districts. School boards are elected. School boards must adopt school budgets. Only elected officials can raise taxes. All of this is in place; the accoutrements of democracy and political accountability are in place. But the participation rates suggest the public lacks ownership of it all. Few attend school board meetings, Parent-Teacher Association meetings, parent-teacher meetings. Voter turnout for local elections is sparse. People complain about taxes but pay them. In some places, public resentment of public education has supplanted public ownership of it. In others, the disconnect between the people and their schools has led to the same sort of neglect that toppled the housing projects of the 1960s. But due to the size and resource base of the public school system, it will not topple from neglect. It will continue in place. It will simply not provide what it was created to provide. This will continue until alternatives become so popular that the resource base begins to erode. And that will happen as families and communities seek to regain ownership of the education of their children.

So, what can be said about ownership in this inner-city school? The school is in a neighborhood, but the majority of children attending it come from a number of other neighborhoods. Many are bussed in from these areas in order to answer concerns about diversity and equality. The district assigned the teachers in this school according to a collective bargaining agreement ironed out by district officials and the local teachers' union. Veteran teachers can select where they want to teach, and most, quite understandably and predictably, seek to work in "good" schools, where students achieve and discipline is hardly an issue. Less senior teachers go where they are assigned, and many at this inner-city school have been assigned to teach here. That does not mean they do not care about their students; this school is just not where they want to be, where they want to spend their professional careers. Many will move on the following year. Some will stay. Some will leave the profession. They do not feel they control their professional destinies. They do not have ownership over their careers. And so they will not permit themselves to become personally vested in them.

The principal in this inner-city school does feel a sense of ownership— but it is only a veneer of ownership. Higher-ups in the district's administration make most of the day-to-day management decisions affecting the school. The principal's job is to carry out their instructions. Her sense of ownership flows from her years of service at the same school. She identifies with it. But it is a false ownership; appearance belies reality.

And what of the parents, the families, the community: do they own the school? Surely some do. Those who try to contribute and to be partners in the education of the children do so out of a sense of having something at stake in the school. But the school will do what it does whether they are partners or not. And it will do what it does whether parents, families, and the community resist or ignore what it does. Here again there exists a veneer of ownership of the school, which, in truth, operates independently of the families and community it is meant to serve. It reports to the head office. That is where decisions are made. That is where ownership resides.

But there is a deeper problem regarding ownership in the inner-city school. The students will leave there lacking the skills to become full participants in the "ownership society" President Bush spoke of so glowingly. Lacking adequate skills, they will grow up unable to earn the resources needed to own their own homes, automobiles, appliances, and so forth. They may go into great debt to acquire what others own outright. Or they may turn to illegal means to acquire the resources necessary to become owners. In all likelihood, they will grow up resentful of the fact that they cannot have what others have and of a system that failed them and that they failed. Resentment fuels animosities, and animosities can easily turn into hostilities among people. How ironic: public education, once heralded as the key to the maintenance of a civil society and democracy, instead helps sow the seeds of class and race animus. It is, again, as if the system has been turned upside down. Rather than curing what ails society, it contributes to the disease.

If it is about anything, education is about hope. For eternity, it has been the ticket to a better, fuller life. Education can conquer anything; ignorance is an abyss. With an education, a pauper can become a millionaire. Without it, poverty is all but inescapable. Education has always held out the endless possibilities that have ignited the imagination and animated the soul. It has been an essential ingredient in the American promise and ideal. Here, if anywhere, anyone can succeed with an educated mind in a free society. Freedom is essential, but so is education.

For these students in this fourth-grade classroom in this inner-city school, however, education proves evasive. The energy, excitement, and hope these students exude will gradually give way to lethargy, complacency, and despair. Whatever hopes these children have about the lives they might lead and the world they might grow up in will be dashed upon the rocks of ignorance. The hope in their eyes on this bright school day is a hollow hope. Surely some will experience some measure of success, despite the circumstances surrounding their lives. But for many, the hopes and dreams of childhood will give way to the harsh realities of an adulthood of cynicism, boredom, animosity, and resentment. For far too many, the hope that is America is false and empty. America has let these children down, even as Americans speak of the need to help them rise up. The system has let these children down, even as the system was created for them.

Freedom, opportunity, equality, responsibility, ownership, and hope: if American education should advance anything, it surely should be these ideas and ideals. Education should advance them for every student, family, community, and neighborhood. It should advance them for the nation. It should advance the cause of freedom, expand the range of opportunities, move us forward in the march toward equality, help us achieve the promise of self-government, offer all the fulfillment of ownership, and fuel the hopes and dreams of all Americans. Education in America today is falling far short of these goals. The next generation of education in America must accomplish all of them, or the next American generation might be the last.

Education in America is falling far short in many ways, and not just in the nation's urban centers. Students in rural schools are not receiving the education they have been promised and deserve. Native American children enrolled in schools administered by the Department of Interior's Bureau of Indian Affairs are not getting the education they have been promised and deserve. Most of the nation's Hispanic students are underserved. For far too many students with special needs, education remains something of an afterthought. The data is compelling and stunning. Dropout rates in some communities and among some demographic groups approach 50 percent. High school graduation rates sometimes dip below 50 percent. Sure, there are some very good schools, and the nation's best-performing students can compete with students anywhere in the world. But these are the exceptional schools and exceptional students, and that is not the promise of public education. The promise of public education is for every child to learn. The fact that the No Child Left Behind Act's call to make good on that promise—by having all students proficient in reading and math by 2014—was so controversial says volumes about how Americans, particularly American educators, understand public education today. Large majorities doubt universal proficiency is achievable. And they are no doubt correct. Under the current system of public education in America, that aim surely is not attainable—not because the children cannot learn but because the system cannot deliver.

⸺✺⸺

The great challenge we confront is to think differently about education in America. As stated earlier, an important first step is to understand the distinction between education and schooling and to focus on the former. A necessary second step is to do away with the distinction between public education/schooling and nonpublic or private education/schooling. Why should we care where a child goes to school? Why should we care how a child receives an education? Instead we should care about the quality of the education the child acquires. We must move beyond the tired old debate over public versus private schools; it is distraction put forth by those who seek to maintain the status quo.

The argument is familiar enough. Public dollars should go to public schools. Public dollars should not go to private, parochial, sectarian, or other nonpublic schools. This is essentially an argument about schools, not education and certainly not about students. Variations on this theme are constantly put forth. Public dollars should not go to religiously affiliated schools because that would violate the First Amendment and blur the distinction between church and state. While the Supreme Court put that argument to rest in *Zelman v. Simmons-Harris*, most state constitutions contain provisions that continue to provide fodder for this position. And as long as the focus remains on public dollars and schooling, this will likely continue to be the case. Ironically, the fact that public dollars go to religiously affiliated colleges and universities all across America every day seems not to color the debate in the K–12 world.

Another argument asserts that public money going to nonpublic schools robs public schools of badly needed resources. Public schools are underfunded as it is, so the argument goes, and need every dollar available.

Those who favor school choice, or vouchers, predictably counter by citing the postsecondary-sector argument as well as declaring that the competition school choice would bring to public schools would help them improve and that the status quo is not getting the job done. But as long as both sides focus on schools, this debate will yield little in the way of substantive change in education. The terms of the debate need to be redefined.

The assertion that public money should go only to public schools should be understood for what it really says: government money should go only to government schools. But the whole notion of government money should be challenged, for in a democracy there really is no such thing as "the government's money." That money belongs to the people; the government uses the taxpayers' money to run government schools. With this understanding, we can assert that taxpayers should retain the authority to decide what kind of education they want their children to receive and how. After all, it is their money and their children. Why should government, at any level, retain the authority to make such a fundamental decision? The answer is that it has been given this authority over time, and taxpayers have come to accept it as an appropriate governmental function—almost as an article of faith. It is time to question that assumption. Surely providing an education for the people is a key function of government, but there might be a variety of ways for government to do this. The fact that over time a system of public schooling has been established does not mean it represents the only way to educate the people. Indeed, given the relatively poor performance of the current system despite the resources devoted to it, one is compelled to ask if there is not some better method.

In addition to distinguishing between schooling and education and doing away with the public-private dichotomy, we should question some other assumptions concerning the current system of education in America. There exist about fifteen thousand public school districts in this country, each governed by a school board. Each maintains an operating budget and employs teachers, administrators, and support personnel. What is it about public education that requires the existence of school districts and school boards? Indeed, what is it about public education that requires the existence of elementary, middle, and high schools? Why must a child be enrolled in an elementary school for a certain number of years, then proceed to a middle school, then to a high school? Why must a child reach a certain age before entering school? What makes the system of K–12 schooling so magical that a young person must sit through five years of elementary school or four years of high school? Indeed, why does education require going to school at all?

Consider some other working assumptions of the current system. Students are taught by teachers. Teachers are credentialed by the states after satisfying various requirements relating to their education and preparation for the classroom. They are credentialed according to the grade level or discipline they teach. They are employed by school districts and paid salaries set by locally determined agreements or contracts. They are compensated based primarily upon their seniority, not the results of their labors. Most would argue they are underpaid and underappreciated. What is so sacred about a system that works this way? Why must a teacher work for a district? Where is it written that teachers should be contracted employees tied to a building and a process? Why shouldn't they be independent professionals who contract with families or communities to provide educational services?

Why shouldn't they be able to choose where they want to work, when, and with whom and to freely seek clients who might pay for their services? What about teaching requires state licensure? President Obama is quite right to ask why teacher compensation must be unrelated to student achievement.

Consider the way student achievement is measured. Until the No Child Left Behind Act, a complex, confused, and problem-plagued array of class-room, school, district, and state assessments were supposed to provide students, parents, and taxpayers with a sense of how well the students and schools were doing.

At the most basic level, teachers assess their students all the time, beginning in the earliest years with spelling, math, and reading tests administered in the classroom. This evolves into such traditional teacher-administered assess-ments of student performance as exams, writing assignments, lab projects, and finals in high school. All of these sorts of assessments have one thing in common: the teacher decides what is to be assessed and judges student per-formance. Most adults in this country grew up with this kind of schooling. Grades were administered by teachers who taught students the material they thought students needed to know and then decided how well they knew it.

On top of these sorts of teacher-based evaluations of student performance have come more objective (ideally, anyway) standardized assessments rooted in state-defined academic standards. The standards movement started among the states in the 1990s, fueled by talk of greater account-ability in education. These assessments aimed to facilitate comparisons of student achievement among students, classes, schools, districts, and states. One goal aimed to reduce the relative arbitrariness of a system of student assessment based almost solely on the judgment of teachers. One teacher's sense of an A performance might be another teacher's C. A second goal was to provide greater and more objective comparability of student and school achievement and objectivity. Basing assessments on state academic stan-dards, it was argued, would also help to ensure all students in a state were learning the same thing at the same time. Standards would guide curricula, which would drive instruction, which would drive learning.

As these assessment and accountability systems have matured, the relatively poor performance of America's students and schools has become more difficult to ignore. With academic standards, Americans have a clearer understanding of what children need to know and be able to do. With academic assessments Americans have a clearer understanding of what children do not know and cannot do.

The overall reaction to all of this has been predictable. The majority of educators decry the amount of testing going on, the alleged narrowing of the curriculum to reflect state standards and assessments, and the pressure kids, teachers, and families feel under the weight of state-imposed account-ability systems. The No Child Left Behind Act added even greater weight to the accountability movement and has encountered ever-growing resistance from educators.

Another reaction is troubling but predictable: those with the most at stake have found ways to inflate assessment results to make students, schools, and states look better than they are. Teachers and administrators who feel the pressure to excel have devised methods to make the case to parents and constituents that their children are indeed performing better, even when external indicators such as the National Assessment of Education Performance demonstrate they are not. State departments of education, and in some cases governors, have participated in the hoax, looking to make a state's education system look better compared to other states. Under the guise of accountability, then, some states have participated in a "race to the bottom" rather than upholding high academic standards for kids. Indeed, this problem led Secretary of Education Duncan to create his Race to the Top initiative.

All of this is completely predictable, of course. With so much money pouring into public education and a hot focus on results, those most directly responsible for spending that money and getting results will feel great pressure. When the results are disappointing, there is a tendency to blame the tests, or the accountability system, or the lack of adequate resources to accomplish what really needs to be done. When the stakes are high and the pressure is on, some will always "cheat" in order to come out looking better. In other words, as more accurate measures of student and school performance have become available, those most directly engaged in education have sought ways to blame others and criticize the measures. For the defenders of the status quo, it cannot be the system that is not getting the job done.

One of the great benefits of the No Child Left Behind Act is that it took the discussion of student and school achievement to the national level and heightened national awareness and expectations. But by not speaking to the fundamental architecture, governance, and politics of public education, the law asks of the system more than it can deliver. Thus, either the law must be changed to better conform to what the existing system can do, or the public's frustration with the system will increase until more fundamental, systemic reform is called for. Given that most of us do not like to hear that our children and schools are not as good as they should be or we think they are, the pressure to change the law will grow more rapidly than any pressure to change the system. And given that it is the same system we all grew up with, generally, identify with, and have supported for generations—we all went to school and remember what it was like, know teachers and administrators, and pay school taxes—imagining an alternative is difficult. So the status quo will, in all likelihood, persist, and those who have the resources and opportunities will find other ways to make sure their children get the education they have been promised and deserve. And those who do not have the resources and opportunities will be left behind, victims of a system that is not working, even as Americans know better than ever just how badly it is failing—unless new visions of the next generation of education in America are put forward.

cℭ∞ℭ

Consider how education might look if government played a slightly different role in society. Initially, the framers of the U.S. Constitution envisioned a limited government of enumerated powers only. Even those seeking a stronger central authority than under the Articles of Confederation and to establish order from a loose alliance of states did not want to establish too strong a central government. The framers knew that a government that tries to do too much ends up doing nothing very well.

The notion of a limited national government seems almost quaint against the backdrop of contemporary government and politics in America. Yet, the vision of the Constitution's framers should inform our thinking about the shape of the next generation of education in America.

Imagine an America in which government acts as a facilitator to help people accomplish their goals—a government that helps people get things done as opposed to doing things for them. In theory this makes sense. After all, in a democracy the focus is supposed to be on the people, not the government. Properly understood, public education should be education by and for the people, not education by the government for the people.

In such a scenario, government's doing less does not necessarily mean less gets done. It means the people accomplish more, and government exists to facilitate that process. It is the principled idea that the people should do the work of a democracy. It returns to the people control of their lives and their destinies. And it begins with education—giving back to the people control over the education of their children.

Imagine a state in which there are no school districts or school boards or school-attendance zones. There are schools, surely: they are all independent entities that have sprung up in communities and neighborhoods throughout the state. They vary in size and purpose. Each has a specialty; they are "boutique" schools. Some contain no grades; students are enrolled according to their knowledge and learning levels and proceed at their own pace with the help of instructors. In these schools every student has his own individualized education plan, put together by the staff and his family. The child's academic progress is charted against that plan, which is adjusted periodically. Children attend group instruction sessions, which provide important socialization and group-dynamics skills.

There is no state-imposed school year or school day in these schools; the schools establish these themselves. They seek to distinguish themselves from one another in certain ways. Some meet year-round; others adhere to a more traditional academic calendar. Many meet in the early evenings as well as during the day. Some specialize in weekend learning. Some act as gathering places for group interaction and learning that takes place at scheduled times, since most of the actual instruction takes places online, wherever the student happens to be.

The sizes of the schools vary tremendously, although few are all that large. The facilities vary as well. Each school offers its own array of academic and cocurricular programming, again as a way of distinguishing itself. Some emphasize technology; others eschew it and promote a back-to-basics approach that emphasizes direct instruction.

In this state, families decide where they want to send their children to school, and they have a vast number of choices. Or they can choose not to send their child to school at all and to have the school come to them via visiting-instructor and online learning systems. Indeed, whole classes can gather anytime and anywhere through technology. Interaction among students and teachers happens in real time, and the students can come from anywhere in the state, while the teachers might be in another country.

In this state, each learning opportunity must present a performance plan before being permitted to operate. The plan must explain to the satisfaction of those who might subscribe and enroll their children how their academic progress will be determined. The state has regulations in place to deal with fraud, abuse, mismanagement, and malfeasance. But since no "government money" goes to any school in the state, the provider is really accountable to the client/family. The state does insist that every child get an education and that every family provide for that education, and it provides each family with children an education allotment equal to or greater than the average per-pupil expenditure were the state overseeing a traditional public education system. Parents are free to spend more but not less.

Here education is ubiquitous. It is not confined to schools or buildings or to certain days of the week and hours of the day. Families are engaged constantly in learning. It comes in many dimensions, entails several learning "platforms," and is multidisciplinary and interdisciplinary. A student might watch a program on television that sends him to the computer to solve some mystery. From the computer he might download some game that engages him in mathematical and musical concepts that help frame a theory of organizing resources to combat an environmental threat. Engagement is constant. Students need not visit chemistry labs, although they certainly can. They conduct virtual experiments in virtual laboratories. Through technology they can sail through space, experiencing the physics of weightlessness, visit the world's great museums, and listen to curators discuss masterpieces. They can access online academic assistance in any subject at anytime in almost any language. Indeed, because online learning is ubiquitous and comprehensive, education need not halt when a flu pandemic sweeps the state or a natural disaster disrupts traditional infrastructure.

Here accountability and responsibility in education take on myriad forms and functions. A young child learning to read works with a teacher who can access instantaneous analyses of the student's progress and problems and make adjustments to her instruction accordingly. Handheld devices that record progress and analyze problems replace piles of paperwork. Science and data inform instruction. And like the teacher, the child's parents can access this information so that they can follow along and witness their child's progress. Report cards are gone, but reporting is not. Rather than relying on a periodic statement of where the child stands in a subject at a given time, parents, students, and teachers can access constantly available progress monitoring; valuable educational information delivered in "just-in-time" fashion can inform instruction. When a student masters material, he moves on to other, different, more challenging subject matter. Education is not about seat time in a classroom; it is about learning. Here students do not graduate from high school with a diploma. They receive certifications that attest to their mastery of subjects—certifications that are the currency of accountability in education and learning. They provide potential employers and institutions of higher education with solid indicators of the intellectual and educational attainment of young men and women.

Here the issue is not how much schooling takes place at what cost. That is an old, outdated model from an earlier era. Here the issue is how to invest smartly in the intellectual capital of a country. And a country's intellectual capital is found in its people and ideas. That is what drives public and private investment here: people and ideas. All of the institutions, places, programs, and policies are driven by the pursuit of developing the country's intellectual capital. It is truly a "knowledge economy" in the fullest sense.

But what of those treasured activities associated with going to school? What about sports and band and clubs and dances? Surely a big part of going to school and getting an education in America has always revolved around all those other activities and rituals that take place in the lives of young boys and girls growing into young men and women.

Here these take place, but on different terms and in different locations. Take sports, for example. Rather than being tied to schools, athletics are community and neighborhood based. This is not really all that different from what has always been the case. Communities all across America live and die by the success of their local high school athletic teams. Friday night football is an American ritual. Here the ritual continues; the high school football team is now the town's or the community's football team. Money spent on sports comes from the community and neighborhood, just as in the past. But it is money set aside exclusively for that purpose and not part of some school or school district budget. Athletics remain a part of educating young people in the community, just not part of schooling in the community. This has the added benefit of making it easier for taxpayers—all the members of the community—to follow where their money goes—how it is spent. It makes it easier to reach decisions about community and educational priorities.

Here there is band and theater and proms; all kinds of associations and activities drive a sense of community. In fact, this has always been the case; the schools have merely been the venue and sponsor. Here the community takes on those roles. It makes sense, after all. In an earlier age, communities built schools to educate their children, and those schools developed what were called extracurricular activities organized around each school for its students. Here the activities persist, except the school is no longer the host, sponsor, or organizer.

Indeed, here public funds do not go toward the construction of schools. School construction is financed privately, as with any other business. Schools include in their operating budgets monies to underwrite institutional infrastructure as they calculate their costs and fees.

Such a scenario seems far-fetched for sure. But why should that be? Just because public education has existed in the same form for generations does not mean future generations must follow the same approach. For example, should it not be possible for a market in education to exist in which a variety of education providers might compete for students? Those providers might include local governments or consortia of governments. Traditional providers might exist as well. But a comprehensive "system" of public education will have been replaced by a "nonsystem" market that makes available a diverse number of education providers, one as diverse, perhaps, as the population of learners.

The great challenge to this innovative vision of American education is the current condition of education and community in the United States. Getting where we need to go is made most difficult by where we are today. Much of the challenge has to do with American culture, tradition, and mind-sets. It has as much to do with how much America and American government and politics have changed over time. And it has everything to do with the American people reestablishing ownership of their schools, their communities, and their lives. Such a vision of education in America will require imagination and entrepreneurship, some smart investing, and some risk taking. It will require challenging conventional wisdom, assumptions, and customs. It will require courage and a willingness to take on those interests, organizations, and public and private entities that benefit from the status quo. It will require the character, traits, and talents that gave birth to this nation and have always been behind the great transformations this country has experienced. It will require an American education revolution. Absent that, the very future of our country may be brought into question.

During his time in office, President Obama has spoken frequently about improving America's schools. But in September 2009, he spoke to America's students, delivering a back-to-school speech aimed directly at them, broadcast nationally from a school in northern Virginia. Presidents have spoken at schools forever, it seems. But Obama was the first to take his speech to students to a national audience. President Bush often said that he was not elected superintendent of America. Here was President Obama, teacher in chief. The president's critics made something of a controversy of the event, arguing Obama was politicizing education and trying to "brainwash" young people. But his message was familiar and ageless and important: work hard, be disciplined and responsible, become good citizens, aspire to succeed. It was good stuff.

America loves her children. It is that love, really, that compels Americans to spend money and time and to extend great effort to educate her young. It is that love that sets this country apart from so many others. Here we believe everyone should receive an education and have a chance to achieve the American dream. Indeed, a powerful example of that is President Obama. But with each passing year and each new education-reform strategy, our chances of living up to our own national expectations grow slimmer. Perhaps this stems in part from our great expectations. Perhaps we really do expect too much from our schools, our teachers, our students, and ourselves. But it is also due, at least in part, to a failure of the imagination and our inability to take on the monumental challenge of rethinking education.

As President Obama spoke to America's students, he must have known how important the task of educating them is. He spoke frequently during his campaign and wrote about the audacity of hope. It will require audacity indeed to change the way America educates her children. And that is change we need.

# Notes

## CHAPTER 1

1. See "Is It George Bush Already," *National Review*, December 22, 1997.

2. Clifford J. Levey, "The 2000 Campaign: The Texas Governor; Citing a Crisis, Bush Proposes Literacy Effort," *New York Times*, March 29, 2000, .www.nytimes .com/2000/03/29/us/2000-campaign-texas-governor-citing-crisis-bush-proposes -literacy-effort.html?pagewanted=1?pagewanted=1

3. For example, see Kate Snow, "Bush Hopes to Bring Texas Education Agenda to National Level," CNN.com, September 1, 2000. Bush's emphasis on student and parent responsibility was the focus of an article appearing in the *Boston Globe* on October 3, 2000. His interest in teacher character was reported by CNN.com on September 11, 2000.

4. Bush visited his hundredth school, Springfield High School, in Toledo, Ohio, on August 31, 2000.

5. See "Is It George Bush Already."

6. See Texas State Library and Archives Commission regarding Gov. George Bush and his senior advisors at www.lib.utexas.edu/taro/tslac/30080/tsi-30080.html.

7. Kevin Fullerton, "Extra Credit: Bush's Education Record: Strong Leadership or Just Good Timing?" *The Austin Chronicle* 18, no. 39 (May 28–June 3, 1999), www .austinchronicle.com/issues/vol18/issue39.

8. See www.pbs.org/newshour/bb/election/july-dec00/busheducation.html, 2000.

9. John Mintz's "In Bush's Texas, an Education Miracle or Mirage?" first appeared in the *Washington Post* on Sunday, April 22, 2000, and was published widely. See www.detnews.com/2000/politics.

10. Jay Greene, "Texas Education Miracle is for Real," in the Manhattan Institute's *City Journal*, Summer 2000. See www.Manhattan-Institute.org/html/greene.html#cj. Mr. Greene is currently on the faculty at the University of Arkansas.

11. Fullerton, "Extra Credit."

12. The Rand Report and Vice President Gore's reaction are reported by Jake Tapper, "Gore: Bush Deserves an F, not an A," Salon.com, October 26, 2000, www .salon.com/news/politics/feature/2000/10/26/gore/index.html.

13. All data regarding expenditures, student performance on the NAEP and Trends in International Mathematics and Science Study, enrollments, numbers of schools, and so forth comes from the U.S. Department of Education, National Center for Educational Statistics, at nces.ed.gov.

14. William Bennett, former secretary of education in the Reagan administration, has offered up this observation with some frequency.

15. This is from "An Open Letter to the President," which Paul Houston, executive director of the American Association of School Administrators, published after the selection of Rod Paige to be President George W. Bush's secretary of education. It can be viewed currently at thefreelibrary.com. An open letter to the president, 076497117.

16. The College Board website provides data regarding high school students' average SAT scores and intended field of postsecondary study. In 2008, it reported that high school graduates who said they intended to major in education scored in the bottom third compared to thirty-six other majors. See http://blogs.ttampabay. com/schools/2008/09/sat-scores-of-t-html. "SAT Scores of Teacher Wannabes." See also studies produced by the Mackinac Center in Michigan at www.Mackinac.org/ pubs, "Future Education Majors Score Below State Average on SAT."

## CHAPTER 2

1. All data reported here is available from the U.S. Department of Education website and from the National Center for Education Statistics.

2. This is from a news release posted on the website of the National Education Association on January 19, 2001. Chase had opposed the nominations of John Ashcroft to be attorney general and Linda Chavez to be secretary of labor. When Chavez withdrew and Elaine Chao was nominated, Chase expressed his support for Chao.

3. This is from a statement by Brenda Wellburn of the Association of State Boards of Education that appeared on the association's website, January 2001.

4. The open letter to the president from Paul Houston, executive director of the American Association of School Administrators, appeared on the association's website, January 1, 2001.

5. This is from the introduction to the National Commission on Excellence in Education, *A Nation at Risk*, Ed.gov, April 1983, www.ed.gov/pubs/NatAtRisk/index .html.

6. This is from the Nation Public Education Financial Survey, Common Core of Data, U.S. Department of Education website.

7. See www.childtrendsdatabanc.org.

8. Jay P. Greene, "High School Graduation Rates in the United States," Manhattan Institute, April 2002, www.manhattan-institute.org.

9. Greene, "High School Graduation Rates."

10. See the website of the National Center for Education Statistics, National Assessment of Educational Progress, of the U.S. Department of Education.

11. See the National Center for Higher Education Management System at www.higheredinfo.org.

12. For example, a 2001 National School Boards Associtaion/Zogby International Poll, "School Vouchers: What the Public Thinks and Why," found relatively modest support for school vouchers; indeed, the more people knew about the concept, the less they liked it. Most preferred more traditional education-reform strategies, such as reducing class size. A 2004 study by the Heartland Institute suggests broader support for school vouchers.

13. See www.publicagenda.org.

14. See www.edreform.org.

15. See www.edreform.org.

## CHAPTER 3

1. This is from a study by The Constitution Project at Georgetown University cited by Edward Feulner, in "Shorten the Gauntlet Nominees Run to the Cabinet," March 1, 2005, www.heritage.org/searchch.aspx?.query=Feulner+on+nominees+to+the+cabinet.

2. According to GovernmentExecutive.com, "Answering the Call: An Excerpt from the New Survivor's Guide for Presidential Nominees," one thousand leadership positions in the executive branch existed in November 2000 (see www.govexec.com/features/1100/1100s1.htm).

3. This anecdote was told to me by Bill Bennett.

4. The conversation was between me and Bill Bennett.

5. Novak had been told of the rift by Bennett. The column mistakenly identified Paige's deputy designate. It was I, under secretary designate at the time, who had spoken with Bennett.

6. During his tenure as chief of staff, Card would recount the events of that day time and again before various gatherings of the Bush administration's political appointees.

## CHAPTER 4

1. I attended this meeting.

## CHAPTER 5

1. Interestingly, Bill Gates and Eli Broad, two philanthropists with deep pockets and deep interest in improving education, combined to establish a fund to promote education as a major issue in the 2008 campaign. Dubbed "E'08," it had practically no effect.

2. Bush's last budget called for ongoing increases in education. According to the Department of Education website, spending on No Child Left Behind alone had increased 41 percent since 2001. See "President's FY 2009 Education Budget: Building on Results," Ed.gov, February 2008, www2.ed.gov/about/overview/budget/budget09/factsheet.html.

3. Indeed, Congressman Miller's draft revision of No Child Left Behind sought to soften the impact of the law on suburban schools by creating a new way of recognizing schools that make most of their AYP targets. For example, a school satisfying its performance targets for most of its subgroups might be able to say it made AYP, even though one of the subgroups did not achieve at the target level. Under current law, all subgroups have to make the performance target in order for a school to make AYP.

4. In 2008, something called the Education Equality Project was introduced with such political polar opposites as Newt Gingrich and Al Sharpton signing on. The argument advanced by the project was education as a civil right. It has not garnered much attention however.

5. According to some estimates provided by the U.S. Department of Education, fewer than 20 percent of eligible families take advantage of supplemental educational services. Interestingly, a Rand study released in June 2007 reported that students in underperforming schools benefit from supplemental educational services.

6. According the National Center for Education Statistics, the percentage of high school math teachers who majored in math in college was about 70 percent. The percentage declines in both middle and elementary schools. Many states require a certification in elementary education to teach at that level rather than a certification in subject matter.

7. See the National Center for Education Statistics website at http://nces.ed.gov.

8. See Eugene Hickok and Matthew Ladner, "Reauthorization of No Child Left Behind: Federal Management or Citizen Ownership of K–12 Education," Backgrounder 2047, Heritage Foundation, June 2007, www.heritage.org/Research/Reports/2007/06/Reauthorization-of-No-Child-Left-Behind-Federal-Management-or-Citizen-Ownership-of-K–12-Education.

9. See the fall 2006 issue of *Education Next*, a publication of the Hoover Institution, Stanford University.

10. See "The American Reinvestment and Recovery Act of 2009: Saving and Creating Jobs and Reforming Education," Ed.gov, March 7, 2009, http://ed.gov/policy/gen/leg/recovery/implementation.html.

11. See "Nation Digest," *Washington Post*, August 22, 2009, www.washington-post.com/wp-dyn/content/article/2009/08/21/AR2009082103638.html.

12. See Frank Newport, "Americans Doubt Effectiveness of 'No Child Left Behind,'" Gallup, August 19, 2009, www.gallup.com/poll/122375/americans-doubt-effectiveness-no-child-left-behind.aspx.

13. See "Delaware and Tennessee Win First Race to the Top Grants," Ed.gov, March 29, 2010, www2.ed.gov/news/pressreleases/2010/03/03292010.html.

# Index

# About the Author

Eugene W. Hickok received his Ph.D. in government from the University of Virginia. He was on the faculty of Dickinson College in Carlisle, Pennsylvania, for many years, where he was a professor of political science. While in Carlisle, he served on the school board. In 1995 he was named Secretary of Education for Pennsylvania by Governor Tom Ridge. He served six years in that position before joining the George W. Bush administration as under secretary of education and, later, deputy secretary of education.

He has written and edited a number of books and articles on politics, law, the Constitution, and education reform. He is senior policy director at Dutko Worldwide and WhiteBoard Advisors, an education consulting practice. He lives in Richmond, Virginia, with his wife Kathy.